Ja

THE SCOTTISH
BEAT OFFICER'S
COMPANION

3rd Edition

John Pilkington

Further titles available:

● Part I Promotion Crammer for Sergeants and Inspectors
● Beat Officer's Companion
● Traffic Officer's Companion

To order or for further details phone +44 (0) 20 8700 3700 or

fax +44 (0) 20 8763 1006

© Jane's Information Group 2005

1st edition 1997
2nd edition 2002
3rd edition 2005

ISBN 978-0-7106-2778-0

Jane's Police Review
Jane's Information Group
Sentinel House
163 Brighton Road
Coulsdon
Surrey CR5 2YH

Front cover images © Empics/1131159

Printed and bound in Great Britain by
Biddles Ltd, www.biddles.co.uk

'An invaluable guide
of great clarity for
all police officers'

John T Dickson, OBE, FI Mgt
former Assistant Chief Constable (Operations)
Strathclyde Police

PREFACE

This book, the third edition of the *Scottish Beat Officer's Companion*, is presented in a format similar to the highly successful *Beat Officer's Companion* written by former Warwickshire superintendent, Gordon Wilson. Where appropriate, material from Supt Wilson's work has been used or adopted for the purposes of Scots Law.

The diagrammatic and pictorial format provides an easily read interpretation of those aspects of Scots Law likely to be of practical value to the operational police officer.

The intention of this book is to provide a practical and speedy reference to those aspects of Scots Law that an officer may encounter during the course of his normal duties.

Because the book is simply a guide, its contents have been subjected to a practical interpretation. As a result, it has been necessary to be selective in the material used and the book should not, therefore, be regarded as a definitive work of reference. Nor should it, in any circumstances, be used as a study reference for the purposes of the Police (Scotland) Examinations.

I am indebted to Gordon Wilson for his kind permission to draw upon his work in the preparation of this book.

John Pilkington LLB BA

Former Inspector, Strathclyde Police

Contents

Chapter 1

Scots Criminal Law and Procedures

Human Rights Act, 1998

The Human Rights Act, 1998 has far-reaching implications for almost every aspect of police work. The following provides a very brief explanation of the Act to give you some understanding of the effects.

The Act came into force in Scotland in May 2000 and is intended to be a keystone of the government's policy of constitutional reform. (Note The Scottish Executive implemented the Act in May 2000. However, it did not come into force in the rest of the United Kingdom until 2 October 2000.) The Act applies to all 'public authorities' in the United Kingdom. This includes all government departments, local authorities, quangos, police and non-departmental public bodies.

The purpose of the Act is to provide certain safeguards for the individual citizen and private organisations (such as companies) as against the state and organs of the state. What it does not do, in general terms, is create direct rights for private individuals as against each other.

The effect of the Act is to enable individuals and private organisations to use the European Convention on Human Rights in the courts of the United Kingdom for certain purposes and for limited effects. It also makes unlawful all actions by a public authority which are 'incompatible with a Convention right'.

At the core of the Act are most of the Articles of the 1950 European Convention on Human Rights, which are statements of the fundamental rights and freedoms guaranteed by the Convention.

In summary these are:

Article 2 – Right to life

Article 3 – Prohibition on inhuman and degrading treatment

Article 4 – No slavery or forced labour

Article 5 – No unjustified detention

Article 6 – Right to fair hearing within a reasonable time to civil and criminal matters

Article 7 – No retrospective penalties for criminal offences

Article 8 – Right to respect for home life, privacy, the home and correspondence

Article 9 – Freedom of thought, conscience and religion

Article 10 – Right to freedom of expression

Article 11 – Right to freedom of assembly and association

Article 12 – Right to marry

Article 14 – No discrimination in relation to convention rights

First Protocol: Article 1 – Right to peaceful enjoyment of possessions

First Protocol: Article 2 – Right to education

First Protocol: Article 3 – Right to free elections

Fourth Protocol – No capital punishment

The Human Rights Act, 1998 specifies the way in which the convention rights are to be applied in the United Kingdom.

Key features of how the Human Rights Act, 2000 applies the convention in Scotland and the United Kingdom

- Interpretation – All legislation must be interpreted and applied, so far as it is possible to do so, in a way which is compatible with convention rights.

- Public authority duty – All public authorities must act in a way compatible with convention rights unless primary legislation (for example, Acts of Parliament) makes this impossible.

- Victim – Only a person or organisation who can show that they are a `victim' of a breach of a convention right may rely on the convention in legal proceedings.

- Remedies – A person or private organisation who can show that they are a `victim of a breach' by a public authority of a convention right may complain to the courts or raise that issue in the content of other legal proceedings.

- Power of the courts – If a court or tribunal finds that a breach of a convention right has taken place, it may make any order, within its powers, as it considers just and appropriate. This could involve an award of compensation to the `victim'. The court or tribunal cannot, however, overrule primary legislation; it may only make a declaration of `incompatibility'. It will then be up to the government to put amending legislation to the United Kingdom Parliament if it considers there are compelling reasons for doing so.

- European Convention on Human Rights case-law – Courts and tribunals, when considering any question involving a convention right, must take into account ECHR case-law.

- Limitation – A victim of an alleged breach of convention right must commence proceedings within one year of the alleged breach.

Scots Criminal Law

The Criminal Law of Scotland forms part of a hybrid legal system, which has over the centuries been developed from the concepts of the Great Scots Legal Writers, who were influenced by both Franco-Germanic and Anglo-American legal systems.

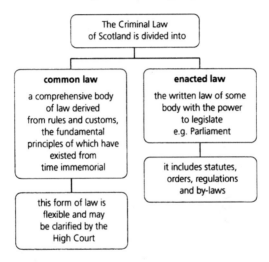

The Criminal Law of Scotland is divided into

common law

a comprehensive body of law derived from rules and customs, the fundamental principles of which have existed from time immemorial

this form of law is flexible and may be clarified by the High Court

enacted law

the written law of some body with the power to legislate e.g. Parliament

it includes statutes, orders, regulations and by-laws

Attempts at crimes/offences
Section 294 Criminal Procedure (Scotland) Act, 1995 states that: `An attempt to commit any crime or offence is itself a crime or offence.'

Criminal liability
Apart from certain immunities, everyone who breaches the Criminal Law of Scotland within the jurisdiction of the Scottish Courts is liable to punishment.

Examples of persons immune from punishment
The Sovereign, Foreign Sovereigns, Heads of Foreign States, certain members of diplomatic missions and certain representatives of Commonwealth countries and the Republic of Ireland.

Exceptions to criminal liability

- Non age – persons under the age of 8 years cannot be guilty of any crime of offence

- Insane persons

- Compulsion – persons compelled to commit crime by direct compulsion, or by threats of death or serious injury

- Non-insane automatism – the inability to form a guilty intention as a result of drugs being administered to the accused without his knowledge and which caused complete loss of self-control

Ignorance of the law will not justify the commission of any crime or offence, nor will the fact that a person committed one offence in an attempt to stop another be accepted as an excuse.

Guilty knowledge

Common law

The essence of all common law crimes is guilty knowledge or guilty intention. Very often this knowledge or intention is presumed from the facts.

Enacted law

Where an enactment imposes an absolute obligation the courts may punish the offender even if he had no guilty knowledge or intention. However, if the enactment uses the word 'knowingly' or a similar expression, guilty knowledge or intention must be proved.

Accession, aiding and abetting

An accessory is a person who aids the perpetrator of a crime with advice or assistance before or at the time of the crime or acts in concert by watching while a crime is committed.

An abettor is a person who incites, instigates, encourages or counsels another to commit a crime or offence.

The Common Law

Makes no distinction between commission and accession. Therefore an accessory or a person aiding or abetting may be convicted as a principal. Indeed an accessory or an abettor may be convicted of the crime even if the person who committed the crime escapes justice.

The Criminal Procedure (Scotland) Act, 1995 provides that a person may be convicted for a contravention of enacted law even if he was only art and part of the offence.

Apart from Treason – Scots Law does not recognise accession after the fact.

Evidence

Introduction
It is not the intention of this book to provide the reader with a comprehensive explanation of the law of evidence in Scotland. Our purpose is simply to briefly explain its meaning, admissibility, the onus of proof and the amount of proof.

Meaning and admissibility
Evidence literally means that which is evident or manifest or which supplies proof.

In *the legal sense* evidence denotes the means by which relevant facts are competently ascertained for judicial purposes.

In Scotland a person accused of a crime can only be convicted upon evidence which is legally admissible and which has been obtained in legal form. This means that only competent evidence will be admitted by the courts. Nevertheless, the rules of evidence in Scotland are flexible and very often one finds that evidence in one set of circumstances may be rejected in another.

The court alone decides what evidence in a particular set of circumstances is admissible. In reaching the decision the court will take into account:

- Fairness to the accused

- The gravity of the crime

- The seriousness or triviality of any irregularity

- The credibility of witnesses

- Relevance to the matter at issue

Onus of proof

Scots Law operates on the principle that an accused is innocent until proved guilty beyond all reasonable doubt. As a result, apart from a few statutory exceptions, the onus of proving guilt rests on the prosecution.

Therefore the prosecutor must satisfy the court beyond all reasonable doubt that:

- A crime or offence has been committed

- The charge against the accused is relevant

- The evidence is competent and sufficient

Where a prosecutor fails to prove one of these points the case against the accused will fail.

Amount of proof – Common Law

Under Scots Common Law, the evidence of a single witness, however credible, is not sufficient to prove such a charge against an accused or to establish any critical or material fact.

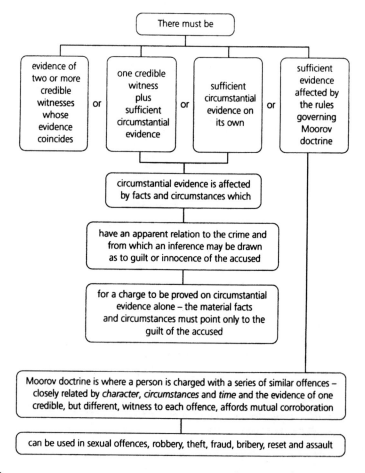

There must be

evidence of two or more credible witnesses whose evidence coincides

or

one credible witness plus sufficient circumstantial evidence

or

sufficient circumstantial evidence on its own

or

sufficient evidence affected by the rules governing Moorov doctrine

circumstantial evidence is affected by facts and circumstances which

have an apparent relation to the crime and from which an inference may be drawn as to guilt or innocence of the accused

for a charge to be proved on circumstantial evidence alone – the material facts and circumstances must point only to the guilt of the accused

Moorov doctrine is where a person is charged with a series of similar offences – closely related by *character*, *circumstances* and *time* and the evidence of one credible, but different, witness to each offence, affords mutual corroboration

can be used in sexual offences, robbery, theft, fraud, bribery, reset and assault

Amount of proof – Under statute

The common law principles relating to the amount of proof also apply to statutory offences *unless* the statute contravened contains a specific provision that the accused may be convicted on the evidence of one credible witness alone

in a case where the statute permits conviction on the evidence of one credible witness, it may happen that two witnesses are called and one contradicts the other. Nevertheless, a conviction can be obtained if the court believes the evidence of one witness

attention will be drawn to any statutory offence contained in this book which only requires one credible witness to convict

Powers of arrest

Common Law – Arrest without warrant

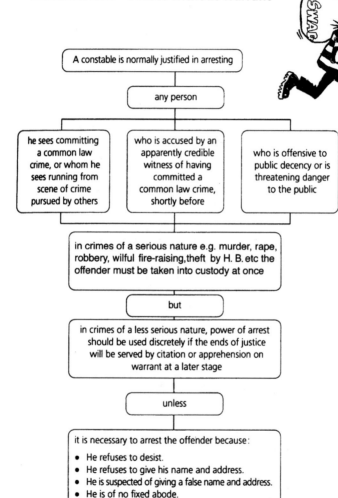

A constable is normally justified in arresting

any person

| he sees committing a common law crime, or whom he sees running from scene of crime pursued by others | who is accused by an apparently credible witness of having committed a common law crime, shortly before | who is offensive to public decency or is threatening danger to the public |

in crimes of a serious nature e.g. murder, rape, robbery, wilful fire-raising, theft by H. B. etc the offender must be taken into custody at once

but

in crimes of a less serious nature, power of arrest should be used discretely if the ends of justice will be served by citation or apprehension on warrant at a later stage

unless

it is necessary to arrest the offender because:

- He refuses to desist.
- He refuses to give his name and address.
- He is suspected of giving a false name and address.
- He is of no fixed abode.
- It is in his own interest or the interests of public safety.

Statutory power of arrest without warrant

Statutory powers of arrest vary considerably – much depends on the specific wording of the legislation contravened. Where an Act authorises a constable to arrest a 'person reasonably suspected of having committed the offence', this does not empower the officer to arrest any person merely because he bona fide suspects the person of having committed the offence. The constable must have reasonable suspicion before he can arrest. However, in general terms the powers of arrest granted by a statute will fall into one of the following categories:

- **Unconditional**
  A constable may arrest where the offender contravenes statute
- **Conditional**
  A constable may arrest only if the offender fails to comply with a specific request or condition of statute
- **Silent**
  The statute makes no reference to a power of arrest

Where a statute gives unconditional or conditional power of arrest it is recommended that arrest should only be exercised when it is in the interests of justice to do so. In cases of conditional powers of arrest where the specific request or condition contained in the statute is not breached by the offender or where the statute is silent, a constable may still arrest the offender if it is necessary to do so in the interests of justice (for example, the offender refuses to desist).

Passage of time
As a general rule the power of arrest without warrant weakens with the passage of time.

In minor crimes, arrest without warrant may be effected within an hour or two and in serious crimes possibly within a day or two, unless the interests of justice dictate otherwise. For example, the accused is in hiding, or he shows an intention to abscond or his identity cannot be established.

Use of force to arrest

Force should not be used to effect an arrest unless it is absolutely necessary to restrain the prisoner – then only the minimum force required may be used.

Arrest by plain clothes officers

An offender arrested by an officer in plain clothes must be informed immediately, if necessary, by production of a warrant card, that he is dealing with the police.

Arrest of HM Forces personnel

Where a member of HM Forces in uniform is arrested he should be conveyed in a closed vehicle to the police station and must not be marched through the streets.

Arrest under warrant

Where a constable is aware that a person is wanted on warrant, he may arrest that person, even when he is not in possession of the warrant. However, as soon as possible thereafter the warrant should be read to the accused.

A constable may effect entry to a house or building in order to enforce the provisions of an arrest warrant.

If admittance is refused, and the constable is **in actual possession of the arrest warrant** (does not apply to Extract Conviction and Means Enquiry Warrants) he may force entry to the premises and is not answerable for any damages caused in forcing entry even if the accused is not or has never been there. Before taking this action the constable must reveal his identity and state the nature of his business.

Assistance Given to the Police
When making an arrest, a constable may command the assistance of bystanders. It is not clear what penalty is at Common Law for failure or neglect to respond to the constable's request.
- Only make this request in extreme cases
- When requiring such assistance the request should be made in such a way that the person requested cannot later make the excuse that he thought the constable was making the request to someone else
- Remember that some people may not respond to the request through fear of injury and in such cases they might not be held liable if they summoned help from others or acted in a way which clearly showed that they were not helping the prisoner to escape

Citizen's Power of Arrest
At Common Law a private citizen has certain powers of arrest, but these must be exercised with care in order to avoid claims for damages in the event of a wrongful arrest.
- A private citizen should only exercise his power of arrest when the crime is a serious one and not merely for Breach of the Peace
- The private citizen affecting an arrest must be certain that an offence has been committed e.g. he witnessed the crime or was a victim of it

Forced entry should only be carried out as a last resort.

Arrest of persons under 16 years of age

CRIMINAL PROCEDURE (SCOTLAND) ACT, 1995

Age of criminal responsibility S 41

In Scotland the age of criminal responsibility is 8 years. Under that age a child cannot be guilty of a crime or offence. (Note: At the time of writing the Scottish Parliament is considering changing the age of criminal responsibility upwards.)

Arrest S 43

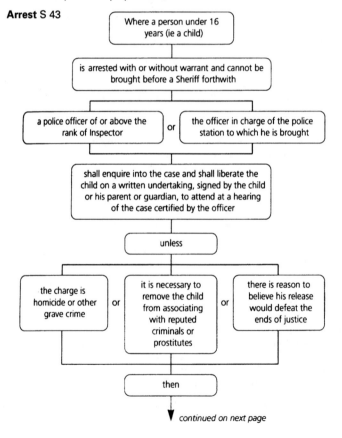

Where a person under 16 years (ie a child)

is arrested with or without warrant and cannot be brought before a Sheriff forthwith

a police officer of or above the rank of Inspector

or

the officer in charge of the police station to which he is brought

shall enquire into the case and shall liberate the child on a written undertaking, signed by the child or his parent or guardian, to attend at a hearing of the case certified by the officer

unless

the charge is homicide or other grave crime

or

it is necessary to remove the child from associating with reputed criminals or prostitutes

or

there is reason to believe his release would defeat the ends of justice

then

continued on next page

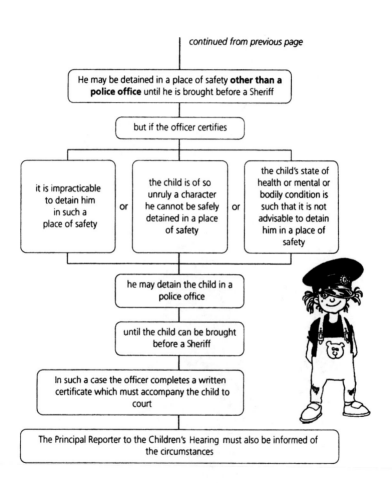

continued from previous page

He may be detained in a place of safety **other than a police office** until he is brought before a Sheriff

but if the officer certifies

| it is impracticable to detain him in such a place of safety | or | the child is of so unruly a character he cannot be safely detained in a place of safety | or | the child's state of health or mental or bodily condition is such that it is not advisable to detain him in a place of safety |

he may detain the child in a police office

until the child can be brought before a Sheriff

In such a case the officer completes a written certificate which must accompany the child to court

The Principal Reporter to the Children's Hearing must also be informed of the circumstances

Restrictions on prosecution of children

SECTION 42 CRIMINAL PROCEDURE (SCOTLAND) ACT, 1995

A child under 16 years cannot be prosecuted for any crime or offence except on the instructions of the Lord Advocate, or at his instance, and no courts other than the High Court and the Sheriff Courts, shall have jurisdiction over a child under 16 years.

Arrest – Police powers

Common Law

A person who has been arrested and is in custody

may be finger printed, etc without his consent and without warrant

See Section 18 on following page

may be required to take part in an identification parade without his consent and without warrant

should the prisoner decline, it is undesirable to use compulsion as this may make him conspicuous

in such cases it is possible to let witnesses see the prisoner, preferably along with others, but in the last resort on his own, in a place of detention

may be photographed, stripped of his clothing and subjected to search, and scrapings of his fingernails taken without his consent and without warrant

See Section 18 on following page

a warrant would be required for blood samples and for dental impressions, etc if the prisoner did not consent

Under statute
Section 18 Criminal Procedure (Scotland) Act, 1995 has supplemented the common law as follows:

• Where a person has been arrested and is in custody, a constable may take from that person fingerprints, palm prints and other such prints and impressions of an external part of the accused's body, as the constable may, having regard to the circumstances of the suspected offence, reasonably consider it appropriate to take

Note: These must be destroyed immediately if criminal proceedings are not instituted or at the conclusion of criminal proceedings unless the accused is convicted or is subject of an Absolute Discharge order or Probation order.

• An Inspector or above may authorise the taking of:
   a) hair from an external part of the body, by means of cutting or combing a sample of hair or other material
   b) a sample of nail or other material from a fingernail, toenail or from under such nails
   c) from an external part of the body, by means of swabbing or rubbing a sample of blood or other body fluid, of body tissue or of other material, from an accused person in custody

• A constable may use reasonable force in exercising the above mentioned powers

• Nothing in Section 18 shall prejudice:
   a) any power of search
   b) any power to take possession of evidence where there is imminent danger of it being lost or destroyed
   c) any power to take prints, impressions or samples under the authority of a warrant

Note: The provisions of Section 18 also apply to persons detained under Section 14 Criminal Procedure (Scotland) Act, 1995.

Rights of person under arrest

SECTION 15 AND 17 CRIMINAL PROCEDURE (SCOTLAND) ACT, 1995

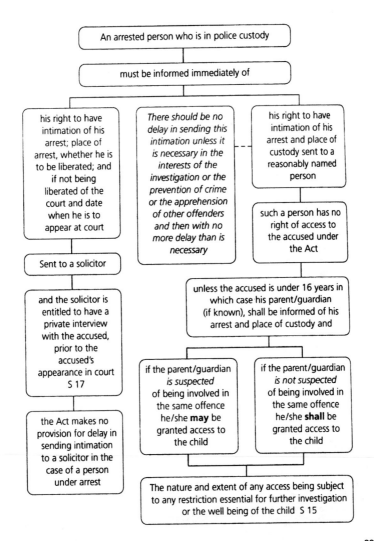

An arrested person who is in police custody

must be informed immediately of

his right to have intimation of his arrest; place of arrest, whether he is to be liberated; and if not being liberated of the court and date when he is to appear at court

There should be no delay in sending this intimation unless it is necessary in the interests of the investigation or the prevention of crime or the apprehension of other offenders and then with no more delay than is necessary

his right to have intimation of his arrest and place of custody sent to a reasonably named person

such a person has no right of access to the accused under the Act

Sent to a solicitor

and the solicitor is entitled to have a private interview with the accused, prior to the accused's appearance in court S 17

the Act makes no provision for delay in sending intimation to a solicitor in the case of a person under arrest

unless the accused is under 16 years in which case his parent/guardian (if known), shall be informed of his arrest and place of custody and

if the parent/guardian *is suspected* of being involved in the same offence he/she **may** be granted access to the child

if the parent/guardian *is not suspected* of being involved in the same offence he/she **shall** be granted access to the child

The nature and extent of any access being subject to any restriction essential for further investigation or the well being of the child S 15

Duty of suspect and witness to identify themselves

SECTION 13 CRIMINAL PROCEDURE (SCOTLAND) ACT, 1995

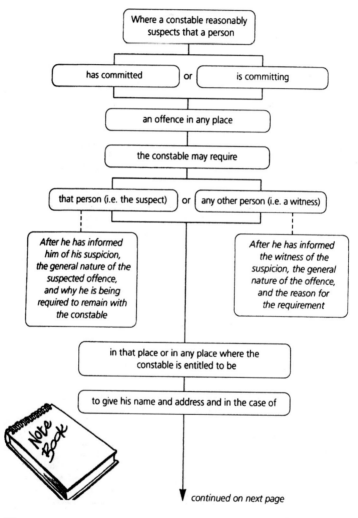

Where a constable reasonably suspects that a person

has committed | or | is committing

an offence in any place

the constable may require

that person (i.e. the suspect) | or | any other person (i.e. a witness)

After he has informed him of his suspicion, the general nature of the suspected offence, and why he is being required to remain with the constable

After he has informed the witness of the suspicion, the general nature of the offence, and the reason for the requirement

in that place or in any place where the constable is entitled to be

to give his name and address and in the case of

continued on next page

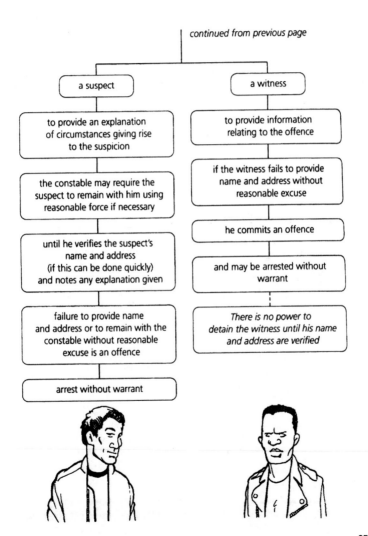

continued from previous page

a suspect

a witness

to provide an explanation of circumstances giving rise to the suspicion

to provide information relating to the offence

the constable may require the suspect to remain with him using reasonable force if necessary

if the witness fails to provide name and address without reasonable excuse

until he verifies the suspect's name and address (if this can be done quickly) and notes any explanation given

he commits an offence

and may be arrested without warrant

failure to provide name and address or to remain with the constable without reasonable excuse is an offence

There is no power to detain the witness until his name and address are verified

arrest without warrant

Detention of a suspect

SECTION 14 CRIMINAL PROCEDURE (SCOTLAND) ACT, 1995

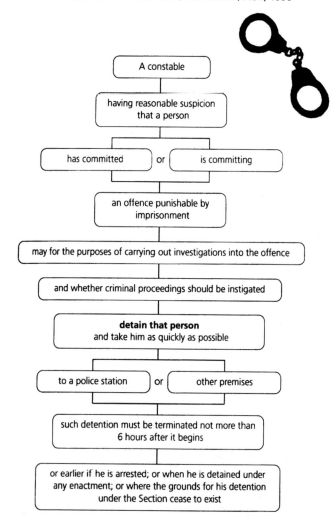

A constable

having reasonable suspicion that a person

has committed   or   is committing

an offence punishable by imprisonment

may for the purposes of carrying out investigations into the offence

and whether criminal proceedings should be instigated

detain that person
and take him as quickly as possible

to a police station   or   other premises

such detention must be terminated not more than 6 hours after it begins

or earlier if he is arrested; or when he is detained under any enactment; or where the grounds for his detention under the Section cease to exist

A suspect detained under Section 14 may not be detained again on the same grounds or on any grounds arising from the same circumstances.

Information given to suspect and notes to be made

SECTION 14 CRIMINAL PROCEDURE (SCOTLAND) ACT, 1995

When a person is detained under Section 14 the constable must inform him:

- Of his suspicion

- The general nature of the offence in question

- The reason for the detention

The constable shall record:

- The place where the detention begins, the police station or other premises where suspect is taken

- Any other place to which suspect is taken during his detention

- The general nature of the suspected offence

- The time when detention begins, the time of arrival at the police station or other premises

- The time the suspect is informed of his rights and the identity of the officer informing him of his rights

- Where the suspect requests a solicitor or that a reasonably named person be informed, the time the request is made and the time when the request is complied with

- The time of the suspect's release from detention and/or of his arrest

Suspects – Police powers

SECTION 14 AND 18 CRIMINAL PROCEDURE (SCOTLAND) ACT, 1995

A constable may:

- Without prejudice to any relevant rule of law regarding the admissibility in evidence of any answers given put questions to the suspect in relation to the suspected offence. S 14

- Search the suspect S 14

- Use reasonable force, if necessary to detain the suspect and/or search him S 14

- Take fingerprints, palm prints and such other prints and impressions from external parts of the suspect's body as may be considered reasonably necessary S 18

- On the authority of an Inspector or above, take hair samples from an external part of suspect's body; samples of fingernails and toenails; and from an external part of suspect's body, by means of swabbing or rubbing samples of blood, other body fluids, tissues and so on. S 18

Note 1: Reasonable force may be used to obtain fingerprints and samples detailed in Section 18.

Note 2: If no criminal proceedings are instituted against a person detained under Section 14, all prints and impressions taken from the suspect must be destroyed immediately following the decision not to institute proceedings.

Detainee's obligations

A suspect detained under Section 14 is under no obligation to answer any question other than provide his name and address and must be informed of this both at the time of his detention and on arrival at the police station or other premises. S 14 (a)

A suspect detained under Section 14 is under no obligation to take part in an identification parade, but if he consents the police are entitled to hold a parade.

Detainee's rights

SECTION 15 CRIMINAL PROCEDURE (SCOTLAND) ACT, 1995

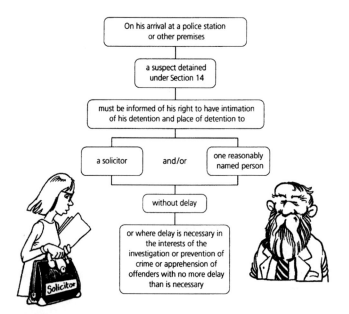

On his arrival at a police station or other premises

a suspect detained under Section 14

must be informed of his right to have intimation of his detention and place of detention to

a solicitor — and/or — one reasonably named person

without delay

or where delay is necessary in the interests of the investigation or prevention of crime or apprehension of offenders with no more delay than is necessary

Note 1: In the case of a detainee requesting that a solicitor be informed, it should be noted that the solicitor has no right of access to the detainee during the detention.

Note 2: The reasonably named person has no right of access to an adult detainee during the period of detention.

*Note 3: Where the detainee is under 16 years of age his parent or guardian, if known, must be informed of the child's detention and if the parent/guardian is reasonably suspected of having been involved in the same offence, he/she **may** be permitted access to the child; and in any other case the parent/guardian **shall** be permitted access to the child.*

Note 4: The nature and access to the child being subject to any restriction essential to the furtherance of the investigation or the well being of the child.

Questioning suspects/accused persons

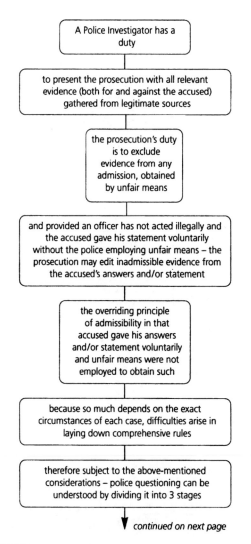

A Police Investigator has a duty

to present the prosecution with all relevant evidence (both for and against the accused) gathered from legitimate sources

the prosecution's duty is to exclude evidence from any admission, obtained by unfair means

and provided an officer has not acted illegally and the accused gave his statement voluntarily without the police employing unfair means – the prosecution may edit inadmissible evidence from the accused's answers and/or statement

the overriding principle of admissibility in that accused gave his answers and/or statement voluntarily and unfair means were not employed to obtain such

because so much depends on the exact circumstances of each case, difficulties arise in laying down comprehensive rules

therefore subject to the above-mentioned considerations – police questioning can be understood by dividing it into 3 stages

continued on next page

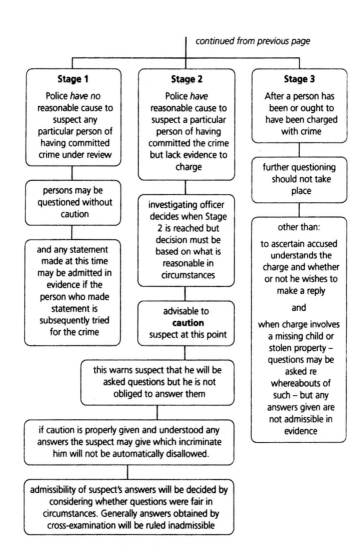

continued from previous page

Stage 1

Police *have no* reasonable cause to suspect any particular person of having committed crime under review

persons may be questioned without caution

and any statement made at this time may be admitted in evidence if the person who made statement is subsequently tried for the crime

Stage 2

Police *have* reasonable cause to suspect a particular person of having committed the crime but lack evidence to charge

investigating officer decides when Stage 2 is reached but decision must be based on what is reasonable in circumstances

advisable to **caution** suspect at this point

Stage 3

After a person has been or ought to have been charged with crime

further questioning should not take place

other than:

to ascertain accused understands the charge and whether or not he wishes to make a reply

and

when charge involves a missing child or stolen property – questions may be asked re whereabouts of such – but any answers given are not admissible in evidence

this warns suspect that he will be asked questions but he is not obliged to answer them

if caution is properly given and understood any answers the suspect may give which incriminate him will not be automatically disallowed.

admissibility of suspect's answers will be decided by considering whether questions were fair in circumstances. Generally answers obtained by cross-examination will be ruled inadmissible

Voluntary statements from accused persons

You will have read previously the limitations imposed on police questioning of an accused once Stage 3 is reached. Nevertheless, this does not prevent the police from obtaining a voluntary statement from an accused who expresses a wish to provide such of his own free will. The following is a general guide to the taking of Voluntary Statements. However, you should always consult your Force Instructions on this matter.

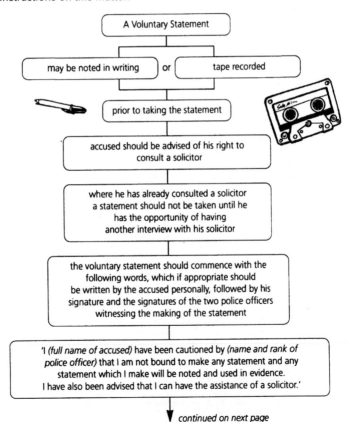

A Voluntary Statement

may be noted in writing | or | tape recorded

prior to taking the statement

accused should be advised of his right to consult a solicitor

where he has already consulted a solicitor a statement should not be taken until he has the opportunity of having another interview with his solicitor

the voluntary statement should commence with the following words, which if appropriate should be written by the accused personally, followed by his signature and the signatures of the two police officers witnessing the making of the statement

'I *(full name of accused)* have been cautioned by *(name and rank of police officer)* that I am not bound to make any statement and any statement which I make will be noted and used in evidence. I have also been advised that I can have the assistance of a solicitor.'

continued on next page

continued from previous page

the accused should conclude the above by indicating one of the following:

- I do not wish the assistance of a solicitor at present
- I have had the assistance of a solicitor and I do not wish him to be present
- I have had the assistance of a solicitor who is now present

the accused's statement then follows

this may be written by the accused or one of the police officers present

the police are not permitted to question the accused other than to clarify points of ambiguity

at the conclusion of the statement the accused should be allowed to read it and insert any corrections he may wish to make

where he does not read it, it should be read to him and any corrections he wishes should be made

the following words should then be added at the end of the statement: 'This statement, written on this and previous pages *(insert numbers of previous pages)* has been read by me (or where appropriate) read over to me and I do not wish to make any changes (except those noted and signed by me on pages...)'

the accused should then sign the statement as should the two police witnesses. A record should also be kept of the times when the statement commences and is concluded

Fairness to accused/suspect

It must always be shown that the police were fair in their dealings with an accused or suspect. The following gives some indication of the standard of fairness the courts will require:

- When a person under 16 is arrested – his parent or guardian should be given the opportunity to accompany him to the police station – otherwise any voluntary statement provided by the accused may be ruled as having been unfairly obtained

- Always consider using solicitors, social workers and so on as independent witnesses when obtaining a voluntary statement from accused persons who are children or mentally handicapped adults, as the courts may take the view that such persons were unable to properly understand their rights, and therefore their statements were unfairly obtained

- When an accused represented by a solicitor is detained in prison, the police must communicate with him only via his solicitor

- Where an accused is a foreigner and cannot speak English or has limited command of the English language, he should be informed of his right to legal advice and be cautioned and charged through an interpreter. (This principle should also be used when dealing with persons who are deaf or mute.)

- Prolonged questioning of a person under 16, even in the presence of a parent/guardian, may be held by the court to be unfair

- Failure to allow an accused to have a private interview with his solicitor may so prejudice his defence that it would be contrary to justice to try and convict him

Search of persons

Powers of search at Common Law

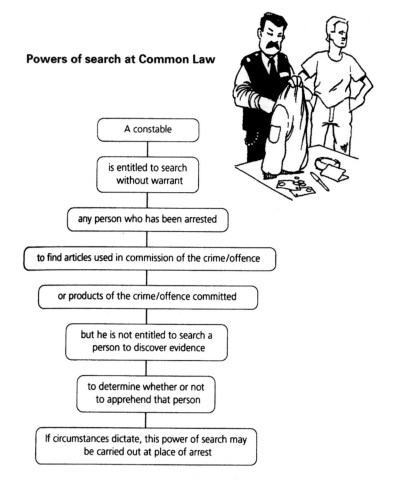

A constable

is entitled to search without warrant

any person who has been arrested

to find articles used in commission of the crime/offence

or products of the crime/offence committed

but he is not entitled to search a person to discover evidence

to determine whether or not to apprehend that person

If circumstances dictate, this power of search may be carried out at place of arrest

Note: Section 60 Civic Government (Scotland) Act, 1982 supplements the common law and permits a constable, having reasonable suspicion that a person is in possession of stolen property, to search that person, and so on.

Searching prisoners

A prisoner arrested for a crime of dishonesty or on suspicion of having committed a crime of dishonesty should be searched as soon as possible after his arrest. However, this should not be done in public view nor until a credible witness is present to provide corroboration.

Searches should be thorough, and tact should be used. Females should not be searched by a male and vice versa.

Search of buildings, and so on

Power of search at Common Law

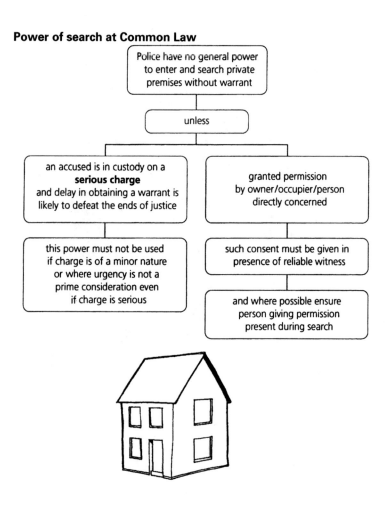

Police have no general power to enter and search private premises without warrant

unless

an accused is in custody on a **serious charge** and delay in obtaining a warrant is likely to defeat the ends of justice

granted permission by owner/occupier/person directly concerned

this power must not be used if charge is of a minor nature or where urgency is not a prime consideration even if charge is serious

such consent must be given in presence of reliable witness

and where possible ensure person giving permission present during search

Entry into buildings, and so on

Power of entry at Common Law

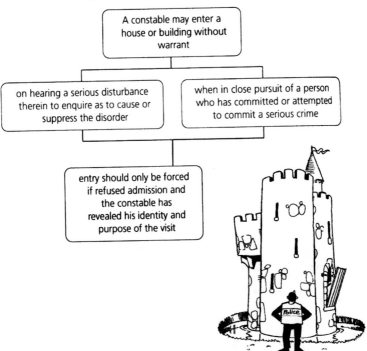

A constable may enter a house or building without warrant

on hearing a serious disturbance therein to enquire as to cause or suppress the disorder

when in close pursuit of a person who has committed or attempted to commit a serious crime

entry should only be forced if refused admission and the constable has revealed his identity and purpose of the visit

Statutory powers

Police powers of entry into premises under statute without warrant are determined by specific statutes. However, generally speaking, only Section 60 Civic Government (Scotland) Act, 1982 and Section 30 Fire Services Act, 1947 give the police power to actually force entry to premises without warrant, when they have been refused entry.

Search warrants

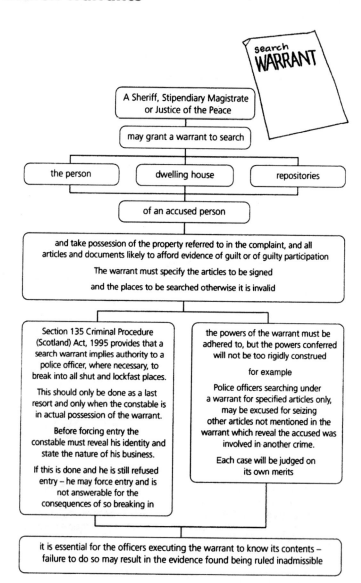

search
WARRANT

A Sheriff, Stipendiary Magistrate or Justice of the Peace

may grant a warrant to search

the person | dwelling house | repositories

of an accused person

and take possession of the property referred to in the complaint, and all articles and documents likely to afford evidence of guilt or of guilty participation

The warrant must specify the articles to be signed

and the places to be searched otherwise it is invalid

Section 135 Criminal Procedure (Scotland) Act, 1995 provides that a search warrant implies authority to a police officer, where necessary, to break into all shut and lockfast places.

This should only be done as a last resort and only when the constable is in actual possession of the warrant.

Before forcing entry the constable must reveal his identity and state the nature of his business.

If this is done and he is still refused entry – he may force entry and is not answerable for the consequences of so breaking in

the powers of the warrant must be adhered to, but the powers conferred will not be too rigidly construed

for example

Police officers searching under a warrant for specified articles only, may be excused for seizing other articles not mentioned in the warrant which reveal the accused was involved in another crime.

Each case will be judged on its own merits

it is essential for the officers executing the warrant to know its contents – failure to do so may result in the evidence found being ruled inadmissible

Bail conditions

SECTION 24 CRIMINAL PROCEDURE (SCOTLAND) ACT, 1995
(AS AMENDED BY THE BAIL, JUDICIAL APPOINTMENTS ETC
(SCOTLAND) ACT, 2000)

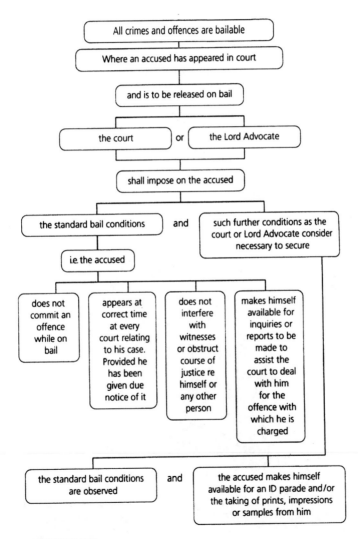

All crimes and offences are bailable

Where an accused has appeared in court

and is to be released on bail

the court   or   the Lord Advocate

shall impose on the accused

the standard bail conditions   and   such further conditions as the court or Lord Advocate consider necessary to secure

i.e. the accused

| does not commit an offence while on bail | appears at correct time at every court relating to his case. Provided he has been given due notice of it | does not interfere with witnesses or obstruct course of justice re himself or any other person | makes himself available for inquiries or reports to be made to assist the court to deal with him for the offence with which he is charged |

the standard bail conditions are observed   and   the accused makes himself available for an ID parade and/or the taking of prints, impressions or samples from him

Breach of bail conditions

SECTION 27 CRIMINAL PROCEDURE (SCOTLAND) ACT, 1995

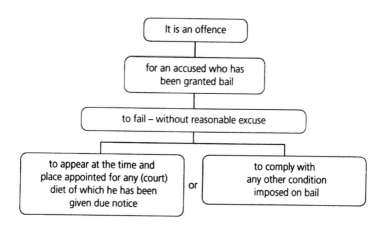

It is an offence

for an accused who has been granted bail

to fail – without reasonable excuse

to appear at the time and place appointed for any (court) diet of which he has been given due notice

or

to comply with any other condition imposed on bail

Breach of bail – police powers

SECTION 28 CRIMINAL PROCEDURE (SCOTLAND) ACT, 1995

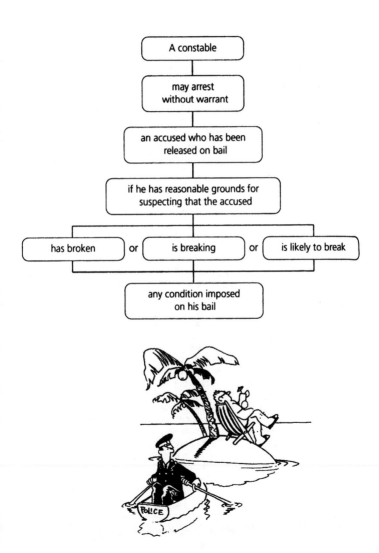

A constable

may arrest without warrant

an accused who has been released on bail

if he has reasonable grounds for suspecting that the accused

has broken or is breaking or is likely to break

any condition imposed on his bail

Powers of arrest – cross-border

SECTION 137 JUSTICE AND PUBLIC ORDER ACT, 1994

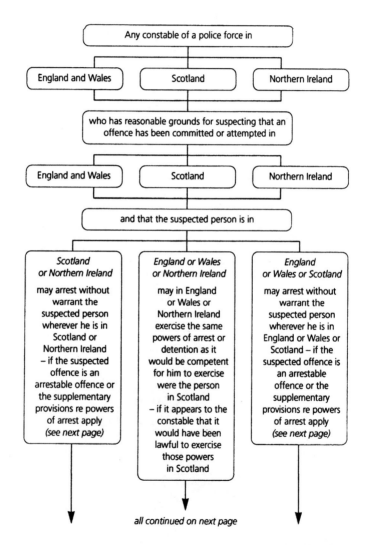

Any constable of a police force in

| England and Wales | Scotland | Northern Ireland |

who has reasonable grounds for suspecting that an offence has been committed or attempted in

| England and Wales | Scotland | Northern Ireland |

and that the suspected person is in

Scotland or Northern Ireland

may arrest without warrant the suspected person wherever he is in Scotland or Northern Ireland – if the suspected offence is an arrestable offence or the supplementary provisions re powers of arrest apply *(see next page)*

England or Wales or Northern Ireland

may in England or Wales or Northern Ireland exercise the same powers of arrest or detention as it would be competent for him to exercise were the person in Scotland – if it appears to the constable that it would have been lawful to exercise those powers in Scotland

England or Wales or Scotland

may arrest without warrant the suspected person wherever he is in England or Wales or Scotland – if the suspected offence is an arrestable offence or the supplementary provisions re powers of arrest apply *(see next page)*

all continued on next page

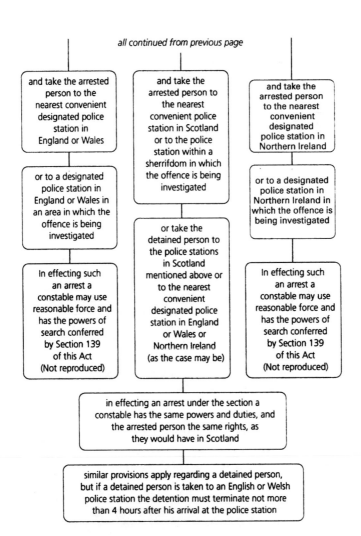

all continued from previous page

and take the arrested person to the nearest convenient designated police station in England or Wales

or to a designated police station in England or Wales in an area in which the offence is being investigated

In effecting such an arrest a constable may use reasonable force and has the powers of search conferred by Section 139 of this Act (Not reproduced)

and take the arrested person to the nearest convenient police station in Scotland or to the police station within a sherrifdom in which the offence is being investigated

or take the detained person to the police stations in Scotland mentioned above or to the nearest convenient designated police station in England or Wales or Northern Ireland (as the case may be)

and take the arrested person to the nearest convenient designated police station in Northern Ireland

or to a designated police station in Northern Ireland in which the offence is being investigated

In effecting such an arrest a constable may use reasonable force and has the powers of search conferred by Section 139 of this Act (Not reproduced)

in effecting an arrest under the section a constable has the same powers and duties, and the arrested person the same rights, as they would have in Scotland

similar provisions apply regarding a detained person, but if a detained person is taken to an English or Welsh police station the detention must terminate not more than 4 hours after his arrival at the police station

Supplementary provisions: powers of arrest

SECTION 138 CRIMINAL JUSTICE AND PUBLIC ORDER ACT, 1994

Identity	That the name of the relevant person is unknown to, and cannot be readily ascertained by, the constable; or
	that the constable has reasonable grounds for doubting whether a name furnished by the relevant person is his real name

Address for Service	That the relevant person has failed to furnish a satisfactory address for service; or
	the constable has reasonable grounds for doubting whether an address furnished by the relevant person is a satisfactory address for service.
	'Satisfactory for Service' means that the relevant person will be at that address sufficiently long to serve a summons; or that some other specified person will accept service for him

Preventative Measures	That the constable has reasonable grounds for believing that arrest is necessary to prevent that relevant person
	causing physical injury to himself or any other person.
	Suffering physical injury.
	Causing loss of or damage to property.
	Committing an offence against public decency where members of the public could not be expected to avoid him.
	Causing an unlawful obstruction of the highway or road.

Protection	That the constable has reasonable grounds for believing that arrest is necessary to protect a child or other vulnerable person from the relevant person

CHAPTER 2
Crime

Theft

Theft at Common Law

Definition

Theft is the taking and appropriating of property without the consent of its rightful owner or other lawful authority.

Essentials

- Dishonest intent to deprive owner

- Appropriation to the thief's use

Where property is taken under a claim of right made in good faith or under a reasonable belief that owner had granted permission – it is not theft.

Gain and deprivation

In theft the taking need not be for the sake of gain. The essence of the crime is the intent to deprive the owner of property in the knowledge that this is wrongful.

The deprivation need only be temporary, and subsequent return of the property does not cancel out the crime.

Meaning of property

The thing taken must be the property of another and be capable of appropriation. For example, a wild animal cannot be stolen unless it has been killed, caught or confined so as to be under the control of the possessor.

Property includes the dead bodies of humans prior to burial and children under the age of puberty (girls under 12 years, boys under 14 years). In the case of children under the age of puberty being abducted/stolen this form of theft is known as **plagium**.

Property that has been abandoned, falls to the Crown and is therefore capable of being stolen. However, in the case of Kane v Friel 1997 – two brothers were found crossing waste ground: one was carrying a sink, the other had lengths of copper piping in a bag. When questioned, they stated that they had found the items and were going to a local scrap merchant to try to sell them for £10. It was held on appeal that they were not guilty of theft since they could have thought the property had been abandoned. The court decided that there was no justification for inferring that the appellant must have known that the items were property which someone intended to retain: the appellants had not lied about the property or where they had found it when questioned, and there was nothing about the condition or value of the property from which dishonest intention could be inferred. Lost property may also be stolen where the finder, knowing who the owner is, appropriates the property. If the finder does not know who the owner is, it is not theft unless he appropriates it forthwith or within a short period. A finder who fails to report or hand over found property to the police, without reasonable excuse (but has no intent to thieve), commits an offence under Section 67 Civic Government (Scotland) Act 1982.

Meaning of owner

It is immaterial to whom the property belongs, whether the Crown, a society, club, corporation, company or an individual, or even to some person unknown.

Use of violence

If a thief obtains property without violence then uses violence in an effort to retain it, he would commit theft and assault rather than robbery. Plagium accompanied by violence to the child, is theft (and assault on the child), but not robbery as the force is not used towards the person possessing the child.

Removal of property

In theft there must not only be the taking, but also the removal of property, from its place of keeping. Theft is complete whenever the thief has obtained complete possession of the property, even though this may be only for an instant. (See case of Carmichael v Black and Prenrice 1992 later in this chapter, where actual physical removal is not required.)

Recent possession

Theft may be proved where it is shown property was stolen and a short time later it was traced to the possession of the accused, without him being able to give a reasonable explanation of his possession.

Clandestine possession (common law)

Clandestinely taking possession of and using another person's property in the knowledge that the owner has not given permission and would not have given permission is a crime at common law but is not theft.

Taking motor vehicles without authority
(Statutory clandestine possession)
SECTION 178 ROAD TRAFFIC ACT, 1988

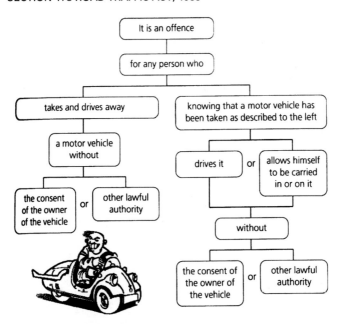

An offence under Section 178 may only be committed in respect of motor vehicles (such as mechanically propelled vehicles intended or adapted for use on the roads). A person who takes and drives away a mechanically propelled vehicle (not intended or adapted for use on the roads) without the consent of the owner and so on would commit theft or clandestine possession.

A constable may arrest without warrant any person he reasonably suspects of having committed or having attempted to commit this offence.

Note 1: An accused who proves he acted in the reasonable belief that he had lawful authority or that the owner of the motor vehicle would, in the circumstances, have given consent if he had been asked for it, shall not be convicted.

Note 2: Section 178 is generally intended to deal with cases where motor vehicles are taken, driven away and then abandoned. If, however, the vehicle were abandoned in a place where it is unlikely to be found, the offender may be held to have committed theft, rather than a contravention of Section 178.

Note 3: Where the police trace the vehicle, while still in the possession of the person(s) who took and drove it away without authority, it is normal to charge the offender(s) with theft, rather than a contravention of Section 178. However, the final decision as to the charge rests with the Procurator Fiscal.

Recent developments in the law of theft

On page 5 we discussed the flexible nature of Scots Common Law. In recent years the law of theft has been extended by the courts into areas previously regarded as civil law disputes. This is clearly demonstrated in the following cases, where it has been decided that temporary appropriation for a nefarious purpose is theft.

Milne v Tudhope 1981

In this case, a builder, carrying out work on a house on a fixed-price contract, refused to carry out remedial work without further payment, and removed parts of the house without consent of the owner, informing the owner that he would not return them unless he received more money.

Held: The builder was guilty of theft on the grounds that clandestine (that is, a secretive) taking, aimed at achieving a nefarious purpose, constitutes theft, even if the taker intended all along to return the thing when his purpose was achieved.

Kidston v Annon 1984

In this case, the owner of a television set handed over the set to a TV repairer for the purpose of estimating the cost of repair. The repairer exceeded his instructions and repaired the TV without authority. He then refused to return the TV to its owner unless he received payment for the repair.

Held: The repairer was convicted of theft. He appealed and the High Court, disallowing the appeal, held that he was holding the TV set to ransom and was therefore guilty of theft.

Carmichael v Black and Prenrice 1992

In this case the two accused were employed to place wheel clamps on cars that were parked in a private car park without authority. They also attached notices on the cars stating that a levy of £45 would be charged for the release of the vehicle. The accused were convicted of theft and extortion.

Held on appeal: The purpose and effect of the wheel clamping was to immobilise the vehicles and deprive their owners of the possession and use of their vehicles. The physical element of appropriation was present and there was no need for physical removal of the vehicle, as deliberate appropriation in the knowledge of its consequence was sufficient to prove theft. The High Court also rejected the accuseds' appeal against their convictions for extortion.

Attempt to steal

Although theft cannot be completed unless the thief obtains possession of property, an attempt to commit the crime may be proved independently of any transfer of property, or indeed, of there being any property to transfer. For example, a pickpocket putting his hand into an empty pocket with the intention of stealing commits the crime of attempted theft.

Aggravations of theft

Housebreaking

Is not by itself a crime – there must be in addition an intention to steal. In the case of H.M.A. v Forbes 1994 – Forbes was charged with "housebreaking with intent to commit rape". The court held that, with the exception of housebreaking with intent to commit theft, it was not a crime to break into premises for the purpose of crime but that such circumstances could be charged as an attempt to commit that crime.

Note: The term 'house' applies to any dwelling house and any other roofed building, finished or unfinished, or to any part of a building used as a separate dwelling, which is secured against intrusion by unauthorised persons.

Theft by housebreaking

Occurs whenever the security of a 'house' is overcome and an article is abstracted or removed for the purpose of being carried off. The thief need not physically enter the building, the theft is complete, for example, if he draws an article towards him with an implement even though he does not lay hands on the article.

Housebreaking with intent to steal

Occurs when a person breaks into a 'house' with the intention of stealing property from therein. The felonious purpose is inferred from the circumstances in which the building was entered.

Attempted housebreaking with intent to steal

Occurs when a person attempts to break into a 'house' with the intention of stealing property. The felonious intent is inferred from the circumstances.

Modes of entry

Housebreaking takes place whenever the security of a 'house' is overcome and entry is effected by what is not the usual or intended means of entry; for example:

- Opening a secured outer door by force or with a false key or a true key dishonestly obtained

- Forcing, raising or opening a window, but not simply entering by means of a ground floor window – which has been left open and requires no further raising or opening to gain entry

- An arrangement with an inmate of a 'house' who leaves it insecure

- Tampering with the fastening while within a 'house' and returning later and obtaining entry

- Ringing a door bell, for example, and rushing in or forcing way past person opening door

- Any unusual method of entry, for example climbing down a chimney or crawling through a sewer

Opening lockfast places

Like housebreaking, opening lockfast places is not a substantive crime – it must be accompanied by either theft or an intention to steal.

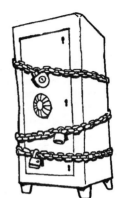

Lockfast places

Includes rooms, cupboards, drawers, safes, desks, cash-boxes, show-cases and any other receptacle the contents of which are protected by lock and key.

Theft by opening lockfast places

Is committed when security of the lockfast place is overcome and the contents are stolen.

Opening lockfast places with intent to steal

Is committed when the security of the lockfast place is overcome with the intention of stealing. Guilty intention is inferred from the circumstances.

Attempted opening lockfast places with intent to steal

Is committed when a person attempts to force entry to a lockfast place with the intention of stealing. Guily intention is inferred from the circumstances.

Note: It is not theft by opening lockfast places to steal the lockfast receptacle from its place of keeping and break into elsewhere. In such cases the charge would simply be theft of the receptacle and its contents.

Association with housebreaking

Frequently a theft from a lockfast place is associated with a housebreaking; in such cases, the crime committed would be theft by housebreaking and opening lockfast places.

Theft under statute

Theft of mail
Any person stealing mail in the course of postage commits an offence under the Post Office Act, 1953.

Theft of gas and electricity
May be prosecuted under the Gas Act, 1986 in the case of gas and under the Electricity Act, 1989 in the case of electricity. However, the common practice is to prosecute offenders for theft at common law.

Venue
SECTION 11 CRIMINAL PROCEDURE (SCOTLAND) ACT, 1995 AND CLAUSE 5 IRISH FREE STATE (CONSEQUENTIAL ADAPTATION OF ENACTMENTS) ORDER 1923

A person who is in possession, in Scotland, of property stolen elsewhere in the United Kingdom or in the Republic of Ireland may be tried and punished in a Scots Court.

Theft and other crimes of dishonesty
SCHEDULE 3 CRIMINAL PROCEDURE (SCOTLAND) ACT, 1995

A person charged with theft may be convicted of reset, embezzlement or fraud, and a person charged with embezzlement, fraud or robbery may be convicted of theft.

Common law power of arrest applies to common law theft, attempted theft and their aggravations.

Breach of Trust and Embezzlement

A crime at common law. This crime is generally referred to as embezzlement.

Definition
Embezzlement is the dishonest appropriation of property entrusted to the accused with certain powers of management or control.

An accused must have received either:

- Limited ownership of the property; or

- Actual possession of the property with a liability to account for it to the owner

Usual mode of commission
Normally embezzlement is regarded as a white-collar crime committed by persons such as company treasurers, solicitors, factors and public officials who feloniously appropriate money entrusted to them in their official capacities. Frequently the crime is accompanied by false entries or omissions in books or documents. However, the crime is complete as soon as appropriation takes place, whether or not books contain false entries.

Distinction between embezzlement and theft
In cases where limited ownership is conferred by loan or hire, it is often hard to determine whether theft or embezzlement is committed when property is dishonestly taken.

The test you should apply is:

- **Embezzlement** is committed where property on loan or hire for an indefinite period and not for a specified purpose is feloniously appropriated by the limited owner.

- **Theft** is committed where property on loan or hire:
  a) for a limited purpose and for a specified purpose; or
  b) for a limited purpose without specification of purpose, is appropriated after the date fixed by the owner for return of his property

Hire purchase

Theft takes place when the hirer appropriates the property immediately or soon after it is received. However, where the hirer does not appropriate the property until after a considerable amount of time has elapsed and a considerable part of the price has been paid, the crime is embezzlement.

Scots Law

Contains provisions for a person charged with embezzlement to be convicted of theft and vice versa.

COMMON LAW
POWER OF
ARREST

Fraud

Fraud at common law
There is no succinct definition to embrace all the criminal forms of cheating. However, if the following three elements are present in a cheat the crime of fraud is complete.

Falsehood
False representations by words, or writing or conduct.

Fraud
Intention to deceive or defraud.

Wilful imposition
The cheat designed has been successful to the extent of gaining benefit or advantage, or of prejudicing or tending to prejudice the interests of another person.

Most common modes of commission

Goods – Board and Lodging Frauds	Personation	Inferior Goods
These occur where a person pretends to be a bona-fide customer of good credit and obtains goods or board and lodgings without paying or intending to pay	Fraud is committed by impersonating another or by falsely assuming a certain position or status in order to obtain gain, benefit or advantage	It is fraud, if a seller with intent to cheat or defraud a buyer, delivers as the article purchased or selected an article inferior in quality to, and less in volume than such article

Goods must be obtained by False Representation to obtain goods without false representations and then tender a worthless cheque, knowing it to be worthless is not fraud

Accused need not gain
In order to establish a fraud, it is not necessary for an accused to gain or for a victim of the fraud to have suffered a loss. A fraud will be complete when a definite practical result is achieved.

Attempted fraud
Where a fraudulent scheme is carried into effect by an overt act (such as there is a falsehood and a fraud) but no wilful imposition is achieved, the crime committed is attempted fraud.

Scots Law
Contains provisions to allow for a person charged with fraud to be convicted of theft or vice versa.

> COMMON LAW
> POWER OF
> ARREST

Forgery and Uttering

Definition at common law

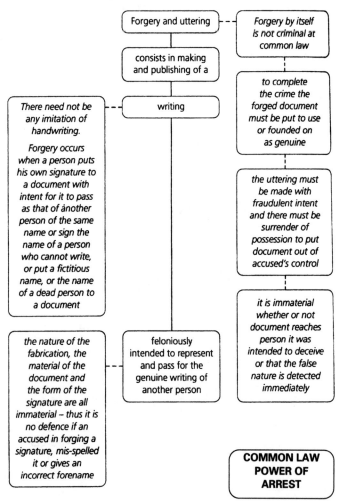

Forgery and uttering - - Forgery by itself is not criminal at common law

consists in making and publishing of a

writing

There need not be any imitation of handwriting.

Forgery occurs when a person puts his own signature to a document with intent for it to pass as that of another person of the same name or sign the name of a person who cannot write, or put a fictitious name, or the name of a dead person to a document

to complete the crime the forged document must be put to use or founded on as genuine

the uttering must be made with fraudulent intent and there must be surrender of possession to put document out of accused's control

the nature of the fabrication, the material of the document and the form of the signature are all immaterial – thus it is no defence if an accused in forging a signature, mis-spelled it or gives an incorrect forename

feloniously intended to represent and pass for the genuine writing of another person

it is immaterial whether or not document reaches person it was intended to deceive or that the false nature is detected immediately

COMMON LAW POWER OF ARREST

Modes of Forgery

Examples of how forgery may be committed:

- Fabricating whole documents including signature

- Adding a false signature to a false document

- Transferring a genuine signature from a genuine document to a false one

- Altering a document to change its character or meaning without the knowledge or consent of the original author

- Placing writing above a genuine signature without the authority of the person who provided the genuine signature

Robbery

Definition at common law

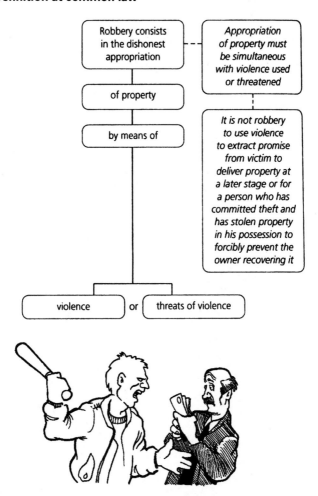

Robbery consists in the dishonest appropriation

Appropriation of property must be simultaneous with violence used or threatened

of property

It is not robbery to use violence to extract promise from victim to deliver property at a later stage or for a person who has committed theft and has stolen property in his possession to forcibly prevent the owner recovering it

by means of

violence   or   threats of violence

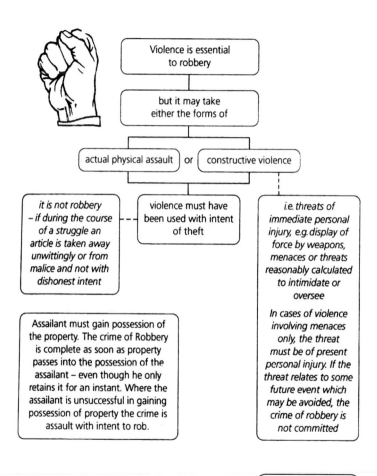

Violence is essential
to robbery

but it may take
either the forms of

actual physical assault | or | constructive violence

it is not robbery
– if during the course
of a struggle an
article is taken away
unwittingly or from
malice and not with
dishonest intent

violence must have
been used with intent
of theft

i.e. threats of
immediate personal
injury, e.g. display of
force by weapons,
menaces or threats
reasonably calculated
to intimidate or
oversee

In cases of violence
involving menaces
only, the threat
must be of present
personal injury. If the
threat relates to some
future event which
may be avoided, the
crime of robbery is
not committed

Assailant must gain possession of
the property. The crime of Robbery
is complete as soon as property
passes into the possession of the
assailant – even though he only
retains it for an instant. Where the
assailant is unsuccessful in gaining
possession of property the crime is
assault with intent to rob.

Scots Law allows for a person charged with
robbery to be convicted of theft or reset.

**COMMON LAW
POWER OF
ARREST**

Reset

EXTENDED BY CRIMINAL PROCEDURE (SCOTLAND) ACT, 1995

Definition at common law

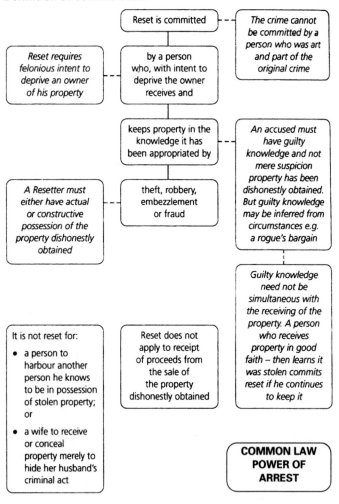

Reset is committed - - - The crime cannot be committed by a person who was art and part of the original crime

Reset requires felonious intent to deprive an owner of his property - - - by a person who, with intent to deprive the owner receives and

keeps property in the knowledge it has been appropriated by - - - An accused must have guilty knowledge and not mere suspicion property has been dishonestly obtained. But guilty knowledge may be inferred from circumstances e.g. a rogue's bargain

A Resetter must either have actual or constructive possession of the property dishonestly obtained - - - theft, robbery, embezzlement or fraud

Guilty knowledge need not be simultaneous with the receiving of the property. A person who receives property in good faith – then learns it was stolen commits reset if he continues to keep it

It is not reset for:

- a person to harbour another person he knows to be in possession of stolen property; or
- a wife to receive or conceal property merely to hide her husband's criminal act

Reset does not apply to receipt of proceeds from the sale of the property dishonestly obtained

COMMON LAW POWER OF ARREST

Criminal Damage

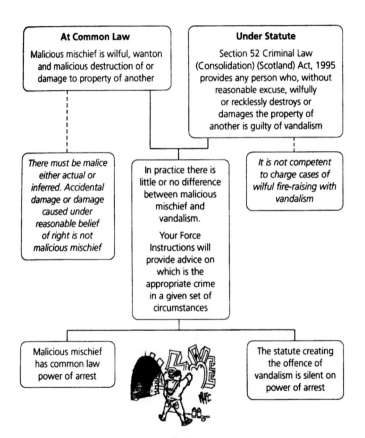

At Common Law

Malicious mischief is wilful, wanton and malicious destruction of or damage to property of another

Under Statute

Section 52 Criminal Law (Consolidation) (Scotland) Act, 1995 provides any person who, without reasonable excuse, wilfully or recklessly destroys or damages the property of another is guilty of vandalism

There must be malice either actual or inferred. Accidental damage or damage caused under reasonable belief of right is not malicious mischief

In practice there is little or no difference between malicious mischief and vandalism.

Your Force Instructions will provide advice on which is the appropriate crime in a given set of circumstances

It is not competent to charge cases of wilful fire-raising with vandalism

Malicious mischief has common law power of arrest

The statute creating the offence of vandalism is silent on power of arrest

Typical modes of commission include breaking windows, injuring growing trees, killing or maiming animals, running to waste any liquid, tearing up plants or switching off a power supply causing economic loss.

Fire-Raising

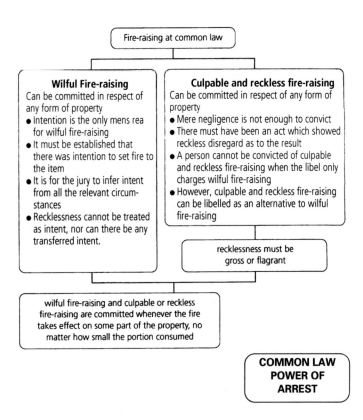

Fire-raising at common law

Wilful Fire-raising
Can be committed in respect of any form of property
- Intention is the only mens rea for wilful fire-raising
- It must be established that there was intention to set fire to the item
- It is for the jury to infer intent from all the relevant circumstances
- Recklessness cannot be treated as intent, nor can there be any transferred intent.

Culpable and reckless fire-raising
Can be committed in respect of any form of property
- Mere negligence is not enough to convict
- There must have been an act which showed reckless disregard as to the result
- A person cannot be convicted of culpable and reckless fire-raising when the libel only charges wilful fire-raising
- However, culpable and reckless fire-raising can be libelled as an alternative to wilful fire-raising

recklessness must be gross or flagrant

wilful fire-raising and culpable or reckless fire-raising are committed whenever the fire takes effect on some part of the property, no matter how small the portion consumed

COMMON LAW POWER OF ARREST

Note 1: Where no recklessness is involved and non-heritable property is deliberately ignited then the accused would be charged with Malicious Mischief or Vandalism under Section 52 of the Criminal Law (Consolidation) (Scotland) Act, 1995.

Note 2: Where a person sets fire to property with the intention of defrauding insurers, he will be guilty of fraud.

Fire-Raising – Under Statute

Section 60 Post Office Act, 1953 makes it an offence to place or attempt to place any fire, match, light, etc, in or against any Post Office letter box

Statute silent on power of arrest

Assault

Definition at common law

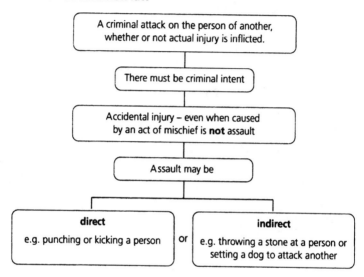

A criminal attack on the person of another, whether or not actual injury is inflicted.

There must be criminal intent

Accidental injury – even when caused by an act of mischief is **not** assault

Assault may be

direct
e.g. punching or kicking a person

or

indirect
e.g. throwing a stone at a person or setting a dog to attack another

Doctrine of Transferred Intent

- Where A intends to assault B and strikes C instead, by the doctrine of transferred intent, he is guilty of assaulting C.

Assault by menaces

Verbal threats alone are not assault, but threatening gestures whether or not words of menace are used, are assault, if they induce a state of bodily fear – for example, aggressively pointing a knife at a person within reach.

Provocation

Insults or provocative words do not justify assault, but may reduce the penalty imposed on the accused.

Indecent assault

Indecent assault is not a specific crime, it is assault accompanied by indecency. To have intercourse with a woman who had made herself so drunk as to be incapable of consent, is indecent assault. (Sweeney and Another v X 1982). To attempt to have intercourse with a sleeping woman is also indecent assault (Rodgers v Hamilton 1994).

Aggravated assault

The crime of assault may be aggravated by:

- Intent – for example, to kill or rob and so on

- Mode of perpetration – for example, with the use of a weapon

- Extent of injuries – for example, serious injury, including broken bones

- Place of assault – for example, in the presence of the Sovereign or in a church and so on

- Character of victim – for example, a pregnant woman, a wife, a very young child

> **COMMON LAW POWER OF ARREST**

Justifiable assault

Assault may be justified if it is shown to be done under the authority of the law or in self-defence and if a minimum amount of force was used.

Note: The term 'self-defence' also covers acts of force used in defence of others.

Assault on the Police
SECTION 41 POLICE (SCOTLAND) ACT, 1967

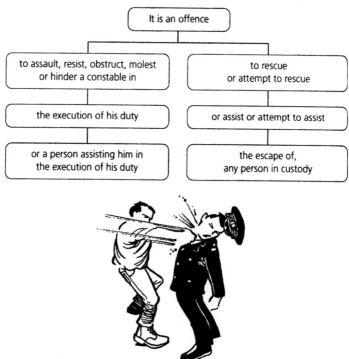

```
                    It is an offence
```

to assault, resist, obstruct, molest or hinder a constable in	to rescue or attempt to rescue
the execution of his duty	or assist or attempt to assist
or a person assisting him in the execution of his duty	the escape of, any person in custody

In custody means:

- In the lawful custody of a constable or any person assisting the constable in the execution of his duty

- In the act of eluding or escaping from such custody, whether or not one has actually been arrested

Homicide

Definition
Homicide is committed when a human being is killed by another human being.

Essential
It is essential that the victim be self-existent and not an unborn child who has not begun to breathe.

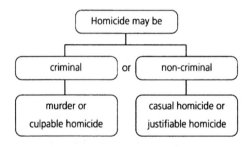

Criminal homicide

Murder
Crime at common law is committed when a person is killed without a necessary cause. There must be:

- An intention to kill
- A wilful act which shows utter disregard for the consequences

Culpable homicide
Is a crime at common law, and the means of committing it will fall into one of the following categories:

- Intentional killing – where death is caused in circumstances which are neither murder nor justifiable, for example, killing someone in the heat of passion following provocation
- Unlawful act – where death results from an unlawful act although death was not intended or probable; for example, killing someone with a single punch
- Negligence – where death results from undue negligence or gross carelessness in the performance of a lawful act or duty, for example, a chemist carelessly selling poison in mistake for medicine, resulting in the death of a person

Non-criminal homicide

Casual homicide
Where death results from pure misadventure, without any intention of harm, during the performance of a lawful act in a proper manner.

Justifiable homicide
This is committed where there is an intention to kill or cause serious injury, but the circumstances excuse the killer, for example, a person killing another in self-defence provided the force used was the minimum necessary in the circumstances.

Abduction

Definition at common law

Abduction is the carrying off or confining of a person forcibly and without lawful authority.

Note: Abduction of children under the age of puberty is charged as plagium, which is a theft-related offence.

Motive

Abduction at common law is unlikely to be committed without an underlying motive. However, the prosecution is not required to prove a motive; it is only necessary to prove that unlawful removal and illegal detention took place.

Abduction – under statute

a) Section 8 Criminal Law (Consolidation) (Scotland) Act 1995 – Abduction of an unmarried girl, under 18 years, with intent that she should have unlawful sexual intercourse with any man

b) Section 115 Representation of the People Act 1983 – Abduction to impede or prevent the free exercise of the franchise of an elector or proxy for an elector

Threats

Definition at common law

Threats, whether verbal or written, are criminal if they menace some substantial injury to the recipient or his property.

Where the threat is contained in a document – the crime is complete whenever the document is dispatched – it is not required to reach the person for whom it is intended.

If the threat contains a demand for money or other advantage – the crime is known as extortion.

Extortion at common law

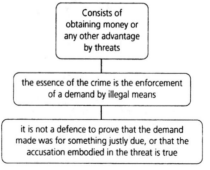

Consists of obtaining money or any other advantage by threats
the essence of the crime is the enforcement of a demand by illegal means
it is not a defence to prove that the demand made was for something justly due, or that the accusation embodied in the threat is true

See case of Carmichael v Black and Prenrice 1992 earlier in this book – under Theft – this case also involved extortion.

Culpable and Reckless Discharge of Firearms

Crime at Common Law

even where actual injury is not caused

the essence of the crime is wanton disregard for the safety of others

Being in Building, Intending to Commit Theft

SECTION 57 CIVIC GOVERNMENT (SCOTLAND) ACT, 1982

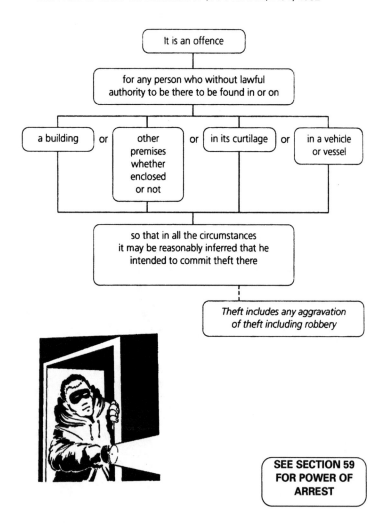

It is an offence

for any person who without lawful authority to be there to be found in or on

a building — or — other premises whether enclosed or not — or — in its curtilage — or — in a vehicle or vessel

so that in all the circumstances it may be reasonably inferred that he intended to commit theft there

Theft includes any aggravation of theft including robbery

SEE SECTION 59 FOR POWER OF ARREST

Convicted Thief in Possession

SECTION 58 CIVIC GOVERNMENT (SCOTLAND) ACT, 1982

Any person who has two or
more (non spent) convictions for
theft commits an offence if

he has or has recently had in his possession
any tool or other object – the possession of which
may reasonably be inferred that he has committed
theft or intended to commit theft and

is unable to demonstrate satisfactorily that his
possession of the tool or object is or was not for
the purposes of committing theft

*Theft includes any aggravation
of theft and robbery*

*Note: A person shall have recently had possession of a tool or other
object if he had possession of it within 14 days before the date of:*

- his arrest without warrant for the offence of having so possessed it in contravention of the above subsection; or

- the issue of a warrant for his arrest for that offence; or

- if earlier, the service upon him of the first complaint alleging that he has committed that offence.

**SEE SECTION 59
FOR POWER OF
ARREST**

Powers of Search and Seizure

SECTION 60 CIVIC GOVERNMENT (SCOTLAND) ACT, 1982

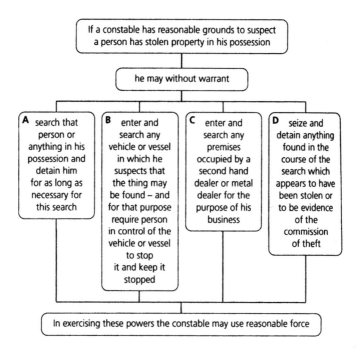

If a constable has reasonable grounds to suspect a person has stolen property in his possession

he may without warrant

A search that person or anything in his possession and detain him for as long as necessary for this search

B enter and search any vehicle or vessel in which he suspects that the thing may be found – and for that purpose require person in control of the vehicle or vessel to stop it and keep it stopped

C enter and search any premises occupied by a second hand dealer or metal dealer for the purpose of his business

D seize and detain anything found in the course of the search which appears to have been stolen or to be evidence of the commission of theft

In exercising these powers the constable may use reasonable force

A constable not in uniform is not entitled to exercise the powers stated in **A**, **B** and **C** until he has proved his identification to the person he is going to search or to the person in charge of the vehicle, vessel or premises and to any other person in or on vehicle, vessel or premises, who having reasonable cause to do so, requests to see it.

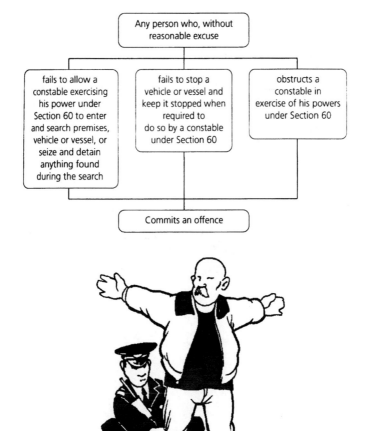

Any person who, without reasonable excuse

- fails to allow a constable exercising his power under Section 60 to enter and search premises, vehicle or vessel, or seize and detain anything found during the search
- fails to stop a vehicle or vessel and keep it stopped when required to do so by a constable under Section 60
- obstructs a constable in exercise of his powers under Section 60

Commits an offence

Power of Arrest

SECTION 59 CIVIC GOVERNMENT (SCOTLAND) ACT, 1982

A constable may, where in the interests of justice finds it necessary, arrest without warrant a person committing offences under Sections 57, 58 and 60 of the Act.

A constable not in uniform must produce his identification if required to do so by the person he is arresting.

The owner, tenant or occupier of property in respect of which an offence under the Act is being committed or any person authorised by the owner, tenant or occupier of such premises may apprehend any person committing the offence and detain him until delivered into the custody of the police.

Drugs

The Misuse of Drugs Act, 1971 creates a number of offences relating to controlled drugs.

Controlled drugs

This means any substance or product listed in one of the three classes (A, B or C) in Schedule 2 to the Act.

While drugs are listed in their basic form it is clear that other forms of the drug and esters or salts are also included. Both the natural substances and any substance resulting from chemical transformation are controlled drugs.

Note: When exercising your powers under Section 23 (2), avoid the use of the word 'arrest', as it has been held that the use of this word conveys the message that the suspect is under arrest rather than simply being detained for the purpose of search, and that such an arrest would be unlawful.

Import and export
SECTION 3 MISUSE OF DRUGS ACT, 1971

The import or export of controlled drugs is prohibited unless authorised under the regulations.

Being concerned with the improper import or export, or the fraudulent evasion of prohibition or restriction, are all offences under the Customs and Excise Management Act 1979, S 50.

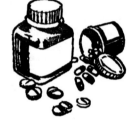

Production
SECTION 42(2) MISUSE OF DRUGS ACT, 1971

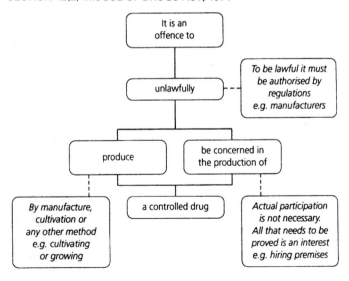

It is an offence to

unlawfully — *To be lawful it must be authorised by regulations e.g. manufacturers*

produce

be concerned in the production of

By manufacture, cultivation or any other method e.g. cultivating or growing

a controlled drug

Actual participation is not necessary. All that needs to be proved is an interest e.g. hiring premises

Supply
SECTION 4(3) MISUSE OF DRUGS ACT, 1971

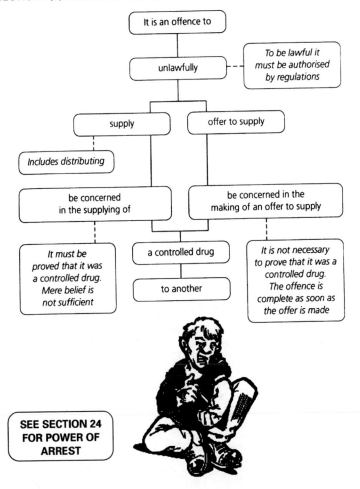

It is an offence to

unlawfully

To be lawful it must be authorised by regulations

supply

offer to supply

Includes distributing

be concerned in the supplying of

be concerned in the making of an offer to supply

It must be proved that it was a controlled drug. Mere belief is not sufficient

a controlled drug

to another

It is not necessary to prove that it was a controlled drug. The offence is complete as soon as the offer is made

SEE SECTION 24 FOR POWER OF ARREST

Possession
SECTION 5(2) MISUSE OF DRUGS ACT, 1971

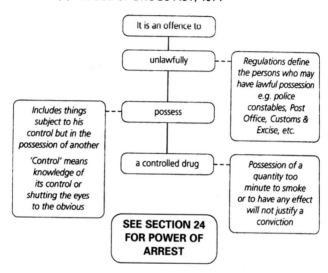

It is an offence to

unlawfully

possess

a controlled drug

Regulations define the persons who may have lawful possession e.g. police constables, Post Office, Customs & Excise, etc.

Includes things subject to his control but in the possession of another

'Control' means knowledge of its control or shutting the eyes to the obvious

Possession of a quantity too minute to smoke or to have any effect will not justify a conviction

SEE SECTION 24 FOR POWER OF ARREST

Defence
SECTION 5(4) MISUSE OF DRUGS ACT, 1971

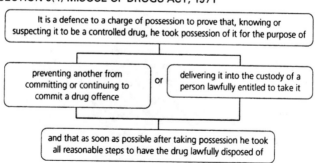

It is a defence to a charge of possession to prove that, knowing or suspecting it to be a controlled drug, he took possession of it for the purpose of

preventing another from committing or continuing to commit a drug offence

or

delivering it into the custody of a person lawfully entitled to take it

and that as soon as possible after taking possession he took all reasonable steps to have the drug lawfully disposed of

Possession with intent to supply
SECTION 5(3) MISUSE OF DRUGS ACT, 1971

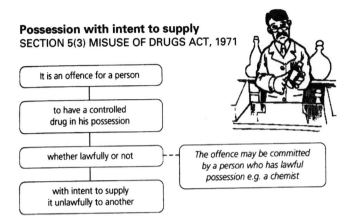

It is an offence for a person

to have a controlled drug in his possession

whether lawfully or not

The offence may be committed by a person who has lawful possession e.g. a chemist

with intent to supply it unlawfully to another

Cannabis – cultivating
SECTION 6(2) MISUSE OF DRUGS ACT, 1971

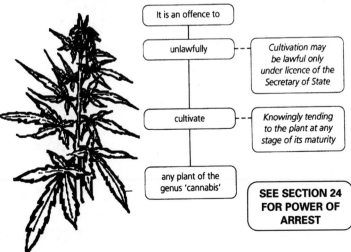

It is an offence to

unlawfully

Cultivation may be lawful only under licence of the Secretary of State

cultivate

Knowingly tending to the plant at any stage of its maturity

any plant of the genus 'cannabis'

SEE SECTION 24 FOR POWER OF ARREST

Premises
SECTION 8 MISUSE OF DRUGS ACT, 1971

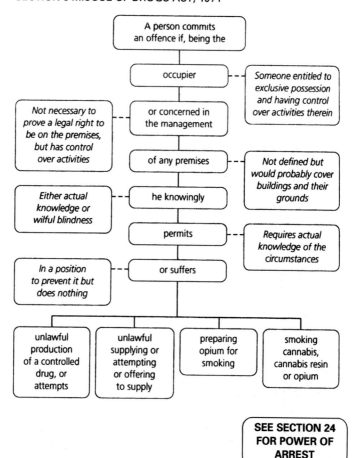

A person commits an offence if, being the

occupier — *Someone entitled to exclusive possession and having control over activities therein*

Not necessary to prove a legal right to be on the premises, but has control over activities — or concerned in the management

of any premises — *Not defined but would probably cover buildings and their grounds*

Either actual knowledge or wilful blindness — he knowingly

permits — *Requires actual knowledge of the circumstances*

In a position to prevent it but does nothing — or suffers

| unlawful production of a controlled drug, or attempts | unlawful supplying or attempting or offering to supply | preparing opium for smoking | smoking cannabis, cannabis resin or opium |

SEE SECTION 24 FOR POWER OF ARREST

Opium
SECTION 9 MISUSE OF DRUGS ACT, 1971

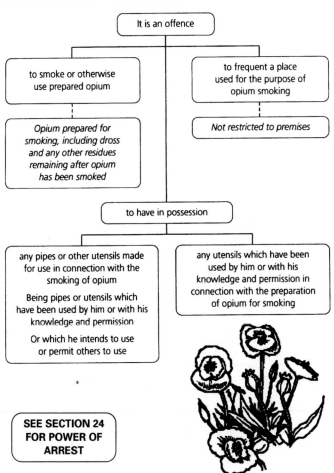

It is an offence

to smoke or otherwise use prepared opium

Opium prepared for smoking, including dross and any other residues remaining after opium has been smoked

to frequent a place used for the purpose of opium smoking

Not restricted to premises

to have in possession

any pipes or other utensils made for use in connection with the smoking of opium

Being pipes or utensils which have been used by him or with his knowledge and permission

Or which he intends to use or permit others to use

any utensils which have been used by him or with his knowledge and permission in connection with the preparation of opium for smoking

SEE SECTION 24 FOR POWER OF ARREST

Drugs - Police Powers

Search
SECTION 23(2) MISUSE OF DRUGS ACT, 1971

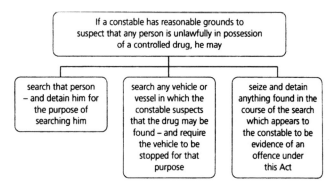

Note: When exercising your powers under Section 23(3), avoid the use of the word 'arrest' as it has been held that the use of this word conveys the message that the suspect is under arrest rather than simply being detained for the purpose of search and that such an arrest would be unlawful.

Arrest
SECTION 24 MISUSE OF DRUGS ACT, 1971

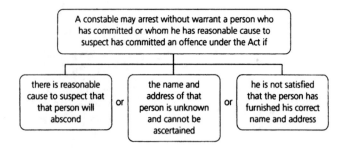

CHAPTER 3
Sexual Offences

Rape

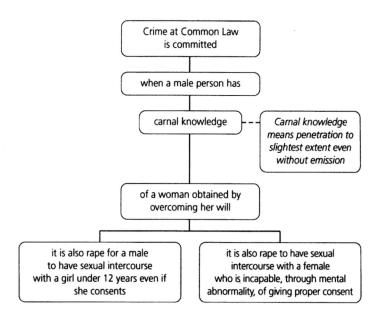

Crime at Common Law
is committed

when a male person has

carnal knowledge

*Carnal knowledge
means penetration to
slightest extent even
without emission*

of a woman obtained by
overcoming her will

it is also rape for a male
to have sexual intercourse
with a girl under 12 years even if
she consents

it is also rape to have sexual
intercourse with a female
who is incapable, through mental
abnormality, of giving proper consent

Note: Prostitutes may be raped - but proof may be more difficult.

**COMMON LAW
POWER OF
ARREST**

Overcoming woman's will
Physical violence is not essential – threats or administration of drugs may be used.

The victim need not offer physical resistance – the important element is that a woman was an unwilling party throughout the act.

Husband and wife
A husband may be convicted of raping his wife, if the wife did not consent to intercourse (Stollard v HMA 1989).

Rape under statute
SECTION 7(3) CRIMINAL LAW (CONSOLIDATION) (SCOTLAND) ACT, 1995

It is rape for a man to induce a married woman to have sexual intercourse by impersonating her husband.

Important decisions
It is an indictable crime, **but not rape**, to have carnal knowledge with a woman when she is asleep and without her consent by a male who is not her husband. (Sweenie - 1858).

It is an indictable crime **but not rape** for a man to have sexual intercourse with a woman in a state of insensibility or unconsciousness from the effects of alcohol. However, it would be rape if the man had plied the woman with alcohol, the nature of which was concealed from her, in order to overcome her resistance (HMA v Logan 1836).

It is indecent assault to have intercourse with a woman, who has made herself so drunk as to be incapable of giving consent (Sweeney and Another v X 1982).

Matters Relating to the Investigation of Rape SUMMARY OF 1985 SCOTTISH OFFICE CIRCULAR

1. Treat a woman who complains of sexual assault with tact, understanding and full regard for her well being.

2. Establish if a victim is in need of immediate medical care and if necessary take her to hospital.

3. Where a victim is distressed or in shock – unless there are compelling reasons to the contrary – limit the enquiry to an initial statement and a medical examination at early stage of enquiry.

4. Explain to a victim (and to parents or guardian if victim is a child or young person) the need for a medical examination.

5. Where the victim is under 12 years – permission of a parent or guardian for the medical examination should be obtained. In the event of refusal or if the available parent/guardian is the alleged perpetrator, the interest of the girl will prevail.

6. Where the girl is under 18 years but over 12 years the permission of the parent or guardian for a medical examination is desirable, but the girl's permission alone is sufficient if she wishes to keep the matter confidential.

7. The victim should be given the choice of being examined by a female doctor and her preference should be respected unless this is impracticable.

8. Detailed questioning of the victim should be conducted by an officer who has the necessary skills and is trained in dealing with such cases.

9. As highly personal questions may have to be asked of the victim, the officer asking such questions must exercise tact and discretion.

10. Generally there is no need to elicit information regarding a victim's previous sexual history, morals or any sexual relationship which has no bearing on the subject matter of the charge.

11. All victims should be informed of their right to Criminal Injuries compensation and given address of the Criminal Injuries Compensation Board (CICB). Details of Rape Crisis Centres and Victim Support Schemes where appropriate should be given to victim.

Sexual Intercourse with a Girl Under Age

CRIMINAL LAW (CONSOLIDATION) (SCOTLAND) ACT, 1995 SECTION 5

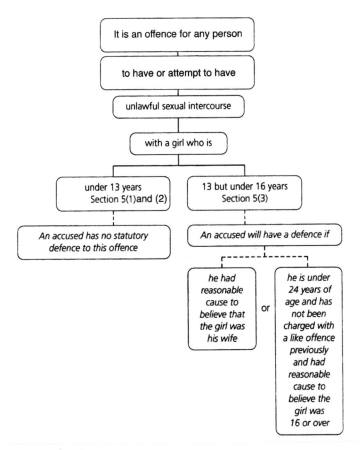

Power of arrest
These are Schedule 1 offences under the Criminal Procedure (Scotland) Act, 1995, and the offender may be arrested in circumstances specified in Section 21 of that Act.

Incest

SECTION 1 CRIMINAL LAW (CONSOLIDATION) (SCOTLAND) ACT, 1995

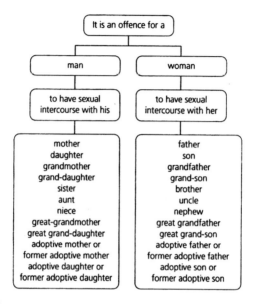

It is an offence for a

man	woman
to have sexual intercourse with his	to have sexual intercourse with her
mother	father
daughter	son
grandmother	grandfather
grand-daughter	grand-son
sister	brother
aunt	uncle
niece	nephew
great-grandmother	great grandfather
great grand-daughter	great grand-son
adoptive mother or former adoptive mother	adoptive father or former adoptive father
adoptive daughter or former adoptive daughter	adoptive son or former adoptive son

Defence

An accused has a defence if he/she proves that:

- He/she did not know and has no reason to believe that the person with who he/she has sexual intercourse was related in a degree specified

- He/she did not consent to have sexual intercourse, or to have sexual intercourse with that person

- He/she was married to that person at the time when sexual intercourse took place, by a marriage entered into outside Scotland and recognised as valid by Scots Law

Power of arrest

Section 1 is a Schedule 1 offence under the Criminal Procedure (Scotland) Act, 1995 and an offender may be arrested in the circumstances detailed in Section 21 of that Act.

Intercourse with Step-Child

SECTION 2 CRIMINAL LAW (CONSOLIDATION) (SCOTLAND) ACT, 1995

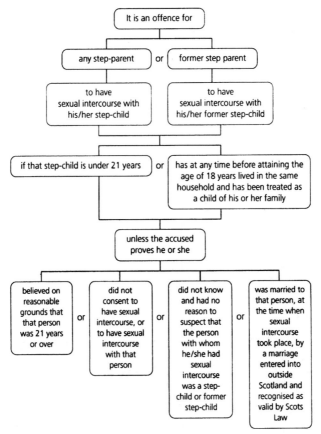

It is an offence for

any step-parent or former step parent

to have sexual intercourse with his/her step-child

to have sexual intercourse with his/her former step-child

if that step-child is under 21 years or has at any time before attaining the age of 18 years lived in the same household and has been treated as a child of his or her family

unless the accused proves he or she

believed on reasonable grounds that that person was 21 years or over

or did not consent to have sexual intercourse, or to have sexual intercourse with that person

or did not know and had no reason to suspect that the person with whom he/she had sexual intercourse was a step-child or former step-child

or was married to that person, at the time when sexual intercourse took place, by a marriage entered into outside Scotland and recognised as valid by Scots Law

Power of arrest

This is a Schedule 1 Offence under the Criminal Procedure (Scotland) Act, 1995, and an offender may be arrested in the circumstances detailed in Section 21 of that Act.

Intercourse by Person in Position of Trust with Person who is Under 18 and in Full Time Education or Residential Care

SECTION 3 SEXUAL OFFENCES (AMMENDMENT) ACT, 2000

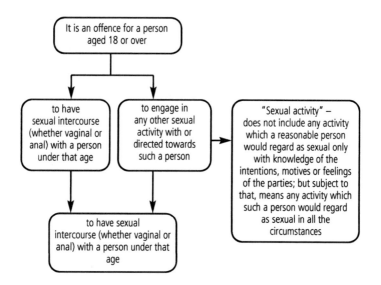

It is an offence for a person aged 18 or over

to have sexual intercourse (whether vaginal or anal) with a person under that age

to engage in any other sexual activity with or directed towards such a person

"Sexual activity" – does not include any activity which a reasonable person would regard as sexual only with knowledge of the intentions, motives or feelings of the parties; but subject to that, means any activity which such a person would regard as sexual in all the circumstances

to have sexual intercourse (whether vaginal or anal) with a person under that age

Defence

Where an accused charged with an offence under this section it shall be a defence for him to prove that, at the time of the intercourse or activity

- he did not know, and could not reasonably have been expected to know, that the person on whom the offence was committed was under 18; or

- he did not know, and could not reasonably have been expected to know, that the person on whom the offence was committed was a person in relation to whom he was in a position of trust; or

- he was lawfully married to the person on whom the offence was committed

Position of Trust

In respect of the Sexual Offences (Amendment) Act, 2000, means a person aged 18 or over (hereafter referred to as A) is in a position of trust in relation to a person under that age (hereafter referred to as B) if any of the four conditions set out below, or any condition specified in an order made by the Secretary of State by Statutory instrument, is fulfilled.

1. A looks after persons under 18 who are detained in an institution by virtue of an order of a Court or under an enactment, and B is so detained in that institution.

2. A looks after persons under 18 who are resident in a home or other place in which accommodation is provided by an authority under section 26(1) of the Children (Scotland) Act, 1995, and B is resident, and is so provided with accommodation and mainte-nance or accommodation, in that place.

3. A looks after persons under 18 who are accommodated and cared for in an institution which is
   a) a hospital;
   b) a residential care home, nursing home, mental nursing home or private hospital;
   c) a community home, voluntary home, children's home or resi-dential establishment;
   and B is accommodated and cared for in that institution.

4. A looks after persons under 18 who are receiving full-time educa-tion at an educational institution, and B is receiving such educa-tion at that institution.

Intercourse of Person in Position of Trust with Child Under 16

SECTION 3 CRIMINAL LAW (CONSOLIDATION) (SCOTLAND) ACT, 1995

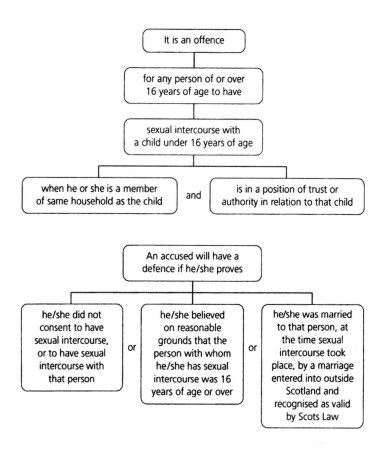

It is an offence

for any person of or over 16 years of age to have

sexual intercourse with a child under 16 years of age

when he or she is a member of same household as the child

and

is in a position of trust or authority in relation to that child

An accused will have a defence if he/she proves

he/she did not consent to have sexual intercourse, or to have sexual intercourse with that person

or

he/she believed on reasonable grounds that the person with whom he/she has sexual intercourse was 16 years of age or over

or

he/she was married to that person, at the time sexual intercourse took place, by a marriage entered into outside Scotland and recognised as valid by Scots Law

Power of arrest

Section 3 is a Schedule 1 Offence under the Criminal Procedure (Scotland) Act, 1995 and an accused may be arrested in circumstances detailed in Section 21 of that Act.

Schedule 1 Offences – Power of Arrest

SECTION 21 CRIMINAL PROCEDURE (SCOTLAND) ACT, 1995

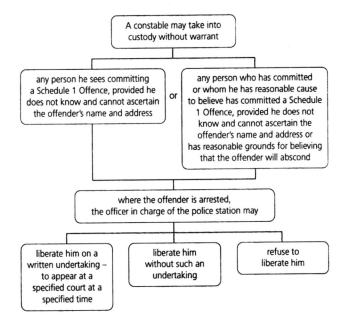

Schedule 1 offences under Criminal Procedure (Scotland) Act, 1995

1. Any offence under Part 1 of the Criminal Law (Consolidation) (Scotland) Act, 1995

2. Any offence under Sections 12 (Cruelty), 15 (Begging), 22 (Burning) or 33 (Dangerous Performance) of the Children and Young Persons (Scotland) Act, 1937

3. Any other offence involving bodily injury to a child under 17 years of age

4. Any offence involving the use of lewd, indecent or libidinous practice or behaviour towards a child under 17 years of age.

Lewd, Indecent and Libidinous Practices

At common law

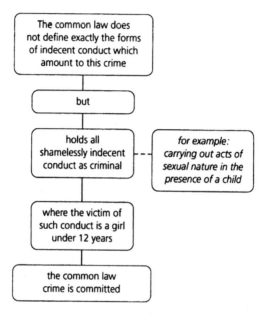

The common law does not define exactly the forms of indecent conduct which amount to this crime

but

holds all shamelessly indecent conduct as criminal

for example: carrying out acts of sexual nature in the presence of a child

where the victim of such conduct is a girl under 12 years

the common law crime is committed

Under statute
SECTION 6 CRIMINAL LAW (CONSOLIDATION) (SCOTLAND) ACT, 1995

It is an offence

to use lewd, indecent and libidinous practices

towards a girl aged over 12 and under 16 years

whether consent is granted or not

Power of arrest
At common law the police may arrest the offender without warrant, no matter the age or sex of the victim – if the common law charge is preferred.

Also note where the victim is a person aged under 17 years, both the common law crime and the statutory offence under Section 6 above are Schedule 1 Offences – see Section 21 of the Criminal Procedure (Scotland) Act, 1995 for powers of arrest.

In practice where common law crime is committed police normally exercise power of arrest at common law.

Statement of victim
Any statement made by victim to the first person met, or at the earliest reasonable opportunity, is admissible evidence. This does not provide corroboration but may assist in credibility.

Note: The common law crime is not restricted to girls under 12 years. Apart from the provisions of the statutory offence – the common law crime may be applied irrespective of the age or sex of the victim.

Indecent Exposure

Indecent exposure at common law

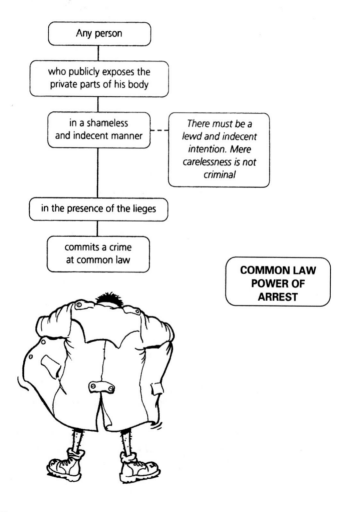

Any person

who publicly exposes the private parts of his body

in a shameless and indecent manner

There must be a lewd and indecent intention. Mere carelessness is not criminal

in the presence of the lieges

commits a crime at common law

COMMON LAW POWER OF ARREST

Sodomy

Sodomy at common law

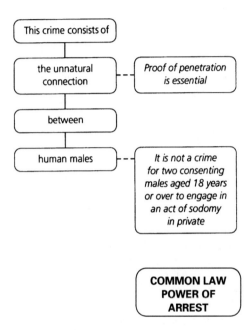

This crime consists of

the unnatural connection --- *Proof of penetration is essential*

between

human males --- *It is not a crime for two consenting males aged 18 years or over to engage in an act of sodomy in private*

COMMON LAW POWER OF ARREST

Homosexual Offences

SECTION 13 CRIMINAL LAW (CONSOLIDATION) (SCOTLAND) ACT, 1995 AS AMENDED BY THE SEXUAL OFFENCES (AMENDMENT) ACT, 2000 AND THE CONVENTION RIGHTS (COMPLIANCE) (SCOTLAND) ACT, 2001

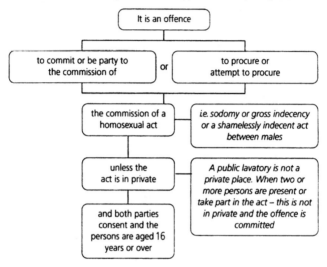

Note 1: If one of the consenting parties suffers from a mental deficiency and in law is regarded as incapable of giving consent – the other party would commit the above offence – unless he proves he did not know and had no reason to suspect that the male was suffering from a mental deficiency.

Note 2: It is also an offence under Section 13 to procure or attempt to procure the commission of a homosexual act between two other males – Section 13(6).

Statutory defence

It is a defence to a charge under Section 13(5) for an accused to prove he was under 24 years of age – he had not previously been charged with a like offence and had reasonable cause to believe that the other male was aged 16 years or more.

Power of arrest

An offence under Section 13 is included in Schedule 1 Criminal Procedure (Scotland) Act, 1995 and an offender may be apprehended in the circumstances specified in Section 21 of the above Act.

Mental Defectives

MENTAL HEALTH (SCOTLAND) ACT, 1984

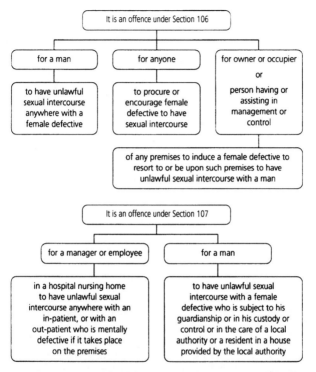

Defective means a state of arrested or incomplete development of mind which includes severe impairment of intelligence and social functioning.

Consent does not provide a defence, but lack of knowledge of the condition and having no reason to suspect it is a defence.

In Section 107 reference to having unlawful sexual intercourse with a female shall include a reference to committing a homosexual act such as sodomy, acts of gross indecency or shameless indecency by one male to another male.

Prostitution
SECTION 46 CIVIC GOVERNMENT (SCOTLAND) ACT, 1982

It is an offence for a prostitute

The term prostitute is not defined in the Act, but it has been held by the courts that prostitution means the offering, for reward, by a female, of her body. Commonly, for the purpose of general lewdness. It now appears that under this Act the term prostitute can be applied to males who offer their bodies for reward, etc.

male or female

Need not be accompanied by words, gestures or conduct – any form of tempting or alluring would suffice

to loiter or solicit or importune

in a public place

Any place (whether a thoroughfare or not) to which the public have unrestricted access and includes:

the doorways or entrances of premises abutting on any such place

any common passage, close, court, stair, garden or yard pertinent to any tenement or group of separately owned houses

any place to which at the material time the public are permitted to have access, whether on payment or otherwise

any public conveyance other than a taxi or hire car

if the person solicited is in a street or public place it is not necessary that the woman is also in such place – she may, for example, be at the window of a house, or a balcony

for the purpose of prostitution

A constable may where it is necessary in the interests of justice to do so arrest without warrant a person whom he finds committing this offence Section 59

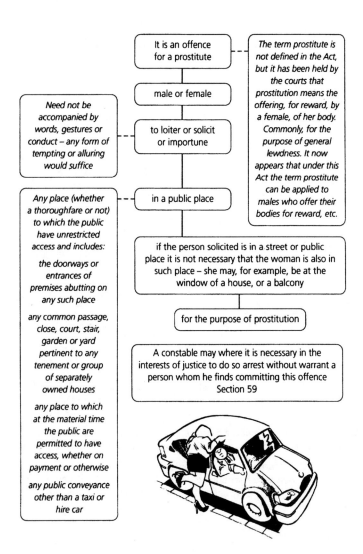

Trading in prostitution
SECTION 11 CRIMINAL LAW (CONSOLIDATION) (SCOTLAND) ACT, 1995

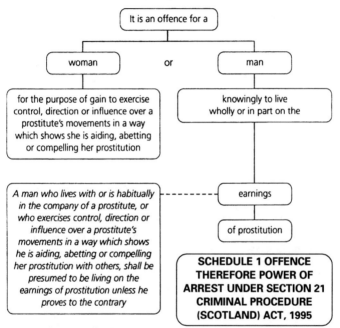

It is an offence for a

woman or man

for the purpose of gain to exercise control, direction or influence over a prostitute's movements in a way which shows she is aiding, abetting or compelling her prostitution

knowingly to live wholly or in part on the

A man who lives with or is habitually in the company of a prostitute, or who exercises control, direction or influence over a prostitute's movements in a way which shows he is aiding, abetting or compelling her prostitution with others, shall be presumed to be living on the earnings of prostitution unless he proves to the contrary

earnings

of prostitution

SCHEDULE 1 OFFENCE THEREFORE POWER OF ARREST UNDER SECTION 21 CRIMINAL PROCEDURE (SCOTLAND) ACT, 1995

Procuring prostitution
SECTION 7 CRIMINAL LAW (CONSOLIDATION) (SCOTLAND) ACT, 1995

It is an offence to procure or attempt to procure a woman or girl to become a prostitute or to leave the UK to become an inmate of, or frequent, a brothel for prostitution abroad.

It is also an offence to procure or attempt to procure any woman under 21 years of age or a girl to have unlawful sexual intercourse with any other person or persons in any part of the world.

Traffic In Prostitution etc

SECTION 22 CRIMINAL JUSTICE (SCOTLAND) ACT, 2003

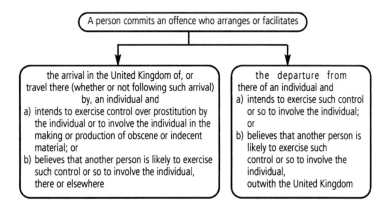

A person commits an offence who arranges or facilitates

the arrival in the United Kingdom of, or travel there (whether or not following such arrival) by, an individual and
a) intends to exercise control over prostitution by the individual or to involve the individual in the making or production of obscene or indecent material; or
b) believes that another person is likely to exercise such control or so to involve the individual, there or elsewhere

the departure from there of an individual and
a) intends to exercise such control or so to involve the individual; or
b) believes that another person is likely to exercise such control or so to involve the individual, outwith the United Kingdom

For the purposes this section a person exercises control over prostitution by an individual if the person exercises control, direction or influence over the prostitute's movements in a way which shows that the person is aiding, abetting or compelling the prostitution.

The Section applies to anything done in the United Kingdom or outwith the United Kingdom-
1. by an individual who is
    a) a British citizen;
    b) a British overseas territories citizen;
    c) a British national (overseas);
    d) a British overseas citizen;
    e) a person who is a British subject under the British Nationality Act 1981; and
    f) a British protected person within the meaning of that Act; or

2. by a body incorporated under the law of a part of the United Kingdom.

If an offence under this section is committed outwith the United Kingdom, proceedings may be taken in any place in Scotland and the offence may, for incidental purposes, be treated as having been committed in that place.

Brothel Keeping

SECTION 11 CRIMINAL LAW (CONSOLIDATION) (SCOTLAND) ACT, 1995

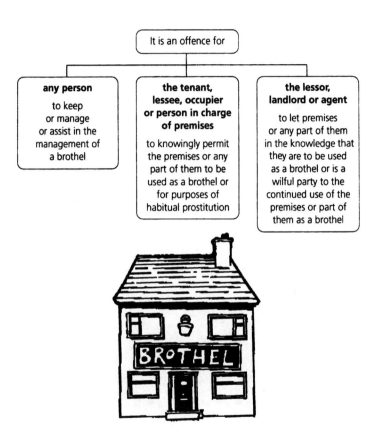

It is an offence for

any person	**the tenant, lessee, occupier or person in charge of premises**	**the lessor, landlord or agent**
to keep or manage or assist in the management of a brothel	to knowingly permit the premises or any part of them to be used as a brothel or for purposes of habitual prostitution	to let premises or any part of them in the knowledge that they are to be used as a brothel or is a wilful party to the continued use of the premises or part of them as a brothel

The Act does not define the term 'brothel' but the courts would probably accept a brothel to be a place where people of the opposite sex resort for illicit intercourse, whether or not the women are common prostitutes, provided the premises are not used by one woman alone for the purpose of prostituting herself.

Indecent Photographs

SECTION 52 CIVIC GOVERNMENT (SCOTLAND) ACT, 1982

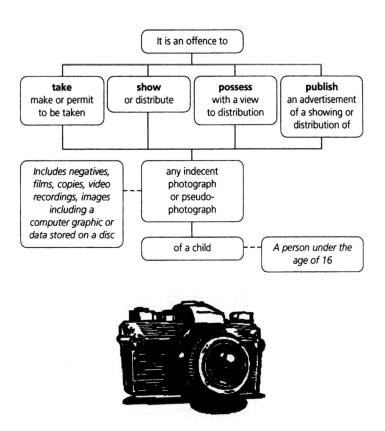

It is an offence to

take
make or permit
to be taken

show
or distribute

possess
with a view
to distribution

publish
an advertisement
of a showing or
distribution of

*Includes negatives,
films, copies, video
recordings, images
including a
computer graphic or
data stored on a disc*

any indecent
photograph
or pseudo-
photograph

of a child

*A person under the
age of 16*

**A CONSTABLE MAY, WHERE IT IS NECESSARY IN THE
INTERESTS OF JUSTICE TO DO SO, ARREST WITHOUT WARRANT
A PERSON HE FINDS COMMITTING THIS OFFENCE – SECTION 59**

A defence to indecent photographs

In relation to these offences it shall be a defence if the accused proves that:

- There is a legitimate reason for distribution or possession

- He had not seen the photographs and neither knew nor suspected they were indecent

SECTION 52A CIVIC GOVERNMENT (SCOTLAND) ACT, 1982 (INSERTED BY SECTION 161 CRIMINAL JUSTICE (SCOTLAND) ACT, 1988 AND AMENDED BY CRIMINAL JUSTICE AND PUBLIC ORDER ACT, 1994 AND THE CRIMINAL JUSTICE (SCOTLAND) ACT, 2003.

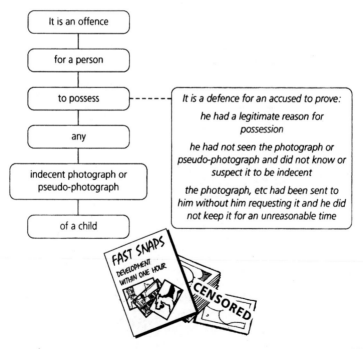

It is an offence

for a person

to possess

any

indecent photograph or pseudo-photograph

of a child

It is a defence for an accused to prove:

he had a legitimate reason for possession

he had not seen the photograph or pseudo-photograph and did not know or suspect it to be indecent

the photograph, etc had been sent to him without him requesting it and he did not keep it for an unreasonable time

Indecent displays
SECTION 1 INDECENT DISPLAYS (CONTROL) ACT, 1981

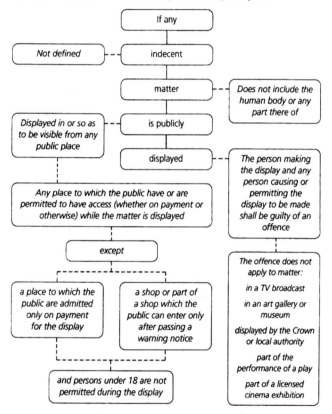

Indecent displays – police powers
A constable may seize any article which he has reasonable grounds for believing to be indecent matter used in the commission of an offence.

Obscene Publications

(At Common Law)

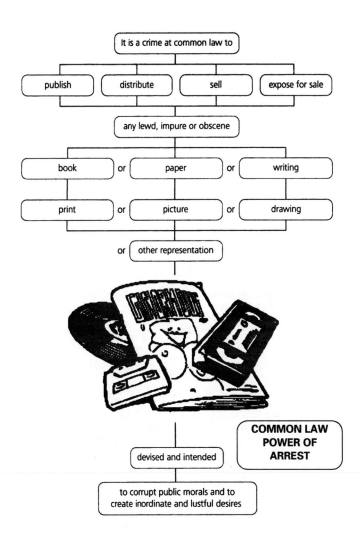

It is a crime at common law to

| publish | distribute | sell | expose for sale |

any lewd, impure or obscene

| book | or | paper | or | writing |
| print | or | picture | or | drawing |

or other representation

devised and intended

COMMON LAW POWER OF ARREST

to corrupt public morals and to create inordinate and lustful desires

Obscene Material

CIVIC GOVERNMENT (SCOTLAND) ACT, 1982

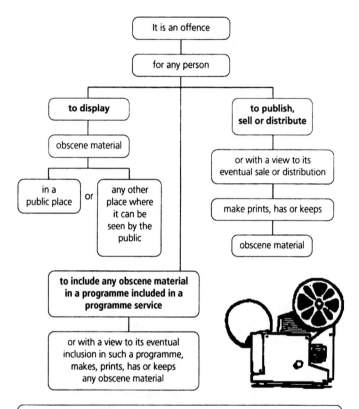

It is an offence

for any person

to display

obscene material

in a public place | or | any other place where it can be seen by the public

to publish, sell or distribute

or with a view to its eventual sale or distribution

make prints, has or keeps

obscene material

to include any obscene material in a programme included in a programme service

or with a view to its eventual inclusion in such a programme, makes, prints, has or keeps any obscene material

Material includes any book, magazine, bill, paper, print, film, tape, disc or other kind of recording (whether of sound or visual images or both), photographs, drawing, painting, representation, model or figure.

Defence

It is a defence for an accused to prove that he used all due diligence to avoid committing the offence.

Harmful Publications

CHILDREN AND YOUNG PERSONS (HARMFUL PUBLICATIONS) ACT, 1955

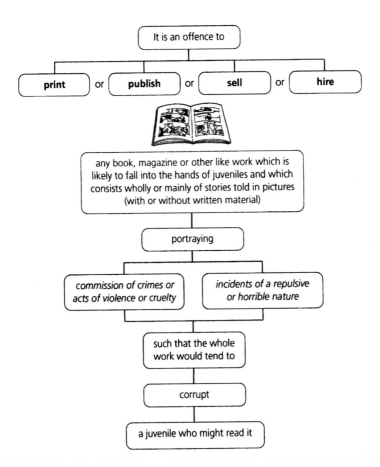

Defence

It is a defence that the accused had not examined the work and had no reasonable cause to suspect that it constituted an offence.

CHAPTER 4
Firearms

Firearms Definitions

SECTION 57 FIREARMS ACT, 1968

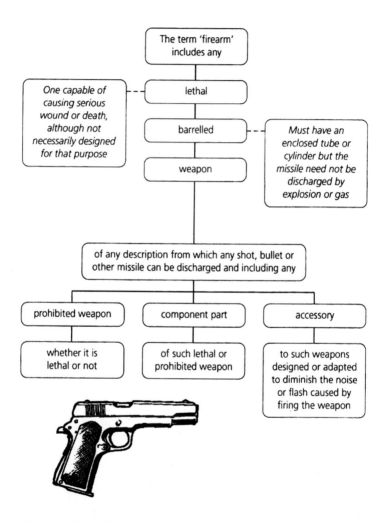

The term 'firearm' includes any

lethal

One capable of causing serious wound or death, although not necessarily designed for that purpose

barrelled

Must have an enclosed tube or cylinder but the missile need not be discharged by explosion or gas

weapon

of any description from which any shot, bullet or other missile can be discharged and including any

prohibited weapon

whether it is lethal or not

component part

of such lethal or prohibited weapon

accessory

to such weapons designed or adapted to diminish the noise or flash caused by firing the weapon

*Note: As to **imitations** see page 126.*

Prohibited Weapons

SECTIONS 5(1) and 5(1A) FIREARMS ACT, 1968

A person commits an offence if, without the authority of the Secretary of State, he has in his possession, or purchases or acquires, or manufactures, sells or transfers, a prohibited weapon.

Note: In the event of the Secretary of State granting authority, an individual would require a firearm certificate to possess and so on, unless exempted.

Prohibited weapons and ammunition
Section 5 (1)
a) any firearm which is so designed or adapted that two or more missiles can be successively discharged without repeated pressure on the trigger.
b) any self-loading or pump-action rifled gun other than one which is chambered for .22 rim-fire cartridges.
c) any firearm which either has a barrel less than 30cm in length or is less than 60cm in length overall, other than an air weapon, a muzzle-loading gun or a firearm designed as signalling apparatus.
d) any self-loading or pump-action smooth bore gun which is not an air weapon or chambered for .22 rim-fire cartridges and either has a barrel less than 24 inches in length or is less than 40 inches in length overall.
e) any smooth bore revolver gun other than one which is chambered for 9mm rim-fire cartridges or a muzzle-loading gun.
f) any rocket launcher, or any mortar, for projecting a stabilised missile, other than a launcher or mortar designed for line throwing or pyrotechnic purposes or as signalling apparatus.
g) any weapon of whatever description designed or adapted for the discharge of any noxious liquid, gas or other thing.
h) any cartridge with a bullet so designed to explode on or immediately before impact, any ammunition containing or designed or adapted to contain any such noxious thing as is mentioned in paragraph b above, and, if capable of being used with a firearm of any description, any grenade, bomb or other like missile, or rocket or shell designed to explode as aforesaid.

Section 5 (1A)
a) any firearm which is disguised as another object (e.g. walking stick).

b) any rocket or ammunition not falling within paragraph c) of subsection (1) of this section which consists in or incorporates a missile designed to explode on or immediately before impact and is for military use.

c) any launcher or other projecting apparatus not falling within paragraph (ae) of that subsection which is designed to be used with any rocket or ammunition falling within paragraph b) above, or with ammunition which would fall within that paragraph but for its being ammunition falling within paragraph c) of that subsection.

d) any ammunition for military use which consists in or incorporates a missile designed so that a substance contained in the missile will ignite on or immediately before impact.

e) any ammunition for military use which consists in or incorporates a missile designed, on account of its having a jacket and hard core, to penetrate armour plating, armour screening or body armour.

f) any ammunition which incorporates a missile designed or adapted to expand on impact.

g) anything which is designed to be projected as a missile from any weapon and is designed to be, or has been, incorporated in –
   1) any ammunition falling within any of the preceding paragraphs; or
   2) any ammunition which would fall within any of those paragraphs but for its being specified in Section 5 (1) above.

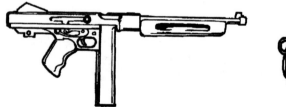

Exemptions

Exemptions exist (but Firearm Certificates are still required) in relation to slaughtering instruments, humane killing of animals, starting pistols, trophies of war acquired before 1 January 1946, part of a collection and manufactured before 1 January 1919, rare or historic importance, shooting vermin or treating animals.

Exemptions also exist in relation to holders of certificates or authority, firearms collectors, bodies concerned in cultural or historical aspects of firearms, slaughtering instruments and registered firearms dealers.

Firearms Certificates

SECTION 1(1) FIREARMS ACT, 1968

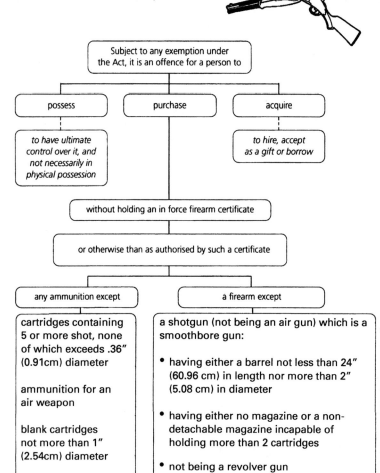

Subject to any exemption under the Act, it is an offence for a person to

possess

to have ultimate control over it, and not necessarily in physical possession

purchase

acquire

to hire, accept as a gift or borrow

without holding an in force firearm certificate

or otherwise than as authorised by such a certificate

any ammunition except

cartridges containing 5 or more shot, none of which exceeds .36" (0.91cm) diameter

ammunition for an air weapon

blank cartridges not more than 1" (2.54cm) diameter

a firearm except

a shotgun (not being an air gun) which is a smoothbore gun:

- having either a barrel not less than 24" (60.96 cm) in length nor more than 2" (5.08 cm) in diameter

- having either no magazine or a non-detachable magazine incapable of holding more than 2 cartridges

- not being a revolver gun

- an air weapon (air rifle, air gun, air pistol not declared by the Secretary of State to be specially dangerous)

Note: It is also an offence to possess, purchase or acquire S1 ammunition in excess of quantities authorised.

Exemptions

In addition to registered firearms dealers, operators of miniature rifle ranges, and persons in the service of the Crown, who may be authorised to possess, purchase and acquire firearms, shotguns and ammunition, provision is made for the following exemptions:

- **Police permit**
  The holder of a police permit may possess a firearm and ammunition in accordance with the terms of his permit. S 7(1)

- **Auctioneer**
  An auctioneer, carrier or warehouseman, or servant of such, may possess a firearm and ammunition in the course of his business. S 9 (1)

  The auctioneer may also sell if he holds a police permit. S 9 (2)

- **Slaughterman**
  A licensed slaughterman may possess a slaughtering instrument and ammunition in a slaughterhouse or knacker's yard where he is employed. (Also applies to the proprietor) S 10 (1) and (2)

- **Sport**
  A person may carry for another a firearm or ammunition, under instruction from, and for the use of, that other person for sporting purposes only. S 11(1)

- **Starter**
  A starter at an athletic meeting may possess a firearm for starting races. S 11(2)

  Persons temporarily in Great Britain for not more than 30 days in the preceding 12 months may purchase a firearm or shotgun from a registered firearms dealer provided it is purchased for the purpose only of being exported from Great Britain without first coming into that person's possession. S18 Firearms (Amendment) Act, 1988

- **Cadet corps**
  A member of a cadet corps approved by the Secretary of State may possess a firearm and ammunition when engaged in drill or target practice. S 11(3)

- **Ranges**
  User of air rifles and miniature rifles (calibre not exceeding 0.58 cm [0.23 in]) at a miniature rifle range or shooting gallery may possess such weapons. S 11(4)

Exemptions continued

- **Clubs**
  A member of a rifle club, miniature rifle club or pistol club approved by the Secretary of State (certain types of weapons may be specified in the approval). S 15 1988 ACT

Private premises
- A person may borrow a shotgun from the occupier of private premises and use it on those premises in the occupier's presence. S 11(5)

- A person over 17 years of age may borrow a rifle from the occupier of private premises if the occupier holds a certificate and he or his servant is present. S 16 1988 ACT

- **Approved**
  A person may use a shotgun at police-approved meetings for shooting at artificial targets S 11(6)

- **Theatres**
  Persons taking part in theatrical performances or rehearsals, or production of films, may possess firearms and, if approved by the Secretary of State, prohibited weapons S 12(1) and (2)

- **Signalling equipment**
  Signalling apparatus on an aircraft or at an aerodrome, or firearms or ammunition on board ship, as equipment of such. S 13 (1)

- **Northern Ireland**
  The holder of a Northern Ireland firearm certificate. S 15

- **Crown service**
  Persons in the service of the Crown (including police officers in their capacity as such). S 54

- **Proof houses**
  Possession of a firearm going to, at, or coming from a specified proof house where they are tested. S 58

- **Visitor's permit**
  The holder of a visitor's firearms or shotgun permit. S 17 1988 ACT

- **Antique firearms**
  See next page.

Shotguns

SECTION 2(1) FIREARMS ACT, 1968

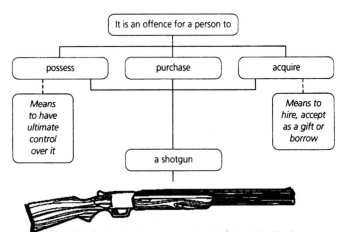

It is an offence for a person to

| possess | purchase | acquire |

possess — Means to have ultimate control over it

acquire — Means to hire, accept as a gift or borrow

a shotgun

A smoothbore gun not being an air gun which has a barrel not less than 24" (60.96 cm) and does not have any barrel with a bore exceeding 2" (5.08 cm) in diameter and either has no magazine or has a non-detachable magazine incapable of holding more than two cartridges and is not a revolver gun. But component parts and sound moderators are not included. It must be a complete shotgun. A certificate would not be required for a part, e.g. a barrel

without holding a certificate authorising him to possess shotguns

Antiques

SECTION 58(2) FIREARMS ACT, 1968

Nothing in the Act relating to firearms shall apply to an antique rifle or shotgun that is sold, transferred, purchased, acquired or possessed as a curiosity or ornament.

The term 'antique' is not defined. But for practical purposes, a breach-loading weapon capable of firing a metallic cartridge would probably not be an antique.

A genuine antique used for target practice would not be possessed as a curio and, therefore, would require a certificate.

Criminal Use of Firearms

FIREARMS ACT, 1968 AS AMENDED BY THE FIREARMS (AMENDMENT) ACT, 1994

The law attempts to prevent the criminal use and possession of firearms and imitation firearms in the following provisions.

Section 16
Possession of a firearm or ammunition with intent to endanger life or cause serious injury to property or enable another to do so (injury not essential).

Section 16A
Possession of a firearm or imitation firearm with intent by means thereof, or to enable another by means thereof, to cause any person to believe that unlawful violence will be used against him or another person.

Section 17(1)
Making use or attempting to make use of a firearm or imitation firearm with intent to resist or prevent arrest or detention of self or another.

Section 17 (2)
Possession of a firearm or imitation firearm at the time of committing or of arrest for a Schedule 2 Offence *(see following page)*.

> **COMMON LAW POWER OF ARREST**

Section 18 (1)
Having with him a firearm or imitation firearm with intent to commit a Schedule 2 Offence or to resist or prevent arrest of self or another.

> **SEE SECTION 50 FOR POWER OF ARREST**

Schedule 2 to the Firearms Act, 1968

The list of offences below are those referred to in section 17(2) and 18(1) of the Firearms Act, 1968.

- Abduction
- Administration of drugs with intent to enable or assist the commission of a crime
- Assault
- House breaking with intent to steal
- Malicious mischief
- Mobbing and rioting
- Preventing the course of justice
- Prison breaking and breaking into prison to rescue prisoners
- Rape
- Robbery
- Theft
- Use of threats with intent to extort
- Wilful fire-raising and culpable and reckless fire-raising
- An offence under Section 57 Civic Government (Scotland) Act, 1982. (Found in property/premises giving reasonable suspicion accused was there to commit theft)
- Offences under Section 2, 3 and 4 of the Explosive Substances Act, 1883 (criminal use of explosives)
- Offence under Section 178 of the Road Traffic Act, 1988 (taking and driving away motor vehicle without consent)
- Offences under Section 41 of the Police (Scotland) Act, 1967 (police assault and so on)
- Any attempt to commit the above crimes and offences

Firearms Dealers

SECTION 3(1) FIREARMS ACT, 1968

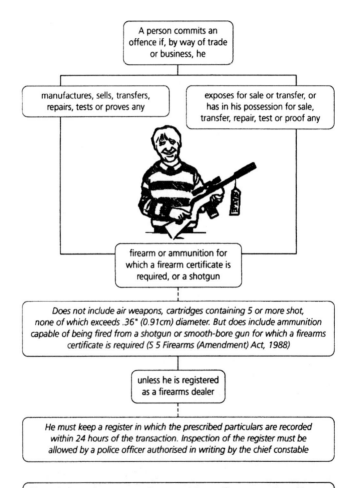

A person commits an offence if, by way of trade or business, he

manufactures, sells, transfers, repairs, tests or proves any

exposes for sale or transfer, or has in his possession for sale, transfer, repair, test or proof any

firearm or ammunition for which a firearm certificate is required, or a shotgun

Does not include air weapons, cartridges containing 5 or more shot, none of which exceeds .36" (0.91cm) diameter. But does include ammunition capable of being fired from a shotgun or smooth-bore gun for which a firearms certificate is required (S 5 Firearms (Amendment) Act, 1988)

unless he is registered as a firearms dealer

He must keep a register in which the prescribed particulars are recorded within 24 hours of the transaction. Inspection of the register must be allowed by a police officer authorised in writing by the chief constable

The main exemptions cover auctioneers, miniature rifle ranges and proof houses

Possession of Firearms
FIREARMS ACT, 1968 (AS AMENDED BY THE FIREARMS (AMENDMENT)
ACT, 1994 AND THE ANTISOCIAL BEHAVIOUR ACT, 2003)

SECTION 19

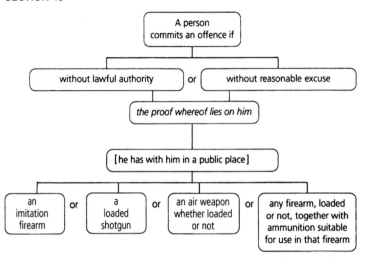

A person commits an offence if

without lawful authority **or** without reasonable excuse

the proof whereof lies on him

[he has with him in a public place]

an imitation firearm **or** a loaded shotgun **or** an air weapon whether loaded or not **or** any firearm, loaded or not, together with ammunition suitable for use in that firearm

A person commits an offence if, while he has a firearm or imitation firearm with him, he enters or is in any building or part of a **building** as a **trespasser** and without reasonable excuse (the proof whereof lies on him). S 20(1)

A person commits an offence if, while he has a firearm or imitation firearm with him, he enters or is on any **land** as a **trespasser** and without reasonable excuse (the proof whereof lies on him). S 20(2)

A person who has been sentenced to serve three years or more **imprisonment** or detention, shall not have a firearm or ammunition in his possession **at any time.** A person who has been sentenced to youth custody or who has been sentenced to be detained in a Detention Centre or in a Young Offenders Institution in Scotland, or to imprisonment for 3 months or more but less than 3 years, shall not have a firearm or ammunition in his possession for **5 years** from the date of his release. S 21

Miscellaneous Firearms Offences

Drunkenness
SECTION 50 GOVERNMENT (SCOTLAND) ACT, 1982

It is an offence for any person to be drunk in a public place while in possession of a firearm (including a crossbow, air gun, air rifle or air pistol).

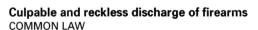

> **SEE SECTION 59 CIVIC GOVERNMENT (SCOTLAND) ACT 1982. FOR POWER OF ARREST**

Culpable and reckless discharge of firearms
COMMON LAW

It is a crime at common law for a person to discharge a firearm in a culpable and reckless manner even where actual injury is not caused.

The essence or the crime is wanton disregard for the safety of others.

> **COMMON LAW POWER OF ARREST**

Shortening barrels
SECTION 4(1) FIREARMS ACT, 1968

It is an offence to shorten the barrel of a shotgun to a length less than 24 in (60.96 cm) (except registered dealers). When less than 24 in (60.96 cm) the shotgun becomes a Section 1 firearm, for which a firearm certificate would be required, and if this certificate is not possessed it becomes an arrestable offence. It is also an offence to possess, purchase or acquire such a weapon. S 6 of the Firearms (Amendment) Act, 1988 creates an offence (unless a dealer) to shorten to less than 24 in (60.96 cm) the barrel of a smoothbore gun for which a firearm certificate is required (other than one with a bore exceeding 2 in [5.08 cm]).

It is an offence (other than as a registered dealer) to convert into a firearm anything which, though having the appearance of being a firearm, is so constructed as to be incapable of discharging any missile through its barrel. S 4 (3)

It is also an offence to possess, purchase or acquire such a weapon.
S 4(4)

> **SEE SECTION 59 FOR POWER OF ARREST**

Firearms – Ages

FIREARMS ACT, 1968

	Under 17 but over 14	Under 15	Under 14
Firearms and ammunition	• May not purchase or hire • Offence to sell or let on hire to, S 22(1), S 24(1) • May accept as a gift or loan if both parties have firearms certificates		• May not possess except as gun bearer, member of rifle club or miniature rifle range or shooting gallery, S 22(2) • Offence to make a gift to, lend to, or part with possession to, S 24(4)
Shotguns	• May not purchase or hire • Offence to sell or let on hire to, S 22(1)	• May not have with him an assembled shotgun except: i) under supervision of a person over 21, or ii) when so covered with a securely fastened gun cover that it cannot be fired, S 22(3) • offence to make a gift to, S 24(3)	
Air weapons	• May not have with him an air weapon or ammunition unless under the supervision of a person over 21; but if on premises may not fire any missile beyond the premises • If over 14 may have with him on private premises with the consent of the occupier but may not fire any missiles beyond the premises • May have with him as a member of an approved rifle club • May use at a shooting gallery if an air rifle or miniature rifle not over .23" calibre • It is an offence to make a gift of an air weapon or ammunition to a person under 17 • It is an offence, except as mentioned above, to part with possession of an air weapon or ammunition to a person under 17		May not have with him an air weapon or ammunition unless under the supervision of a person over 21; but if on premises may not fire any missile beyond the premises

IT IS AN OFFENCE TO SELL OR LET ON HIRE ANY FIREARM OR AMMUNITION TO A PERSON UNDER THE AGE OF 17

Firearms – Police Powers
FIREARMS ACT, 1968

Stop and search Section 47(1)
A constable may require any person whom he has reasonable cause to suspect:-

a) of having a firearm, with or without ammunition, with him in a public place

b) to be committing or about to commit, elsewhere than in a public place an offence of carrying firearms with criminal intent (S 18(1)) or trespassing with a firearm (S 20)

To hand over the firearm or ammunition for examination by the constable.

Note: Failure to do so is an offence under Section 47(2) - see following page.

Production of certificate
S 48(1)

A constable may demand from any person whom he believes to be in possession of a firearm or ammunition for which a certificate is required, or of a shotgun, the production of his firearm certificate or, as the case may be, his shotgun certificate.

Where appropriate the constable may demand the corresponding document issued by another European state. S 48 (1A)

Seizure of weapon
S 48(2)

If the person fails to produce the certificate or to permit the constable to read it, or to show that he is exempt from the requirement to hold one, the constable may seize and detain the firearm, ammunition or shotgun, and demand the person to declare to him immediately his name and address. It is an offence for the person to refuse to declare his name and address or give a false name and address.

It is an offence for a person having a firearm or ammunition with him to fail to hand it over when required to do so by a constable. S 47(2)

Arrest

A constable may arrest without warrant any person whom he has reasonable cause to suspect to be committing an offence under:

- Section 4 – Shortening barrels and so on, without authority
- Section 5 – Possession of prohibited weapons without authority
- Section 18 – Intent to commit Schedule 2 Offence, and so on
- Section 19 – Loaded firearms and so on, in a public place
- Section 20 – Trespass with firearm
- Section 21 – Possession of firearms by prohibited persons
- Section 47(2) – Failing to hand over firearm/ammunition to constable
- Section 48(2) – Refusing to declare name and address and so on

Search Warrants

SECTION 46 FIREARMS ACT, 1968 (AS AMENDED BY FIREARMS (AMENDMENT) ACT, 1997

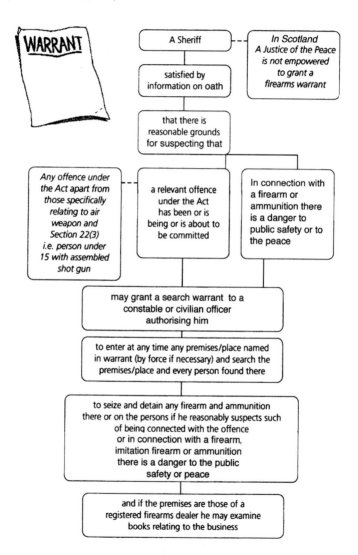

WARRANT

A Sheriff

In Scotland A Justice of the Peace is not empowered to grant a firearms warrant

satisfied by information on oath

that there is reasonable grounds for suspecting that

Any offence under the Act apart from those specifically relating to air weapon and Section 22(3) i.e. person under 15 with assembled shot gun

a relevant offence under the Act has been or is being or is about to be committed

In connection with a firearm or ammunition there is a danger to public safety or to the peace

may grant a search warrant to a constable or civilian officer authorising him

to enter at any time any premises/place named in warrant (by force if necessary) and search the premises/place and every person found there

to seize and detain any firearm and ammunition there or on the persons if he reasonably suspects such of being connected with the offence or in connection with a firearm, imitation firearm or ammunition there is a danger to the public safety or peace

and if the premises are those of a registered firearms dealer he may examine books relating to the business

CHAPTER 5
Licensing

Betting

BETTING, GAMING AND LOTTERIES ACT, 1963

Definition

Although 'betting' is not defined in the statutes it is commonly taken to mean:

- The staking of money or other value on the event of a doubtful issue (whether of a future event or the facts of a past event).

Betting is not in itself unlawful but becomes so in any of four ways:

Unauthorised business S 2

A bookmaker is a person who carries on a business of betting and he must hold a bookmaker's permit. The permit must be produced at the request of a constable.

A person acting as a servant or agent of a bookmaker must:

- Be over 21

- Be authorised in writing by the bookmaker unless he acts only on the bookmaker's premises. The bookmaker must keep a register of persons authorised to act as his servant or agent

Unauthorised premises S 1

Otherwise than on horse racecourses and dog tracks, premises may not be used for betting transactions (see betting offices on following page). But premises may be used if all persons involved in the transaction either reside or work there. An offence is committed by any person who resorts to unauthorised premises for the purpose of betting (proof that he was on the premises will be sufficient until he proves otherwise).

With young persons S 21

It is an offence to have a betting transaction with; to employ to effect betting transactions; or to receive or negotiate a bet through - a person under the age of 18.

In a street or public place S 8

It is an offence to frequent or loiter in a street or public place for betting except on a racecourse.

Betting Offices

SECTION 10 AND SCHEDULE 4 BETTING, GAMING AND LOTTERIES
ACT, 1963 LICENSED BETTING OFFICE (SCOTLAND) REGULATIONS,
1986 (AS AMENDED)

Under 18s
Not permitted. A notice to this effect must be
displayed.

Licence
The betting office licence must be displayed
on the premises.

Encouragement
There must be no encouragement to bet.

Closure
Premises must remain closed Good Friday,
Christmas Day and at such other times, if any,
as may be prescribed.

Permitted opening hours
Between 7am and 10pm each day April to August (inclusive); and
between 7am and 6.30pm each day September to March (inclusive).

Access
Except for the licensee and his employees, no access must be made
available to premises used for other purposes.

Refreshments
The only refreshments allowed are non-alcoholic drinks, pre-packed
sandwiches and snacks including confectionery, biscuits and cakes.

Notice
A notice must be displayed setting out the terms of betting (including
deductions from winnings, any maximum limit on winnings and the
procedure for resolving disputes).

Apparatus

Sound or visual apparatus may only be used to provide information about, and coverage of, a sporting event:

- Betting on such an event
- Other matters, including incidental advertisement
- Betting transactions on the premises
- Results of the event

No visual images may be shown unless they are intended to be received by the general public or other licensees generally. If video recordings are used, identical recordings must be available to other licensees generally.

Advertisements

No advertisement may be published indicating that the premises are a licensed betting office, its location or the facilities offered, except:

- Inside the office; or

- Outside the office (but only the words `licensed betting office' or similar expression such as `bookmaker' or `turf accountant' (limited to three words), the name of the licensee, directions to the office if those premises give access only, the opening hours, the facilities offered, the range of bets available; and information relating to betting transactions in the premises on sporting events, including odds available)

Entertainment

No music, dancing or other entertainment may be provided or allowed except as authorised above.

Betting – Enforcement

BETTING, GAMING AND LOTTERIES ACT, 1963

Licensee S 10(2)

The licensee, his servant or agent may refuse to admit to, or may expel from premises any person who is:

- Drunk
- Violent
- Quarrelsome
- Disorderly
- Likely to subject the licensee to a penalty

Note: Any person who fails to leave when requested commits an offence.

Constable S 10(3)

A constable may, at the request of the licensee, his servant or agent, help to expel from the premises any person whom the constable has reasonable cause to suspect to be liable to be expelled, and such force as may be required may be used for that purpose.

Power of entry S 10(4)

A constable may enter a licensed betting office for the purpose of ascertaining whether provisions are being complied with, and any person who obstructs the constable commits an offence.

Betting – Advertisements and Notices

SECTION 10(5) BETTING, GAMING AND LOTTERIES ACT, 1963
LICENSED BETTING OFFICE (SCOTLAND) REGULATIONS, 1986

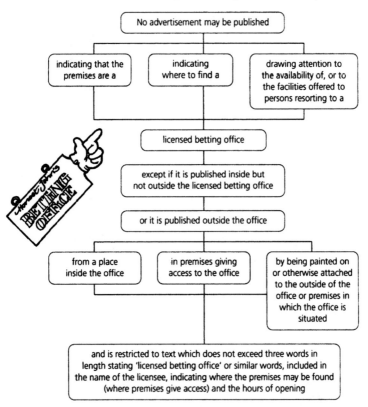

A conspicuous notice must be displayed inside the premises, but not so that it can be read from the outside, setting out the terms on which persons are invited to bet on the premises including the amount of deductions made from winnings, the maximum limit on the amount of winnings and the procedure for the resolution of disputed bets.

Betting office licence to be displayed on the premises.

Gaming

S 52(1) GAMING ACT, 1968

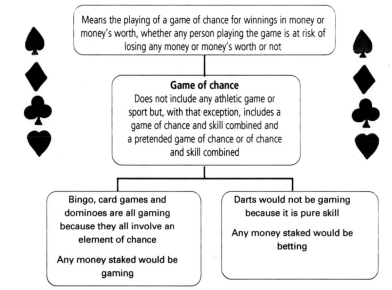

Means the playing of a game of chance for winnings in money or money's worth, whether any person playing the game is at risk of losing any money or money's worth or not

Game of chance
Does not include any athletic game or sport but, with that exception, includes a game of chance and skill combined and a pretended game of chance or of chance and skill combined

Bingo, card games and dominoes are all gaming because they all involve an element of chance

Any money staked would be gaming

Darts would not be gaming because it is pure skill

Any money staked would be betting

'Lotteries' not constituting 'Gaming'. Where the playing of a game of chance constitutes a 'small lottery incidental to certain entertainments' (S 3), a 'private lottery' (S 4), a 'societies' lottery' (S 5) or a 'local lottery' (S 6), and the winner is ascertained by reference to not more than 3 determining factors, the playing of the game will not constitute 'gaming' (S 52(3)).

The Gaming Act,1968 controls gaming
The four parts into which the Act is divided are as follows:

Part 1   Gaming other than on premises licensed or registered under the Act

Part 2   Gaming on premises which have been licensed or registered under this Act

Part 3   Gaming machines

Part 4   Gaming at entertainment not held for private gain

These are now discussed in turn on the following pages.

Gaming Elsewhere than on Premises Licensed or Registered Under the Act

GAMING ACT, 1968

This part of the Act does not apply to gaming machines, entertainment not for private gain, or amusements with prizes.

Certain restrictions are imposed on the gaming which is allowed:

the nature of the game S 2	charges for taking part S 3	levy on stakes or winnings S 4
This restriction does not apply to domestic occasions in a private dwelling, in a hostel, hall of residence or similar place not used as a business, and the players are all inmates or residents	Other than any stakes hazarded, no charge, in money or money's worth, may be made to take part (this would include an admission charge) but this restriction would not apply to member's clubs	A levy may not be charged on any of the stakes or winnings, whether by direct payment, deduction, exchange of tokens at a lower rate than of issue, or any other means

The game shall not involve playing or staking against a bank, whether or not a player holds the bank

The chances must be equally favourable to all players

Where the players are playing against some other person, the chances must not be more favourable to the other person than the players

Public places S 5

No person may take part in gaming in a street or any place to which the public have access on payment or otherwise.

Street includes any bridge, road, lane, footway, etc, which is open to the public, and the doorways and entrances of premises abutting upon, and any ground adjoining and open to, a street.

Licensed premises S 6

Dominoes and cribbage, and any other game authorised by the licensing justices may be played on premises for which a justices' on-licence is in force (other than a restaurant or guest house licence).

Persons Under 18

No person under the age of 18 years may take part in gaming on premises (S 7).

Gaming on Premises Which Have Been Licensed or Registered Under This Act

This part does not apply to gaming by way of gaming machines
S 12 GAMING ACT, 1968

The following restrictions apply to gaming on premises which are either licensed under the Act, or which consist of a club or miners' welfare institute registered under the Act.

Who may take part?

- Only persons who are present on the premises at the time gaming takes place (applies to both Licensed or Registered clubs)
- They must be members of the club in question, or bona fide guests of such a member (applies to both Licensed or Registered clubs)
- Neither the licence holder nor any other person acting on his behalf may take part in the gaming except holding the bank (Licensed clubs only)
- At least 24 hours (for a Licensed club, 48 hours in the case of a Registered club) must have elapsed since application being made for membership and taking part in the gaming
- No person under 18 years shall be present whilst gaming is taking place (except on premises restricted to the playing of bingo) (S 17)

Games which may be played

In licensed clubs, in addition to any game which does not contravene the requirements of 'nature of the game' (see previous page), the following games may be played if they comply with the provisions of the Gaming Clubs (Banker's Games) Regs. 1994:

roulette, dice, baccarat (whether it is baccarat banque, chemin de fer, punto banco, punto 2000 or some other version), the big six, sic bo, three card poker, blackjack, casino stud poker and super pan 9.

In registered clubs, in addition to any game which does not contravene the requirements of 'nature of the game' (see previous page), pontoon and chemin de fer may be played

Charges for taking part

Charges to take part are generally prohibited by S 3 but may be made in the following circumstances:

- **Licensed Clubs** A fixed amount of money may be charged in respect of one or more facilities for 1 person. But if it is a recurring charge, it may not be incurred again by the same person within 1 hour of the last charge (except a series of games of chemin de fer).
- **Registered Clubs** One or more charges may be made in respect of a person if the amount of that charge, or charges in aggregate, does not exceed £2 for that person for that day.

Gaming on Sundays

In licensed premises gaming may not take place between 4am and 2pm on Sundays.

A constable may at any reasonable time enter any premises Licensed under the Act and may inspect the premises, machines or other equipment, and any book or other document on the premises, for the purpose of ascertaining whether any contravention has been committed (S 43).

Bingo Clubs

S 20 GAMING ACT, 1968

Application of section

This section applies to any club licensed under this Act where restrictions have been imposed which limit the gaming which may take place to bingo.

Simultaneous games of bingo

Where a game of bingo is played simultaneously on different bingo club premises, and:

a) all the players take part at the same time and all are present at that time on one or other of those premises;

b) the draw takes place on one or other of those premises while the game is being played; and

c) any claim by a player to have won is indicated to all the players before the next number is called,

then, if the following conditions are fulfilled,

a) the aggregate amount paid as winnings for that game does not exceed the aggregate amount staked by the players in that game, and

b) the aggregate amount paid as winnings for that game, together with the aggregate amount paid as winnings for all games in the same week (7 days beginning Monday) played on any of those premises does not exceed £2,000,000

the requirement for the player to be on the premises when the gaming takes place (S 12) shall have effect as if those different premises were the same premises.

And the requirement to:
- be a member of the club or bona fide guest; and
- the requirement for 24 hours to have elapsed since making the application for membership, and taking part in gaming, will only apply to persons present on the individual premises.

Persons under 18

Where the gaming takes place on bingo club premises persons under 18 will be allowed on the premises while gaming takes place provided they do not take part in the gaming.

Maximum aggregate weekly winnings

Without prejudice to the above, the aggregate amount paid as winnings in respect of all games of bingo in any one week (7 days beginning Monday) on any bingo premises shall not exceed the aggregate amount of the players' stakes by more than £20,000.

Bingo with prizes

See following page.

Gaming With Prizes

S 21 GAMING ACT, 1968

Application of this section
This provision deals with 'gaming' to which this part of the Act applies and in respect of which:

a) the amount paid for a chance to win a prize does not exceed 50p;
b) the aggregate amount of the sale of chances in any 1 game does not exceed £500, and the sale of chances and the declaration of results take place on the same day and time as when the game is played, and on the same premises;
c) any money prize does not exceed £25;
d) the winning of a prize, or the purchase of a chance to win, does not entitle (whether subject to a further payment or not) any person to any further opportunity to take part in any other gaming or lottery; and
e) the aggregate amount or value of prizes on any one game does not exceed £500.

If the above conditions are fulfilled, the following 'relaxations' will apply:

Type of game
If the gaming takes place on licensed premises, the restrictions placed on which type of game may be played (see previous page) will not apply.

Where a condition of a licence for any premises includes a restriction as to the types of games which may be played, those restrictions will not apply.

Charges for taking part
If the gaming takes place on licensed premises, the restrictions on making charges for taking part will not apply (see previous page).

Bingo Clubs
Where the gaming takes place on bingo club premises persons under 18 will be allowed on the premises while gaming takes place provided they do not take part in the gaming.

Where a game of bingo is played for prizes on bingo club premises, the prizes won will be disregarded for the purposes of calculating the aggregate maximum amount paid to players as winnings in any one week.

Gaming Machines on Premises Licensed or Registered Under This Act

GAMING ACT, 1968

For practical purposes, machines are of two types:

JACKPOT MACHINES S 31
- May only be used on premises which are either licensed or registered under the Act for the purpose of gaming or gaming machines (S 35)
- There is a limit to the charge for playing a single game on the machines (currently 50p)
- There is a maximum limit on the winnings which may be paid out on a single game (which must be by way of coins):
  1) for registered premises (club or miners' welfare), £250;
  2) for bingo clubs, £500; and
  3) for any other premises which are licensed, £2,000

(GAMING MACHINES (MAXIMUM PRIZES) REGS. 1998, S I 1998/2150 & 2001/3970)
- Where a percentage of the aggregate value of charges for play is prescribed for any machine on licensed premises, it must not pay out less than that percentage
- A statement must be displayed on the machine giving:
  1) the value of prizes which can be won by playing a single game;
  2) any special circumstances in which that prize cannot be won; and
  3) the percentage of the aggregate value of charges for play paid out as winnings
- The machines may not be used on the premises on any occasion when the public are admitted whether on payment or otherwise
- The maximum number of machines which may be available is:
  a) registered club or miners' welfare, three
  b) bingo clubs, four; and
  c) any other licensed premises, ten

AMUSEMENT MACHINES S 34
- May only be used on premises for which a permit has been granted; on premises used as a pleasure fair for which a permit has been granted; or at a travelling showmen's pleasure fair
- The charge for playing the machine once shall be by coins or tokens to a maximum value of 30p.

Gaming Machines – continued

- Prizes are restricted to one of the following:
  1) Money prize not exceeding £5 or tokens exchangeable for such amount;
  2) Non-money prize not exceeding £8 or tokens exchangeable for such non-money prize.
  3) A mixture of money and non-money prizes which do not exceed the above amounts;
  4) Tokens which can be either used to play further games or be exchanged as above
- In the case of a Betting Office, the maximum charge for playing the machine is 30p and the prize must be monetary, not exceeding £25, delivered by the machine.

USE AT NON-COMMERCIAL ENTERTAINMENTS S 33

Jackpot machines, amusement with prizes machines, or any other type of machine may be used as an incident to non-commercial entertainment if not on premises licensed or registered under the Act, without further authority and without limits on numbers or prizes. This would apply to bazaars, sales of work, fêtes, dinners, dances, sporting or athletic events, etc, whether limited to one day or extended over two or more days. In these cases the whole of the proceeds after deducting expenses must be devoted to other than private gain. The opportunity to win prizes shall not be the only, or only substantial, inducement to attend.

Gaming – Advertisements

S 42 GAMING ACT 1968 (AS AMENDED)

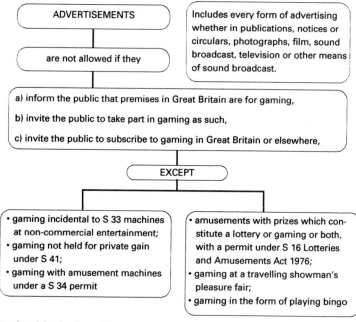

ADVERTISEMENTS

are not allowed if they

Includes every form of advertising whether in publications, notices or circulars, photographs, film, sound broadcast, television or other means of sound broadcast.

a) inform the public that premises in Great Britain are for gaming,

b) invite the public to take part in gaming as such,

c) invite the public to subscribe to gaming in Great Britain or elsewhere,

EXCEPT

- gaming incidental to S 33 machines at non-commercial entertainment;
- gaming not held for private gain under S 41;
- gaming with amusement machines under a S 34 permit

- amusements with prizes which constitute a lottery or gaming or both, with a permit under S 16 Lotteries and Amusements Act 1976;
- gaming at a travelling showman's pleasure fair;
- gaming in the form of playing bingo

But advertising is allowed if:

a) a sign inside or outside of licensed premises indicating that gambling takes place, or

b) a notice required by the Act, or

c) a publication in a newspaper stating that a gaming licence has been granted (but must be within 14 days of the grant), or

d) an advertisement in a publication (not published wholly or mainly for the purpose of promoting gaming premises), relating to licensed premises other than bingo clubs, and which contains no more than the name, logo, address, telephone, fax, ownership and facilities provided, or

e) an advertisement published in a newspaper which circulates wholly or mainly outside Great Britain.

Gaming at Non-commercial Entertainment

S 41 GAMING ACT, 1968

Gaming which:

- is played at entertainment promoted otherwise than for private gain;
- is not gaming to which part 2 (gaming on premises licensed or registered under this Act) or part 3 (gaming machines) of the Act applies; and
- does not constitute 'amusements' with prizes under S 15 or S 16 of the Lotteries and Amusements Act 1976 (see later)

must comply with the provisions listed below.

Provisions

1. **Nature of the game** It must not involve playing against a bank, whether held by one of the players or not; and chances must be equally favourable to all the players.
2. **Payment to take part** In respect of all games, not more than one payment (whether by entrance fee, stake or otherwise) shall be made by each player, and this shall not exceed £4.
3. **Total value of prizes** In respect of all games, the total value of prizes shall not exceed £400.
4. **Proceeds** The whole of the proceeds, less expenses and any cost of providing prizes, shall be applied for purposes other than private gain.
5. **Expenses** shall not exceed a reasonable cost of facilities provided.
6. **Multiple entertainments** Where 2 or more entertainments are provided by the same person on the same premises on the same day, the above provisions will apply to those entertainments collectively as if they were one.
7. **Series of entertainments** Where a series of entertainments is held otherwise than as in paragraph 6, the above provisions will have effect separately in relation to each one; and the total value of prizes is increased to £700 for the final game in a series, if the player qualified to take part by playing in another entertainment held the day before.

Offences

If gaming takes place in contravention of these provisions, every person concerned in the **organisation or management** of the gaming shall be guilty of an offence. A person who takes part in **procuring the assembly** of the players will have been involved in the organisation of the gaming.

Where gaming takes place on any **premises, vessel or vehicle** in contravention of these provisions, any person who knew or had reasonable cause to suspect that they would be used in contravention of the provisions and **allowed them to be used** for gaming, or **let, let on hire or made them available** for gaming, will be guilty of an offence.

Lotteries

S 1 LOTTERIES AND AMUSEMENTS ACT, 1976
READERS DIGEST ASS V WILLIAMS (1976) 3 ALL ER 737

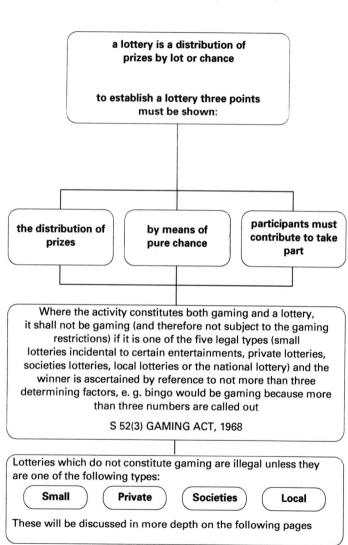

a lottery is a distribution of prizes by lot or chance

to establish a lottery three points must be shown:

the distribution of prizes

by means of pure chance

participants must contribute to take part

Where the activity constitutes both gaming and a lottery, it shall not be gaming (and therefore not subject to the gaming restrictions) if it is one of the five legal types (small lotteries incidental to certain entertainments, private lotteries, societies lotteries, local lotteries or the national lottery) and the winner is ascertained by reference to not more than three determining factors, e. g. bingo would be gaming because more than three numbers are called out

S 52(3) GAMING ACT, 1968

Lotteries which do not constitute gaming are illegal unless they are one of the following types:

Small   Private   Societies   Local

These will be discussed in more depth on the following pages

Small Lotteries Incidental to Exempt Entertainments

S 3 LOTTERIES & AMUSEMENTS ACT, 1976

Exempt Entertainment

Means a bazaar, sale of work, fête, dinner, dance, sporting or athletic event, or other entertainment of similar character, whether for one day or for two or more days.

A lottery promoted as an incident of exempt entertainment will not be unlawful if the conditions below are complied with. If any one of them is contravened, any person concerned in its promotion or conduct will be guilty of an offence.

The conditions are:

- All proceeds less expenses must be devoted to other than private gain
- Prizes must not be money
- Sale of tickets etc, and declaration or result must take place at the entertainment
- The lottery shall not be the only or substantial inducement to attend.

Private Lotteries

S 4 LOTTERIES AND AMUSEMENTS ACTS, 1976

A **private lottery** means one which is promoted:

- for members of one society established and conducted for purposes other than betting, gaming and lotteries;
- for persons who all work on the same premises; or
- for persons who all reside on the same premises,

and the following conditions are met:

- the lottery must be promoted by a person for whom it is promoted and, in the case of a society, is authorised in writing by the governing body; and
- the sale of tickets or chances in the lottery is confined to persons for whom it is promoted and, in the case of a society, to any other person on the society's premises.

'Society' includes any club, institution, organisation or association of persons by whatever name called and any separate branch or section of such a club, etc.

Each local or affiliated branch of a society shall be regarded as a separate and distinct society.

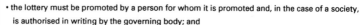

A **private lottery is not unlawful** but the following conditions must be observed:

a) the whole proceeds, less expenses for printing and stationery shall be devoted to the provision of prizes, or, in the case of a society, devoted either to the provision of prizes, or the purposes of the society, or part prizes and part purposes of the society;

b) no written notice or advertisement of the lottery shall be exhibited, published or distributed other than a notice of it exhibited on the premises of the society, or where they work or reside, or an announcement or advertisement of it on the ticket, if any;

c) the price of every ticket or chance shall be the same and the price of a ticket shall be stated on the ticket;

d) every ticket must show the name and address of each of the promoters; a statement of the persons to whom the sale of tickets is restricted; and a statement that no prize will be delivered to persons other than the one to whom the winning ticket is sold;

e) no ticket or chance shall be issued other than by sale and upon receipt of its full price which is non-returnable; and

f) no tickets shall be sent through the post.

Offences

If any of the above conditions is contravened, each of the promoters of the lottery, and any other person breaking a condition, shall be guilty of an offence.

Societies' and Local Lotteries

LOTTERIES & AMUSEMENTS ACT, 1976 AND
LOTTERIES REGULATIONS, 1993

SOCIETIES' LOTTERIES S 5

Promoted by a society established for: charitable purposes, athletic sports or games or culture, other purposes which are not for private gain or commercial

A society's lottery is not unlawful if the following conditions are met:
- Promoted in GB
- Society is registered under the Act and the name of the registration authority must appear on the ticket
- Scheme approved by the society
- Total value of tickets, etc sold is £10,000 or less, otherwise scheme to be registered with the Board before sale of tickets
- All proceeds less expenses to be applied to purposes of the society

LOCAL LOTTERIES S 6

These are lotteries promoted by the local authority

A local lottery is not unlawful if the following conditions are met:
- Promoted in GB
- Promoted in accordance with a scheme approved by the local authority
- Scheme registered with the Board before sale of tickets
- Publicity must be given to the objects of the lottery (S 7)
- All money accruing must be applied to the objects of the lottery (S 8)
- Tickets must specify the name of the promoting authority, the date of the lottery, and the fact that it has been registered with the Board

AND

- No more than 55% of proceeds to be spent on prizes (S 11)
- No ticket to exceed £2 (S 11)
- Full price must be paid for tickets and no refunds (S 11)
- No payment other than the price of a ticket or chance shall be required to take part
- Tickets, etc may not be sold by or to persons under 16 or by machine (Regs 3&5)
- Tickets not to be sold in a street except from a kiosk or shop front (Reg 4)
- Tickets must bear name and address of promoter (in the case of societies), the date of the lottery and the name of the society (S 11)
- The price of every ticket shall be the same and shall be stated on the ticket (S 11)
- The promoter of the lottery must be authorised in writing by the governing body (in the case of societies)
- No prize to exceed £25,000 or 10% of value of tickets sold, whichever is greater
- Total value of tickets sold not to exceed £2,000,000
- Total value of tickets sold in all lotteries in 1 year not to exceed £10,000,000

'Society' – see previous page
'Board' – the Gaming Board of Great Britain

Amusements with Prizes

S 15 & S 16 LOTTERIES AND AMUSEMENTS ACT 1976

An **'amusement with prizes'** may include activities which constitute 'gaming'.

There are basically two types, those which are provided at **'exempt entertainments'**, and those provided at certain **'commercial entertainments'**. In both cases, the conditions to which they are subject apply where amusement is provided which constitutes a lottery or gaming or both, but does not constitute:

• Gaming to which Part 2 of the Gaming Act, 1968 applies; or

• Gaming by means of a machine to which Part 3 of that Act applies.

'Exempt entertainment' means a bazaar, sale of work, fete, dinner, dance, sporting or athletic event or other entertainment of a similar character, whether limited to one day or extending over two or more days.

Both types are subject to different conditions which are detailed below.

Exempt Entertainments (S 15)

Where such amusement constitutes a lottery, the 'lottery offences' under S 2 (see following page) do not apply. Whether it is a lottery or not, the below conditions must be observed:

a) the whole proceeds, less expenses, shall go to other than private gain; and

b) the facilities for winning prizes must not be the only, or the only substantial, inducement to attend.

Commercial Entertainments (S 16)

This section applies where the amusements are provided:

a) on premises for which a permit for the provision of commercial amusements with prizes has been granted under this Act;

b) on premises used mainly for amusements by way of machines and a permit has been granted under S 34 of the Gaming Act, 1968 for the provision of machines for commercial purposes; or

c) at a pleasure fair consisting of amusements provided by travelling showmen, which is held on any day of the year on premises not previously used in that year on more than 27 days for such a purpose.

In these circumstances the 'lottery offences' under S 2 (see following page) do not apply. However, the following conditions must be observed:

a) the amount paid for any 1 chance to win must not exceed 50p;

b) the aggregate amount taken by the sale of chances for any 1 determination shall not exceed £90;

c) the sale of the chances and declaration of the result take place on the same day and on the same premises during the time when the amusement is provided;

d) no money prize may exceed £25;

e) the winning of a prize may not entitle the person, whether or not further payments are made by him, to any further opportunity to take part in any amusement with prizes or in any gaming or lottery; and

f) in the case of a pleasure fair, the opportunity to win prizes is not the only, or the only substantial, inducement to attend the fair.

Lottery Offences

S 2 LOTTERIES AND AMUSEMENTS ACT, 1976

Where a lottery does not come within the aforementioned 'legalised' lotteries, every person who, in connection with any lottery promoted in Great Britain or elsewhere, is involved in any of the following activities, commits an offence.

a) **Printing** – Prints any tickets;

b) **Sale or distribution** – Sells or distributes, or offers or advertises for sale or distribution, or has in his possession for the purpose of sale or distribution, any tickets or chances;

c) **Inducements** – Prints, publishes or distributes or has in his possession for the purpose of publication or distribution, any advertisement, any list of prize winners or winning tickets, or any such matter relating to the lottery, as is calculated to act as an inducement to participate;

d) **Importation** – Brings, or invites any person to send, into Great Britain any ticket or advertisement from a place outside the British Islands and member states, for the purpose of sale or distribution;

e) **Exportation** – Sends or attempts to send out of Great Britain to a place outside the British Islands and member states, any money or valuable thing received in respect of the sale or distribution of any ticket or chance, or any document recording the sale or distribution or identity of the holder of a ticket or chance;

f) **Premises** – Uses any premises, or knowingly causes or permits the use of premises for promoting or conducting the lottery; or

g) **Procuring others** – Causes, procures or attempts to procure any person to do any of the above.

Alcoholic Liquor

SECTION 90 LICENSING (SCOTLAND) ACT, 1976

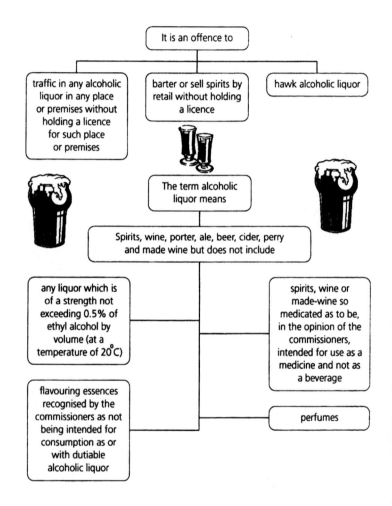

It is an offence to

traffic in any alcoholic liquor in any place or premises without holding a licence for such place or premises

barter or sell spirits by retail without holding a licence

hawk alcoholic liquor

The term alcoholic liquor means

Spirits, wine, porter, ale, beer, cider, perry and made wine but does not include

any liquor which is of a strength not exceeding 0.5% of ethyl alcohol by volume (at a temperature of 20°C)

spirits, wine or made-wine so medicated as to be, in the opinion of the commissioners, intended for use as a medicine and not as a beverage

flavouring essences recognised by the commissioners as not being intended for consumption as or with dutiable alcoholic liquor

perfumes

Alcoholic Liquor – Licensing Board

SECTION 9 LICENSING (SCOTLAND) ACT, 1976

A licensing board has the responsibility for granting licences to persons authorising them to sell by retail or supply alcoholic liquor.

Sale by retail means the sale at any one time to any one person of quantities not exceeding:

- In the case of spirits, wine or made wine - 2 gallons or 1 case

- In the case of beer or cider - 4 gallons or 2 cases

The types of licences

Licences which may be granted by a licensing board under Part 1 of the Licensing (Scotland) Act, 1976 are:

- **Public house**
  Authorises sale for 'on' or 'off' consumption

- **Hotel**
  Authorises sale for 'on' or 'off' consumption

- **Off-sales**
  Authorises sale for 'off' consumption only

- **Restaurant**
  Authorises sale or supply for 'on' consumption only as an ancillary to meals consumed on premises. No bar counter permitted

- **Refreshment**
  Authorises sale or supply for 'on' consumption only in premises
  providing refreshment, including food and non-alcoholic beverages
  for consumption on the premises. No bar counter permitted.

- **Entertainment**
  Authorises sale or supply for 'on' consumption in places of public
  entertainment where the liquor is ancillary to entertainment
  provided.

  *Note: Theatres erected and licensed by a local authority prior to 1
  January 1904 do not require a licence to sell alcoholic liquor.*

- **Restricted hotel**
  Authorises sale or supply for 'on' consumption to persons taking
  table meals on premises as an ancillary to the meal.

  Sale and supply to residents for 'on' consumption.

  Supply to the private friends of residents - bona fide entertained at
  residents' expense - for 'on' consumption.

  Sale and supply to residents, for consumption by residents or
  their private friends - bona-fide entertained at residents' expense
  as an ancillary to a meal supplied at, but to be consumed 'off' the
  premises (for example, picnic meals).

Under part III of the Licensing (Scotland) Act, 1976 a licensing
board may also grant a licence to a:

- **Seamen's canteen**
  Authorises sale or supply for 'on' consumption only.

  *Note: Seamen's Canteens are for Merchant Navy seamen and
  should not be confused with Military Messes.*

Under part VII of the Licensing (Scotland) Act, 1976, Certificates of
Registration for:

- **Registered clubs**
  Are granted, renewed, refused or cancelled by the Sheriff rather
  than the Licensing Board. However, where a registered Club
  makes application for an 'occasional licence' under Section 33 of
  the Act, the application is made to the Licensing Board and not to
  the Sheriff.

Alcoholic Liquor – Permitted Hours

Permitted hours means the hours during which, by virtue of the Licensing (Scotland) Act, 1976, alcoholic liquor may be sold, supplied or consumed in licensed premises.

Normal permitted hours for 'on' consumption
SECTION 53 LICENSING (SCOTLAND) ACT, 1976

- Public House
- Hotels
- Restricted Hotels
- Restaurants
- Refreshment Licences
- Entertainment Licences
- Registered Clubs
- Seamen's Canteens

Weekdays
11 am to 11 pm

Sundays
12.30 pm to 2.30 pm
and
6.30 pm to 11 pm

Note 1: Public Houses and Places holding Refreshment Licences may only open on Sundays if the licensee applies for and is granted permission so to do by the Licensing Board.

Note 2: Normal Permitted Hours may be extended if the Licensing Board agrees to grant an 'Occasional' or 'Regular' Extension of permitted hours under the provisions of Section 64 of the Act.

Note 3: Subject to certain conditions Sections 57 and 58 of the Act may permit premises providing meals to extend 'normal permitted hours' on Weekdays from 11 pm to 1 am and on Sundays from 2.30 pm in the afternoon to 4 pm and from 11 pm in the evening to 1 am if the liquor sold or supplied is an ancillary to the meal.

Alternative 'winter' permitted hours for athletic registered clubs
SECTION 56 LICENSING (SCOTLAND) ACT, 1976

Registered Clubs of a sports nature which have activities taking place out of doors may apply to the Sheriff to have alternative permitted hours on Sundays between 1 October and 31 March.

If granted the alternative hours will be 12.30 pm to 2 pm and 4 pm to 9 pm.

Trading Hours of Off-Sales Premises

SECTION 119 LICENSING (SCOTLAND) ACT, 1976

The trading hours for off-sales premises and those parts of public houses and hotels set aside for the purpose of off-sales are:

Weekdays
8 am to 10 pm

Sundays
12.30 pm to 10 pm

Note: Although those parts of public houses and hotels set aside for the purpose of off-sales are subject to the above-mentioned Trading Hours, these do not prevent 'off-sales' taking place in the other parts of the licensed premises, during the permitted hours operated by those premises.

Exceptions
SECTION 54 LICENSING (SCOTLAND) ACT, 1976

Permitted hours do not apply to:

- **'Drinking up times'**
  During the first 15 minutes after the conclusion of permitted hours, consumption may take place and liquor may be removed from the premises (unless supplied or taken away in an open vessel), provided the alcohol was supplied during permitted hours.

- **After meals**
  During the first 30 minutes after permitted hours, consumption of alcohol is permitted by persons taking meals provided the drink is ancillary to the meal and was supplied during the permitted hours.

- **Residents**
  Sale or supply to a person residing on the premises, for consumption on the premises and/or taking away from the premises by that resident.

- **Private friends**
  A licence holder or a resident on premises may supply alcohol to private friends for consumption on the premises, provided the private friend is being bona-fide entertained by and at the expense of the licensee or resident.

- **Off-sales**
  The ordering of alcohol to be consumed off the premises or the despatch of alcohol so ordered.

- **Traders**
  Sale to a trader for the purposes of his trade, or to a registered club, Government Canteen or Military Mess.

Alcoholic Liquor - Occasional Licences

SECTION 33 LICENSING (SCOTLAND) ACT, 1976

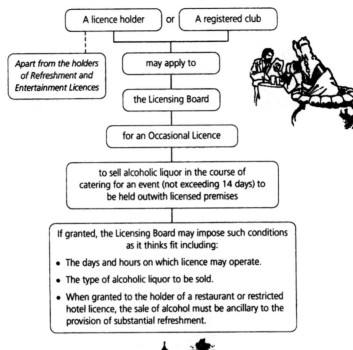

A licence holder   or   A registered club

Apart from the holders of Refreshment and Entertainment Licences

may apply to

the Licensing Board

for an Occasional Licence

to sell alcoholic liquor in the course of catering for an event (not exceeding 14 days) to be held outwith licensed premises

If granted, the Licensing Board may impose such conditions as it thinks fit including:

- The days and hours on which licence may operate.
- The type of alcoholic liquor to be sold.
- When granted to the holder of a restaurant or restricted hotel licence, the sale of alcohol must be ancillary to the provision of substantial refreshment.

Note 1: If the event exceeds 14 days an additional, Occasional Licence(s) will be required.

Note 2: If the holder, his employee or agent contravenes any condition imposed on the Occasional Licence, he commits an offence.

Note 3: If a Registered Club contravenes any condition of the Occasional Licence, then officials, members of the management committee or governing body commit an offence unless they prove the contravention took place without their knowledge or consent.

Alcoholic Liquor – Occasional Permissions SECTION 34 LICENSING (SCOTLAND) ACT, 1976

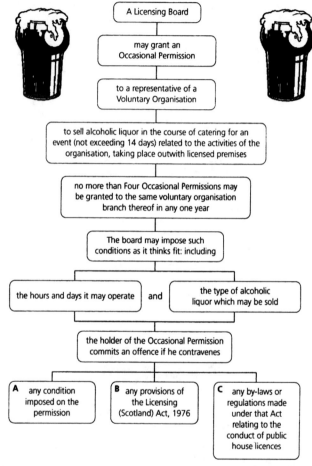

A Licensing Board

may grant an Occasional Permission

to a representative of a Voluntary Organisation

to sell alcoholic liquor in the course of catering for an event (not exceeding 14 days) related to the activities of the organisation, taking place outwith licensed premises

no more than Four Occasional Permissions may be granted to the same voluntary organisation branch thereof in any one year

The board may impose such conditions as it thinks fit: including

the hours and days it may operate **and** the type of alcoholic liquor which may be sold

the holder of the Occasional Permission commits an offence if he contravenes

A any condition imposed on the permission

B any provisions of the Licensing (Scotland) Act, 1976

C any by-laws or regulations made under that Act relating to the conduct of public house licences

Note: In the case of contraventions of b) and c) the holder of the Permission has a defence if he proves he used due diligence to prevent the offence occurring.

Children in Bars

SECTION 69 LICENSING (SCOTLAND) ACT, 1976 (AS AMENDED)

SECTION 69(1)

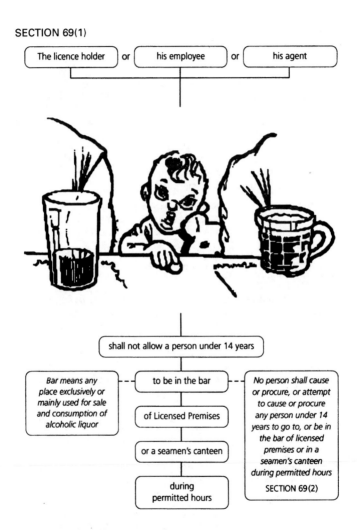

| The licence holder | or | his employee | or | his agent |

shall not allow a person under 14 years

Bar means any place exclusively or mainly used for sale and consumption of alcoholic liquor

to be in the bar

of Licensed Premises

or a seamen's canteen

during permitted hours

No person shall cause or procure, or attempt to cause or procure any person under 14 years to go to, or be in the bar of licensed premises or in a seamen's canteen during permitted hours

SECTION 69(2)

Defences

No offence is committed if the person under 14 years:

- Is a child of the licence holder; or

- Resides in, but is not employed in the licensed premises; or

- Is in the bar of licensed premises or seamen's canteen solely for the purpose of passing to or from some other part of the premise, not a bar or canteen, being apart to or from where is no other convenient means of access or egress; or

- The bar was part of a railway refreshment room or other premises constructed, fitted and intended to be used bona-fide for any purpose the holding of a licence was merely ancillary; or

- Is in the bar of a public house or hotel, granted a Children's Certificate, accompanied by a person aged 18 years or over between 11 am and 8 pm.

Note 1: The holder of a Refreshment Licence, his employee or agent commit an offence if: a) they allow a person under 14 years to be in the premises during permitted hours if not accompanied by a person aged 18 years or over; b) they allow a person under 14 years to remain on the premises after 8 pm. No offence is committed if the person under 14 years is a child of the licence holder or resides in the premises but is not employed there. Section 70 Licensing (Scotland) Act, 1976.

Note 2: Under Section 112 of the Licensing (Scotland) Act, 1976 it is an offence for every official, member of the committee of management or governing body of a Registered Club to allow a child under 14 years to be in a bar of a registered club during permitted hours. Furthermore, it is an offence for any person to cause a child under 14 years to be in a bar of a registered club during permitted hours.

Alcoholic Liquor – Persons Under 18: Sale, Supply and Consumption

SECTION 68 LICENSING (SCOTLAND) ACT, 1976

The licensee or his Employee or Agent SECTION 68(1)

It is an offence for the licence holder, or his employee or agent:

- To sell alcoholic liquor to a person under 18 years in licensed premises.

- To allow a person under 18 years to consume alcoholic liquor in a **bar** of licensed premises.

Note: Where the employee or agent commits these offences the licence holder is also guilty.

Persons under 18 SECTION 68(2)

It is an offence for a person under 18 years:

- To buy or attempt to buy alcoholic liquor in licensed premises.

- To consume alcoholic liquor in a **bar** of licensed premises.

But a person who has attained the age of 16 years can buy beer, wine, made-wine, porter, cider or perry for consumption at a meal in a part of the premises set apart for the service of meals. If in a bar it must be a table meal.

Any person SECTION 68(3)

It is an offence for any person:

- To knowingly act as an agent in the purchase of alcoholic liquor for a person under 18 years.

- To knowingly buy or attempt to buy alcoholic liquor for consumption in a **bar** of licensed premises by a person under 18 years.

Nothing prohibits a person acting as an agent for a person who has attained the age of 16 years in the purchase of beer, wine, made-wine, porter, cider or perry for consumption at a meal.

Delivery to persons under 18 years SECTION 68(5)

It is an offence for the licensee or his employee or agent to deliver (or the licensee to allow any person to deliver) alcoholic liquor sold in licensed premises to a person under 18 years for consumption off the premises except where the delivery is made at the residence or place of work of the purchaser.

Alcoholic Liquor – Employment Restrictions

Employment in bars and seamen's canteens
SECTION 72 LICENSING (SCOTLAND) ACT, 1976
It is an offence for the licensee, his employee or agent to employ a person under 18 years in a bar or a seamen's canteen, at a time when the premises are open for the sale of alcoholic liquor.

Supervision of sale of alcoholic liquor in off-sales
SECTION 97A LICENSING (SCOTLAND) ACT, 1976
It is an offence for a licensee, his employee or agent to cause or permit a person under 18 years to sell alcoholic liquor on off-sales premises or the off-sales part of other licensed premises without that sale having been specifically approved by the licensee or by a person aged 18 or over acting on his behalf.

Employment to serve alcoholic liquor in premises holding refreshment licence
SECTION 73 LICENSING (SCOTLAND) ACT, 1976
It is an offence for any person to employ a person under 18 years in premises holding a Refreshment Licence if the purpose, or one of the purposes of employment, is to serve alcoholic liquor to persons in those premises.

Note: There are no restrictions on persons under 18 years serving alcohol to customers in licensed restaurants or in the restaurant parts of hotels and public houses provided the person is not employed in the bar of hotels and public houses.

Employment in registered clubs
SECTION 113 LICENSING (SCOTLAND) ACT, 1976
A person under 18 years must not be employed in a registered club to serve alcoholic liquor to persons in that club.

Where this section is contravened officials or members of the management committee or governing body are guilty of the offence unless they prove the offence took place without their knowledge or consent.

Statutory defences
It is a defence for any person charged under Sections 68(1), 68(5), 69(1), 70 or 97A of the Licensing (Scotland) Act, 1976 to prove:

- He used due diligence to prevent the occurrence of the offence.

- He had no reason to suspect that the person in relation to whom charge was brought was under 18 or under 14, as the case may be.

Drunks in Licensed Premises

LICENSING (SCOTLAND) ACT, 1976

Permitting drunkenness SECTION 78
A licence holder, his employee or agent shall not permit any breach of the peace, drunkenness, or riotous or disorderly conduct to take place in licensed premises.

Selling to drunks SECTION 76
A licence holder, his employee or agent shall not sell alcoholic liquor to a drunken person.

Procuring alcohol SECTION 75
No person in licensed premises may procure or attempt to procure alcoholic liquor for consumption by a drunken person, nor aid a drunken person to obtain or consume alcoholic liquor.

Power to request person to leave SECTION 79
The occupier or manager of licensed premises, or his employee or agent, or any constable may request any person who is riotous, quarrelsome or disorderly or who refuses to leave premises at the conclusion of permitted hours, to leave the premises.

Failure to leave the premises on being so requested is an offence and a constable may assist in expelling any such person. A constable may also arrest without warrant anyone committing an offence under this Section.

Thieves, prostitutes, and so on SECTION 80
Any person who occupies or keeps licensed premises must not knowingly allow thieves or reputed thieves, or prostitutes or reputed prostitutes, or persons convicted under Section 4 or 5(3) of the Misuse of Drugs Act, 1971, to meet, assemble or remain on those premises; or knowingly permit goods which he has reasonable grounds to believe are stolen to remain on the premises.

Betting and gaming SECTION 81
The licence holder, his employee or agent shall not permit any game to be played on the premises in such circumstances that any offence under the betting, gaming and lotteries legislation is committed.

The playing of dominoes, cribbage and other games authorised by the licensing board may be permitted in public houses and hotels. In such circumstances the licensing board may impose requirements to ensure the gaming does not take place for high stakes and is not the primary inducement for person to resort to the premises.

Alcoholic Liquor – Offences in Relation to Constables SECTION 84

It is an offence for the licence-holder, his employee or agent to

knowingly allow a constable to remain on the premises whilst on duty, except for the purpose of the execution of his duty

knowingly supply any liquor or refreshment to any constable on duty except by the authority of a superior officer of the constable

Alcoholic Liquor – Power of Entry

LICENSING (SCOTLAND) ACT, 1976

Licensed premises SECTION 85

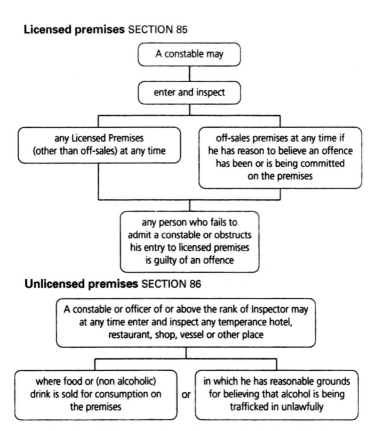

A constable may

↓

enter and inspect

any Licensed Premises
(other than off-sales) at any time

off-sales premises at any time if
he has reason to believe an offence
has been or is being committed
on the premises

any person who fails to
admit a constable or obstructs
his entry to licensed premises
is guilty of an offence

Unlicensed premises SECTION 86

A constable or officer of or above the rank of Inspector may
at any time enter and inspect any temperance hotel,
restaurant, shop, vessel or other place

where food or (non alcoholic)
drink is sold for consumption on
the premises

or

in which he has reasonable grounds
for believing that alcohol is being
trafficked in unlawfully

Officers below the rank of Inspector may exercise the powers granted
under this section if they obtain the written authority of a Justice of
the Peace or of an officer of or above the rank of Inspector.

Such written authority expires after 8 days and may specify the time
or times when the powers may be used.

Alcoholic Liquor – Registered Clubs

SECTION 114 LICENSING (SCOTLAND) ACT, 1976

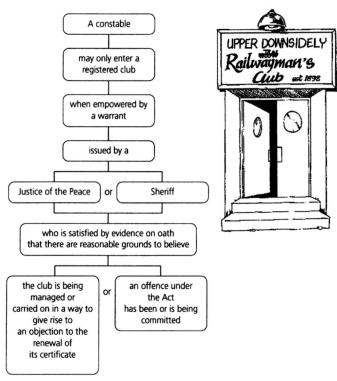

The warrant authorises a constable to enter the premises, by force if necessary, to search and seize documents relating to the club's business; and take the names and addresses of persons found in the premises.

It is an offence for a person to refuse to give his name and address on being requested or to give a false name and address.

Note: There is nothing in Section 114 which prevents a constable entering a registered club when invited to do so by the management or when using his common law power to quell a disturbance taking place on the premises.

Drunkenness

SECTION 50 CIVIC GOVERNMENT SCOTLAND) ACT, 1982

Drunk and incapable in a public place

It is an offence for a person to be drunk and incapable of taking care of himself in a public place (other than in licensed premises), while not in the care and protection of a suitable person.

Children

It is an offence to be drunk in a public place, including licensed premises, while in charge of a child under the age of 10 years.

Firearms and so on

It is an offence to be drunk in a public place, including licensed premises, while in possession of a firearm (including air weapons or a crossbow).

Power of arrest

A constable may, when it is in the interests of justice to do so, arrest without warrant, any person he finds committing the above-mentioned offences.

Note: A constable not in uniform must produce his identification if required to do so.

Drunkenness in licensed premises

SECTION 74 LICENSING (SCOTLAND) ACT, 1976

- **Entering licensed premises**

  It is an offence for any person (other than a resident) to enter or attempt to enter licensed premises while drunk. The offender may be arrested without warrant.

- **Drunk and incapable in licensed premises**

  It is an offence for a person to be drunk and incapable of taking care of himself in licensed premises, while not in the care and protection of a suitable person. The offender may be arrested without warrant.

Drunk Licence Holder, and so on

SECTION 77 LICENSING (SCOTLAND) ACT, 1976

It is an offence for the licence holder or his employee or agent to be drunk in licensed premises.

No Power of Arrest under the Act.

Sale or supply to drunken persons
SECTION 76 LICENSING (SCOTLAND) ACT, 1976

It is an offence for the licence holder or his employee or agent to sell or supply alcohol to a drunken person in licensed premises.

No Power of Arrest under the Act.

Note: Where the offence is committed by the employee or agent, the licence holder also commits the offence as he is responsible for their actions.

Public Charitable Collections

SECTION 119 CIVIC GOVERNMENT (SCOTLAND) ACT, 1982 AND PUBLIC
CHARITABLE COLLECTIONS (SCOTLAND) REGULATIONS, 1984

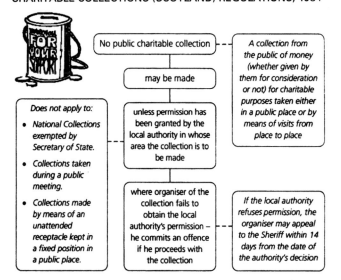

No public charitable collection

may be made

unless permission has been granted by the local authority in whose area the collection is to be made

where organiser of the collection fails to obtain the local authority's permission – he commits an offence if he proceeds with the collection

Does not apply to:

- *National Collections exempted by Secretary of State.*
- *Collections taken during a public meeting.*
- *Collections made by means of an unattended receptacle kept in a fixed position in a public place.*

A collection from the public of money (whether given by them for consideration or not) for charitable purposes taken either in a public place or by means of visits from place to place

If the local authority refuses permission, the organiser may appeal to the Sheriff within 14 days from the date of the authority's decision

Note: Collections may be obtained in sealed envelopes or in collecting boxes.

Some important rules

- Each collector requires a Certificate of Authority from the organiser or his agent, which must be produced on demand to a police constable; persons from whom collector has solicited a contribution or any interested persons. He must also wear a badge bearing the name of the charity which will benefit from the collection.

- No person under 14 years must act as a collector in a street collection and no person under 16 years must act as a collector in a house to house collection.

- Collectors in a sealed envelope collection must only accept contributions in a sealed envelope and in non-envelope collections must only accept contributions by having donors place such in the collecting box.

- Collectors must return their certificates of authority, collecting boxes or envelopes unopened to the organiser or his agent upon ceasing to be a collector or on demand from organiser or his agent.

CHAPTER 6
Animals

Cruelty to Animals

SECTION 1 PROTECTION OF ANIMALS (SCOTLAND) ACT, 1912

Means to cause, permit or in any way be concerned with:

Physical cruelty

To cruelly beat, kick, ill-treat, over-ride, over-drive, over-load, torture, infuriate or terrify any animal, or in any way to cause unnecessary suffering to any animal.

Conveyance

To convey or carry any animal in such a manner or position as to cause any unnecessary suffering.

Abandoning

SECTION 1 ABANDONMENT OF ANIMALS ACT, 1960
Without reasonable cause or excuse, whether temporarily or not, in circumstances likely to cause unnecessary suffering, for example, leaving animals at home while on holiday.

Fighting

The fighting or baiting of any animal.

Drugs

The administration of any poisonous or injurious drug or substance to any animal without reasonable cause or excuse.

Operations

To subject the animal to any operation which is performed without due care and humanity.

Tethering

To tether any horse, ass or mule under such conditions or in such a manner as to cause that animal unnecessary suffering.

Police powers

A police constable may arrest without warrant any person who he has reason to believe to be guilty of this offence either upon his own view or that of a third person. He may take charge of any animal or vehicle. S 11(1)

SECTION 13 PROTECTION OF ANIMALS (SCOTLAND) ACT, 1912

For the purposes of the offence of cruelty to animals:

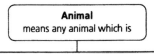

Animal
means any animal which is

Domestic

Horse, ass, mule, bull, sheep, pig, goat, dog, cat, fowl, or any other animal which is tame or has been or is being sufficiently tamed to serve some purpose for the use of man

Note: Does not include invertebrates, for example, worms

Captive

Any animal (not being a domestic animal) including any bird, fish or reptile which is in captivity or confinement, or which is maimed, pinioned or subjected to any appliance for the purpose of hindering or preventing its escape

A wild animal temporarily unable to escape is not a captive animal

The offences created by this Act do not apply:

- To anything done in the course of destruction, or preparation for destruction, of any animal as food for mankind unless unnecessary suffering is inflicted S 1(3)

- To the coursing or hunting of any captive animal, unless such animal is liberated in an injured, mutilated or exhausted condition, or if it is done in an enclosed space from which it has no reasonable chance of escape

- To vivisection carried out under licence provided it complies with the provisions of Animals (Scientific Procedures) Act, 1986.

Cruelty To Wild Mammals

WILD MAMMALS (PROTECTION) ACT, 1996

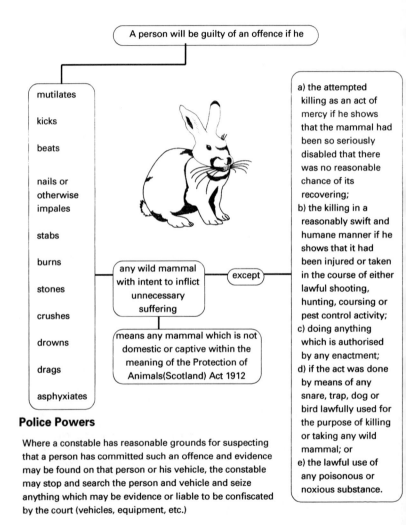

A person will be guilty of an offence if he

mutilates

kicks

beats

nails or otherwise impales

stabs

burns

stones

crushes

drowns

drags

asphyxiates

any wild mammal with intent to inflict unnecessary suffering — except

means any mammal which is not domestic or captive within the meaning of the Protection of Animals(Scotland) Act 1912

a) the attempted killing as an act of mercy if he shows that the mammal had been so seriously disabled that there was no reasonable chance of its recovering;

b) the killing in a reasonably swift and humane manner if he shows that it had been injured or taken in the course of either lawful shooting, hunting, coursing or pest control activity;

c) doing anything which is authorised by any enactment;

d) if the act was done by means of any snare, trap, dog or bird lawfully used for the purpose of killing or taking any wild mammal; or

e) the lawful use of any poisonous or noxious substance.

Police Powers

Where a constable has reasonable grounds for suspecting that a person has committed such an offence and evidence may be found on that person or his vehicle, the constable may stop and search the person and vehicle and seize anything which may be evidence or liable to be confiscated by the court (vehicles, equipment, etc.)

Animal Fights

SECTION 1 & 1A PROTECTION OF ANIMALS (SCOTLAND) ACT, 1912
ADDED BY THE PROTECTION OF ANIMALS (AMENDMENT) ACT, 1988

SECTION 1 COCKFIGHTING ACT, 1952

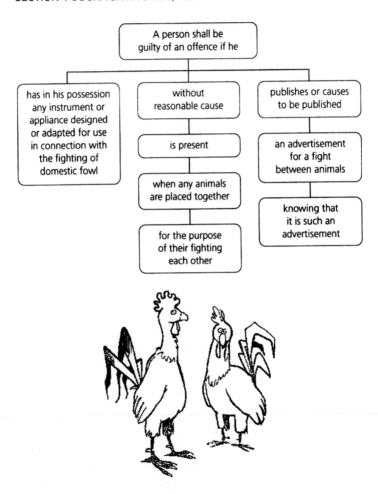

A person shall be guilty of an offence if he

has in his possession any instrument or appliance designed or adapted for use in connection with the fighting of domestic fowl

without reasonable cause

is present

when any animals are placed together

for the purpose of their fighting each other

publishes or causes to be published

an advertisement for a fight between animals

knowing that it is such an advertisement

Injured Animals

SECTION 10 PROTECTION OF ANIMALS (SCOTLAND) ACT, 1912

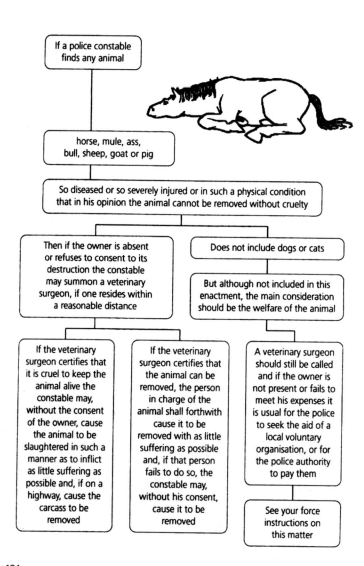

If a police constable finds any animal

horse, mule, ass, bull, sheep, goat or pig

So diseased or so severely injured or in such a physical condition that in his opinion the animal cannot be removed without cruelty

Then if the owner is absent or refuses to consent to its destruction the constable may summon a veterinary surgeon, if one resides within a reasonable distance

Does not include dogs or cats

But although not included in this enactment, the main consideration should be the welfare of the animal

If the veterinary surgeon certifies that it is cruel to keep the animal alive the constable may, without the consent of the owner, cause the animal to be slaughtered in such a manner as to inflict as little suffering as possible and, if on a highway, cause the carcass to be removed

If the veterinary surgeon certifies that the animal can be removed, the person in charge of the animal shall forthwith cause it to be removed with as little suffering as possible and, if that person fails to do so, the constable may, without his consent, cause it to be removed

A veterinary surgeon should still be called and if the owner is not present or fails to meet his expenses it is usual for the police to seek the aid of a local voluntary organisation, or for the police authority to pay them

See your force instructions on this matter

Pets

PET ANIMALS ACT, 1951 AS AMENDED BY THE PET ANIMALS
(AMENDMENT) ACT, 1983

No person shall keep a pet shop except under the authority of a
licence granted by the local authority. S 1

If any person carries on a business of
selling animals as pets in any part of
a street or public place, except at a
stall or barrow in a market, he
shall be guilty of an offence. S 2

If any person sells an animal as a pet
to a person who he has reasonable
cause to believe to be under the age
of 12 years, the seller shall be
guilty of an offence. S 3

Dog Collars

ARTICLE 1 CONTROL OF DOGS ORDER 1992

Every dog while in a highway or place of public resort, shall wear a collar with the name and address of the owner inscribed on the collar or on a plate or badge attached thereto.

Exceptions
* Dogs used on official duties by the armed forces, HM Customs & Excise or the police

* Dogs used for sporting purposes and packs of hounds

* Dogs used for the capture or destruction of vermin

* Dogs used for driving or tending cattle or sheep

* Guide dogs for the blind.

The owner of the dog and any person in charge of it, who, without lawful authority or excuse causes or permits the dog to be on the highway or place of public resort shall be guilty of an offence. Dogs not wearing a collar may be seized as a stray dog. This order will be executed and enforced by officers of a local authority and not by the police.

Dogs Worrying Livestock

SECTION 1 DOGS (PROTECTION OF LIVESTOCK) ACT, 1953 AS
AMENDED

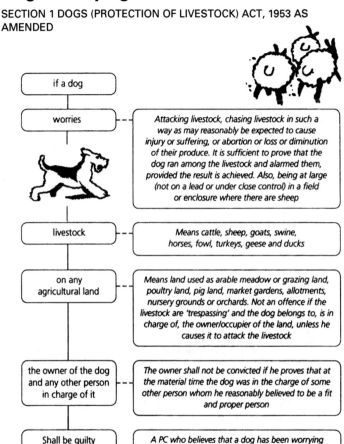

if a dog	
worries	*Attacking livestock, chasing livestock in such a way as may reasonably be expected to cause injury or suffering, or abortion or loss or diminution of their produce. It is sufficient to prove that the dog ran among the livestock and alarmed them, provided the result is achieved. Also, being at large (not on a lead or under close control) in a field or enclosure where there are sheep*
livestock	*Means cattle, sheep, goats, swine, horses, fowl, turkeys, geese and ducks*
on any agricultural land	*Means land used as arable meadow or grazing land, poultry land, pig land, market gardens, allotments, nursery grounds or orchards. Not an offence if the livestock are 'trespassing' and the dog belongs to, is in charge of, the owner/occupier of the land, unless he causes it to attack the livestock*
the owner of the dog and any other person in charge of it	*The owner shall not be convicted if he proves that at the material time the dog was in the charge of some other person whom he reasonably believed to be a fit and proper person*
Shall be guilty of an offence	*A PC who believes that a dog has been worrying livestock as above may seize the dog if no person admits to being the owner or person in charge of it*

Defence

In civil proceedings it is a defence to a charge of killing or injuring a
dog to prove that it was done to protect the livestock and the police
were informed within 48 hours. SECTION 4 ANIMALS (SCOTLAND)
ACT, 1987

Dangerous Dogs

Orders for controlling dangerous dogs

SECTION 2 DOGS ACT, 1871

Where a dog is regarded as being dangerous, either because it has attacked someone, or because it has worried livestock and not kept under proper control, application may be made to the court for an order to be made for the dog to be kept by the owner under proper control or destroyed.

SECTION 1 DANGEROUS DOGS ACT, 1989

Where a court of summary jurisdiction makes an order under Section 2 of the Dogs Act, 1871 directing a dog to be destroyed, it may also:

- Appoint a person to undertake its destruction and require the person having custody of the dog to deliver it up for destruction

- If it thinks fit, make an order disqualifying the owner from having custody of a dog for a specified period.

Any person who fails to comply with an order to keep a dog under proper control or deliver a dog up for destruction commits an offence.

SECTION 1 DANGEROUS DOGS ACT, 1991

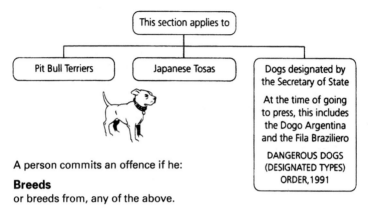

This section applies to

Pit Bull Terriers

Japanese Tosas

Dogs designated by the Secretary of State

At the time of going to press, this includes the Dogo Argentina and the Fila Braziliero

DANGEROUS DOGS (DESIGNATED TYPES) ORDER, 1991

A person commits an offence if he:

Breeds

or breeds from, any of the above.

Sells

or exchanges such a dog or offers, advertises or exposes such a dog for sale or exchange.

Makes a gift

(or offers to do so) of such a dog or advertises or exposes such a dog as a gift.

Allows

such a dog of which he is the owner or of which he is for the time being in charge to be in a **public place** without being **muzzled** and **kept on a lead.** ('Muzzled' means sufficient to prevent it biting someone, and 'kept on a lead' means securely held by a person not less than 16 years.) S 7

Abandons

such a dog of which he is the owner.

Allows such a dog to **stray,** being the owner or for the time being in charge.

Have such a dog in his **possession** or **custody** except under a power of seizure or in accordance with an order for its destruction.

Control of Dangerous Dogs

SECTION 3 DANGEROUS DOGS ACT, 1991

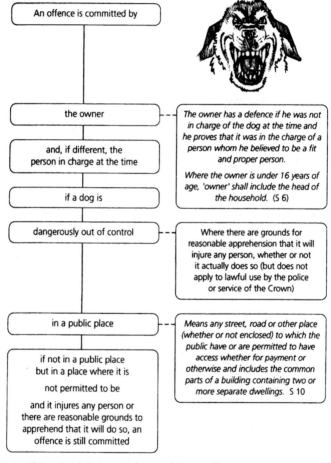

An offence is committed by

the owner

The owner has a defence if he was not in charge of the dog at the time and he proves that it was in the charge of a person whom he believed to be a fit and proper person.

and, if different, the person in charge at the time

Where the owner is under 16 years of age, 'owner' shall include the head of the household. (S 6)

if a dog is

dangerously out of control

Where there are grounds for reasonable apprehension that it will injure any person, whether or not it actually does so (but does not apply to lawful use by the police or service of the Crown)

in a public place

Means any street, road or other place (whether or not enclosed) to which the public have or are permitted to have access whether for payment or otherwise and includes the common parts of a building containing two or more separate dwellings. S 10

if not in a public place but in a place where it is not permitted to be

and it injures any person or there are reasonable grounds to apprehend that it will do so, an offence is still committed

*Note: If the dog **injures someone** while out of control an aggravated offence is committed for which heavier penalties are liable.*

Dangerous Dogs – Police Powers

SECTION 5 DANGEROUS DOGS ACT, 1991

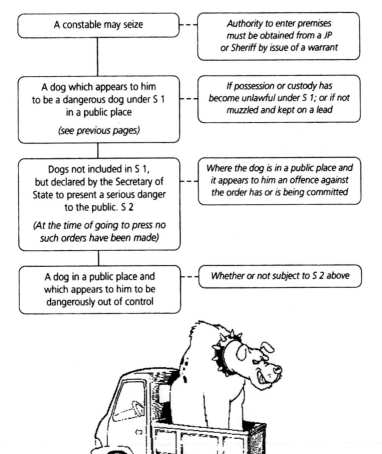

| A constable may seize | | *Authority to enter premises must be obtained from a JP or Sheriff by issue of a warrant* |

| A dog which appears to him to be a dangerous dog under S 1 in a public place *(see previous pages)* | | *If possession or custody has become unlawful under S 1; or if not muzzled and kept on a lead* |

| Dogs not included in S 1, but declared by the Secretary of State to present a serious danger to the public. S 2 *(At the time of going to press no such orders have been made)* | | *Where the dog is in a public place and it appears to him an offence against the order has or is being committed* |

| A dog in a public place and which appears to him to be dangerously out of control | | *Whether or not subject to S 2 above* |

Guard Dogs
SECTION 1 GUARD DOGS ACT, 1975

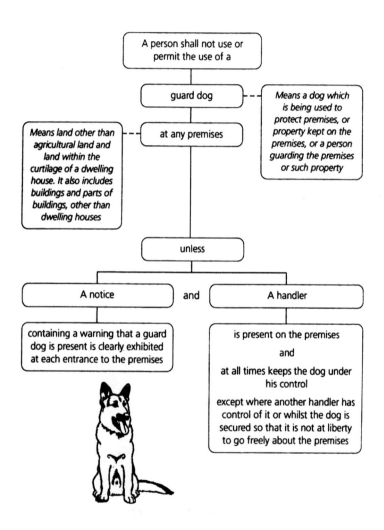

A person shall not use or permit the use of a

guard dog

Means a dog which is being used to protect premises, or property kept on the premises, or a person guarding the premises or such property

at any premises

Means land other than agricultural land and land within the curtilage of a dwelling house. It also includes buildings and parts of buildings, other than dwelling houses

unless

A notice

and

A handler

containing a warning that a guard dog is present is clearly exhibited at each entrance to the premises

is present on the premises

and

at all times keeps the dog under his control

except where another handler has control of it or whilst the dog is secured so that it is not at liberty to go freely about the premises

Dangerous Wild Animals

SECTION 1 DANGEROUS WILD ANIMALS ACT, 1976

No person is allowed to keep a dangerous wild animal unless he has been granted a licence to do so by the local authority. S 1

A `dangerous wild animal' is one which is specifically mentioned in the Act. Many animals are mentioned but the following list gives a guide to the type of animal referred to:

- Alligators
- Crocodiles
- Ostriches
- Apes
- Poisonous snakes
- Lions
- Tigers
- Leopards
- Bears
- Wild dogs
- Wolves.

The provisions of this Act do not apply to:

- Zoos
- Circuses
- Licensed pet shops
- Premises authorised to be used for experiments. S 5

Animals on Roads

SECTION 98 ROADS (SCOTLAND) ACT, 1984

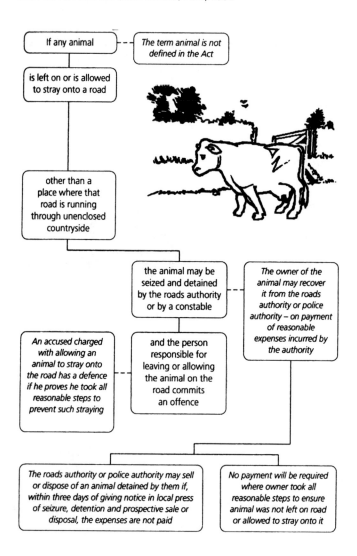

If any animal

The term animal is not defined in the Act

is left on or is allowed to stray onto a road

other than a place where that road is running through unenclosed countryside

the animal may be seized and detained by the roads authority or by a constable

The owner of the animal may recover it from the roads authority or police authority – on payment of reasonable expenses incurred by the authority

An accused charged with allowing an animal to stray onto the road has a defence if he proves he took all reasonable steps to prevent such straying

and the person responsible for leaving or allowing the animal on the road commits an offence

The roads authority or police authority may sell or dispose of an animal detained by them if, within three days of giving notice in local press of seizure, detention and prospective sale or disposal, the expenses are not paid

No payment will be required where owner took all reasonable steps to ensure animal was not left on road or allowed to stray onto it

Diseases of Animals
ANIMAL HEALTH ACT, 1981

Notification S 15(1)
Any person having possession or charge of a diseased animal shall keep it separate from unaffected animals and notify the police with all practicable speed.

`Infected areas'
If necessary, the veterinary inspector who is called to visit the infected place declares the premises and the area surrounding the premises to be an infected area.

Movement
Movement of animals from and to infected areas is then restricted to those authorised by licence. Various powers are then given to the minister and the local authority to make orders and regulations to control the situation.

Power of arrest S 60
If a person is seen or found committing, or is reasonably suspected of being engaged in committing, an act which has been declared to be an offence against the Act or an order of the minister or a regulation of the local authority, a constable may stop and detain him and if his name and address is not given to the satisfaction of the constable, he may be apprehended without warrant.

Animals and property
Irrespective of the stopping or apprehension of the person the constable may stop, detain and examine any animal, vehicle, boat or thing to which the offence relates, and require the same to be returned to any place from which it was unlawfully removed, and he may execute and enforce that requisition.

Obstruction S 60
A person who obstructs or impedes or assists to obstruct or impede a constable or other officer in the execution of this Act or of orders or regulations made in consequence of it, may be arrested, without warrant, by the constable or officer.

Powers of entry
In areas where constables are appointed as local authority inspectors, they also have power to enter land and buildings where they suspect that diseased animals are or have been kept or where provisions of the Act are not being complied with.

Rabies

SECTIONS 15, 61 & 62 ANIMAL HEALTH ACT, 1981

The powers conferred by this Act are without prejudice to powers given on the previous page.

Offences specific to this disease involve landing or attempting to land or importing animals in contravention of the order introduced to prevent the introduction of rabies into Great Britain and the unlawful movement of any animal into, within or out of an infected area or place.

Any person who knows or suspects that an animal is affected with rabies shall give notice of that fact to a constable. S 15

Police powers

A constable may arrest without warrant any person whom he, with reasonable cause, suspects to be in the act of committing or to have committed an offence against this section.

For the purpose of arresting a person a constable may enter (if need be by force) and search any vessel, boat, hovercraft, aircraft or vehicle of any other description in which that person is or where the constable reasonably suspects him to be. The prohibition extends to the Channel Tunnel.

The above power of entry also applies in exercising the power to seize any animal.

Game Licence

SECTION 1 HARES (SCOTLAND) ACT, 1848; SECTION 4 GAME
LICENCES ACT, 1860; SECTION 4 GROUND GAME ACT, 1880

It is an offence, without
having a game licence

1860 ACT

to take, kill or pursue by any means whatever,
or to use any dog, gun, net or other engine for the
purpose of taking, killing or pursuing any

hare, pheasant, partridge, grouse, heath or moor
game, black game, woodcock, snipe, rabbit or deer
except

A game licence is not required for
any of the following purposes:

- Taking woodcock or snipe with
  nets or snares.

- Taking or destroying rabbits by
  the proprietor of a warren or
  grounds, or the tenant of land,
  or by his permission.

- Pursuing hares by coursing with
  greyhounds, or killing hares by
  hunting with beagles or other
  hounds.

- Pursuing and killing of deer by
  hunting with hounds.

- Taking and killing of deer in
  enclosed lands by the owner or
  occupier of lands or by his
  permission.

The following persons are exempt
from the requirement to hold a licence:

- The royal family.

- Any person appointed as
  gamekeeper on behalf of Her
  Majesty.

- A person aiding or assisting the
  holder of a licence.

- A person authorised to kill hares
  under the Hares (Scotland) Act,
  1848.

- The occupier of the land upon
  which the game is taken or killed,
  and persons authorised by him.

Game – Out of Season

SECTION 1 GAME (SCOTLAND) ACT, 1772

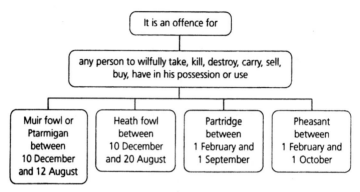

Possession of game by unqualified person
SECTION 3 GAME (SCOTLAND) ACT, 1772

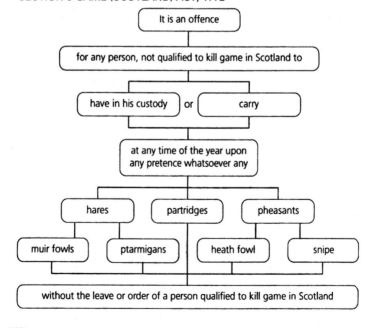

Poaching (by day)

SECTIONS 1, 4-6 GAME (SCOTLAND) ACT, 1832

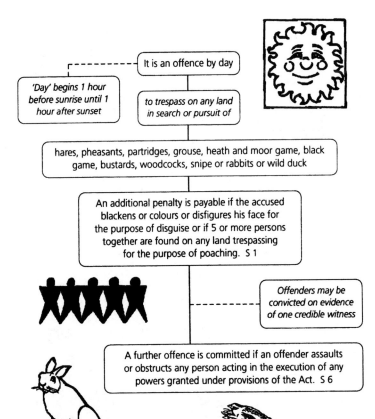

It is an offence by day

'Day' begins 1 hour before sunrise until 1 hour after sunset

to trespass on any land in search or pursuit of

hares, pheasants, partridges, grouse, heath and moor game, black game, bustards, woodcocks, snipe or rabbits or wild duck

An additional penalty is payable if the accused blackens or colours or disfigures his face for the purpose of disguise or if 5 or more persons together are found on any land trespassing for the purpose of poaching. S 1

Offenders may be convicted on evidence of one credible witness

A further offence is committed if an offender assaults or obstructs any person acting in the execution of any powers granted under provisions of the Act. S 6

Exception

The offence of trespassing in pursuit of game does not extend to hunting or coursing with hounds and being in fresh pursuit of any deer, hare or fox already started on other land. S4

Poaching (by night)

SECTION 1 NIGHT POACHING ACT, 1828, AS AMENDED

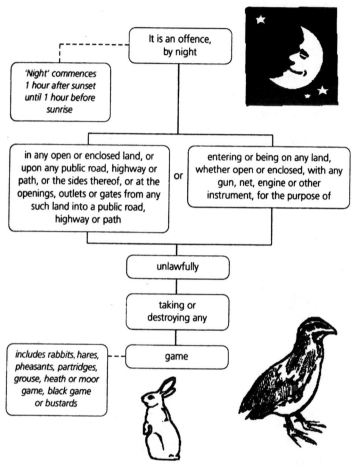

It is an offence, by night

'Night' commences 1 hour after sunset until 1 hour before sunrise

in any open or enclosed land, or upon any public road, highway or path, or the sides thereof, or at the openings, outlets or gates from any such land into a public road, highway or path

or

entering or being on any land, whether open or enclosed, with any gun, net, engine or other instrument, for the purpose of

unlawfully

taking or destroying any

includes rabbits, hares, pheasants, partridges, grouse, heath or moor game, black game or bustards

game

Note: These are the basic elements of poaching by night, but the offence may be aggravated if the circumstances outlined on the following page are present.

SECTIONS 2 & 9 NIGHT POACHING ACT, 1828

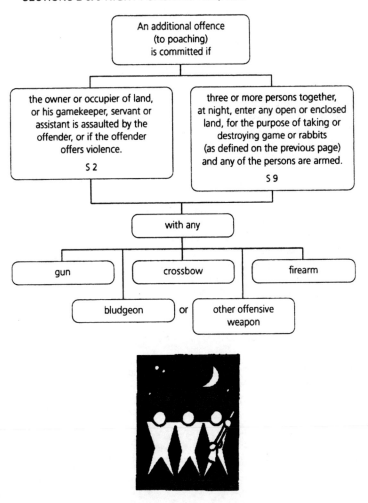

An additional offence
(to poaching)
is committed if

the owner or occupier of land,
or his gamekeeper, servant or
assistant is assaulted by the
offender, or if the offender
offers violence.

S 2

three or more persons together,
at night, enter any open or enclosed
land, for the purpose of taking or
destroying game or rabbits
(as defined on the previous page)
and any of the persons are armed.

S 9

with any

gun

crossbow

firearm

bludgeon

or

other offensive
weapon

Poaching – Police Powers

The Game (Scotland) Act, 1832 and the Night Poaching Act, 1828, give the police in Scotland no direct powers to deal with offenders who contravene the provisions of these two pieces of legislation.

In general terms the legislation empowers owners, and occupiers of land, lords of the manor, gamekeepers and persons assisting gamekeepers and so on, to take the action necessary to bring offenders to justice.

Street or public place
SECTION 2 POACHING PREVENTION ACT, 1862

A constable may, in any public place, **search** any person whom he has good cause to **suspect** of coming from any land where he has been unlawfully in the pursuit of game, and having in his possession any game, gun, ammunition, nets, snares, traps or other device for killing or taking game, and also to **stop** and **search** any cart or other conveyance which the constable has good cause to suspect is carrying any game or article mentioned above, and the constable may **seize** and detain any game or article found on the person or in the conveyance. Proceedings are then taken by **summons**. There is no power of arrest.

Note 1: The evidence of one credible witness is sufficient to gain a conviction.

Note 2: As a preliminary to any criminal proceedings under this Act an oath known as the `Oath of Verity' has to be sworn, before a judge or Justice of the Peace, by the police witnesses. If for any reason the oath were omitted it would be fatal to the proceedings.

Note 3: Under this Act, game means: hares, pheasants, partridges, woodcocks, snipes, rabbits, grouse and black or moor game; and the eggs of pheasants, partridges, grouse and black or moor game.

Poaching of Deer

DEER (SCOTLAND) ACT, 1996

Prohibition of Poaching SECTIONS 17 AND 25

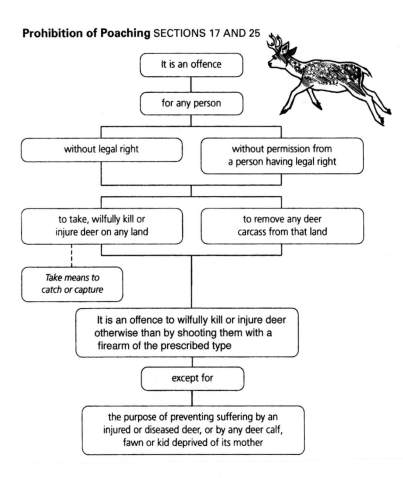

It is an offence

for any person

without legal right

without permission from
a person having legal right

to take, wilfully kill or
injure deer on any land

to remove any deer
carcass from that land

*Take means to
catch or capture*

It is an offence to wilfully kill or injure deer
otherwise than by shooting them with a
firearm of the prescribed type

except for

the purpose of preventing suffering by an
injured or diseased deer, or by any deer calf,
fawn or kid deprived of its mother

*Note: Any deer taken or killed or found in accused's possession may
be forfeited on conviction.*

Deer – Close Season

SECTION 5 DEER (SCOTLAND) ACT, 1996 AND DEER (CLOSE
SEASONS)(SCOTLAND) ORDER, 1984

Subject to certain exemptions contained in Section 26 of the Deer
(Scotland) Act, 1996, it is an offence to take or wilfully kill or injure
any deer during the close season applicable to the species.

Red deer/Sika deer and Sika deer hybrids
(Cervas Elaphus and Cervus Nippon)

Male:	21 October to 30 June inclusive
Female:	16 February to 20 October inclusive

Fallow deer
(Dama dama)

Male:	1 May to 31 July inclusive
Female:	16 February to 20 October inclusive

Roe deer
(Capreolus capreolus)

Male:	21 October to 31 March inclusive
Female:	1 April to 20 October inclusive

Section 26 - makes it lawful in certain circumstances to take, kill and
so on during the close season when they are causing serious damage
to crops.

Taking and Killing Deer at Night

SECTION 18 DEER (SCOTLAND) ACT, 1996

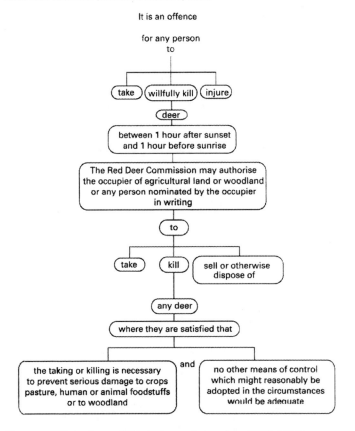

It is an offence

for any person
to

(take) (willfully kill) (injure)

(deer)

between 1 hour after sunset
and 1 hour before sunrise

The Red Deer Commission may authorise
the occupier of agricultural land or woodland
or any person nominated by the occupier
in writing

(to)

(take) (kill) (sell or otherwise
dispose of)

(any deer)

(where they are satisfied that)

the taking or killing is necessary
to prevent serious damage to crops
pasture, human or animal foodstuffs
or to woodland

and

no other means of control
which might reasonably be
adopted in the circumstances
would be adequate

Power of Secretary of State to make orders SECTION 21

- This section empowers the Secretary of State to make orders regarding the classes of firearms, ammunition, sights and other equipment which may be lawfully used and the circumstances in which these may be used to kill or take deer.

  Any person failing to comply with such orders commits an offence under Section 21(3).

- It is also an offence under Section 21(5) for any person to use a firearm or any ammunition for the purpose of wilfully injuring any deer.

Using Vehicles to Drive Deer

SECTION 19 DEER (SCOTLAND) ACT, 1996

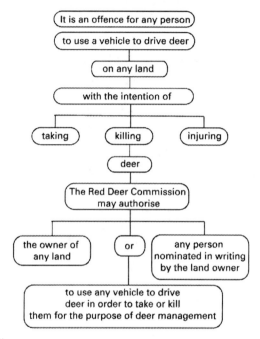

Notes:
a) 'Deer management' does not include driving deer in the course of any sporting activity.
b) The term 'vehicle' does not include any aircraft or hovercraft.

Note 1: `Deer management' does not include driving deer in the course of any sporting activity.

Note 2: The term `vehicle' does **not** include any aircraft or hovercraft.

Moving Vehicles

SECTION 20 DEER (SCOTLAND) ACT, 1996

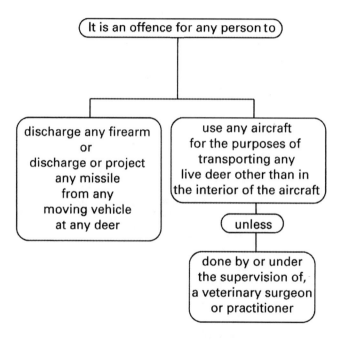

It is an offence for any person to

discharge any firearm
or
discharge or project
any missile
from any
moving vehicle
at any deer

use any aircraft
for the purposes of
transporting any
live deer other than in
the interior of the aircraft

unless

done by or under
the supervision of,
a veterinary surgeon
or practitioner

Deer - Gang Poaching

SECTION 22 DEER (SCOTLAND) ACT, 1996

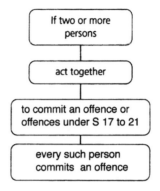

If two or more persons

act together

to commit an offence or offences under S 17 to 21

every such person commits an offence

Deer – Firearms

SECTION 21 DEER (SCOTLAND) ACT, 1996 AND DEER (FIREARMS ETC) (SCOTLAND) ORDER, 1985

No person shall use in connection with the killing or taking of deer any firearm, ammunition or sight except as declared lawful. ARTICLE 2

Failure to comply with this article is an offence under Section 21.

Firearms

It is lawful to use a rifle capable of firing the following ammunition:

- For shooting any species of deer - a bullet of an expanding type designed to deform in a predictable manner of not less than 6.48 g (100 grains) with a muzzle velocity of not less than 746.76 m/s (2,450 ft/s) and a muzzle energy of not less than 2,373 joules (1,750 foot pounds); or

- For shooting roe deer - a bullet of an expanding type designed to deform in a predictable manner of not less than 3.24 g (50 grains) with a muzzle velocity of not less than 746.76 m/s (2,450 ft/s) and muzzle energy of not less than 1,356 joules (1,000 foot pounds). ARTICLE 3

Occupiers

An occupier of agricultural land or enclosed woodlands having reasonable grounds for believing serious damage will be caused to:

- Crops

- Pasture

- Trees

- Human or animal foodstuffs.

On that land if deer are not killed, then it shall be lawful for:

- The occupier; or

- His servants in his ordering service on the land or other person normally resident on the land who are authorised in writing by the occupier for that purpose; or

- Any other person approved in writing by the Red Deer Commission as a fit and competent person for the purpose and who has been authorised in writing by the occupier for that purpose; to use a shotgun not less than 12 bore load with the following lawful ammunition:

a) For shooting deer of any species, a single rifled non-spherical projectile weighing not less than 24.62 g (380 grains); or

b) For shooting deer of any species, a cartridge purporting to contain not less than 35.64 g (550 grains) of shot, none of which is less than 6.81 mm (0.268 in) in diameter (SSG size); or

c) For shooting roe deer, a cartridge purporting to contain not less than 29.16 g (450 grains) of shot, none of which is less than 5.16 mm (0.203 in) in diameter (AAA size).

For the purpose of taking or killing any deer found on any arable land, garden grounds or permanent grass land (other than moorland and unenclosed land) and forming part of that land or on enclosed woodland. ARTICLE 4

Slaughtering instruments
It is lawful to use:

- A slaughtering instrument using any ammunition intended for use in it

- A sight which is not a light-intensifying, heat-sensitive or other special sighting device for night shooting. ARTICLE 5

Scientific purposes
It is lawful for any person authorised by the Secretary of State to take or kill deer for any scientific, veterinary or related purpose by any means specified in the authorisation. ARTICLE 6

Illegal Possession of Deer and Firearms SECTION 23 DEER (SCOTLAND) ACT, 1996

It is an offence for any person

to be in possession of deer, firearms or ammunition

in circumstances which make it reasonable to infer

he obtained the deer or used the firearm or ammunition when committing an offence under Sections 5 or 17 to 22 of the Act

he knew an offence under Sections 5 or 17 to 22 had been committed in relation to the deer or that the firearm or ammunition had been used for the purpose of committing these offences

Note 1: An accused has a defence to offence under Section 23 if he shows that no offence under Sections 5 or 17 to 22 had been committed, or that he had no reason to believe that such an offence had been committed.

Note 2: A person shall not be guilty of an offence under Section 23 in respect of anything done in good faith, including conduct which would otherwise constitute an offence under Section 5 or 17 to 22 in relation to any deer, where what is done is done for purposes connected with the prevention or detection of crime or the investigation or treatment of disease.

*Note 3: A person may be convicted of an offence under this section on the evidence of **one witness**.*

Attempts

SECTION 24 DEER (SCOTLAND) ACT, 1996

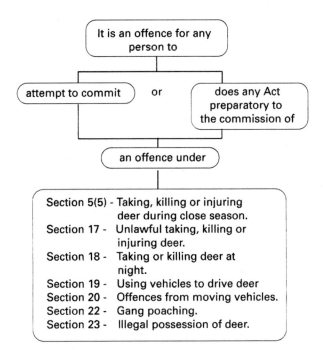

It is an offence for any person to

attempt to commit

or

does any Act preparatory to the commission of

an offence under

Section 5(5) - Taking, killing or injuring deer during close season.

Section 17 - Unlawful taking, killing or injuring deer.

Section 18 - Taking or killing deer at night.

Section 19 - Using vehicles to drive deer

Section 20 - Offences from moving vehicles.

Section 22 - Gang poaching.

Section 23 - Illegal possession of deer.

Deer – Police Powers

SECTIONS 27 AND 28 DEER (SCOTLAND) ACT, 1996

Seizure

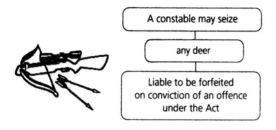

A constable may seize

any deer

Liable to be forfeited
on conviction of an offence
under the Act

SECTION 27 (1)

Warrant

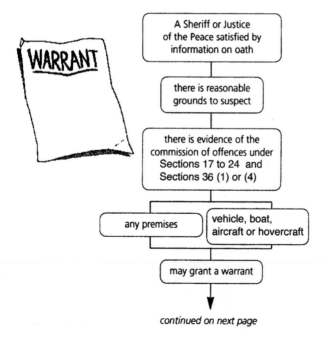

A Sheriff or Justice
of the Peace satisfied by
information on oath

there is reasonable
grounds to suspect

there is evidence of the
commission of offences under
Sections 17 to 24 and
Sections 36 (1) or (4)

any premises

vehicle, boat,
aircraft or hovercraft

may grant a warrant

continued on next page

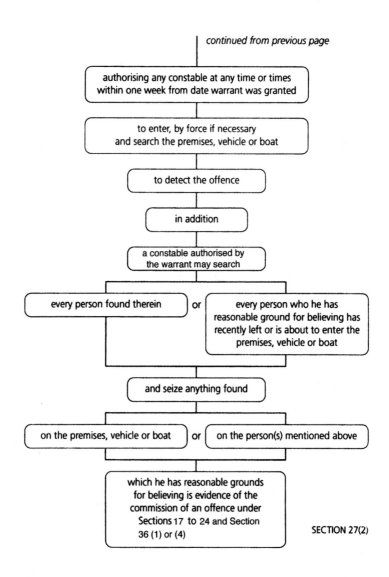

continued from previous page

authorising any constable at any time or times within one week from date warrant was granted

to enter, by force if necessary and search the premises, vehicle or boat

to detect the offence

in addition

a constable authorised by the warrant may search

every person found therein

or

every person who he has reasonable ground for believing has recently left or is about to enter the premises, vehicle or boat

and seize anything found

on the premises, vehicle or boat

or

on the person(s) mentioned above

which he has reasonable grounds for believing is evidence of the commission of an offence under Sections 17 to 24 and Section 36 (1) or (4)

SECTION 27(2)

Urgency

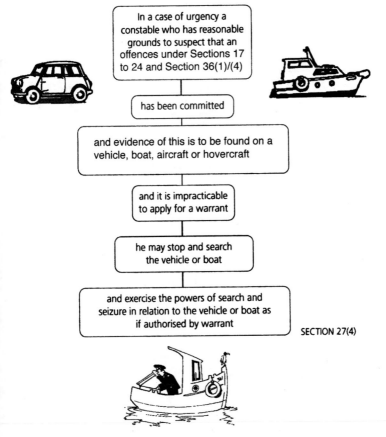

In a case of urgency a constable who has reasonable grounds to suspect that an offences under Sections 17 to 24 and Section 36(1)/(4)

has been committed

and evidence of this is to be found on a vehicle, boat, aircraft or hovercraft

and it is impracticable to apply for a warrant

he may stop and search the vehicle or boat

and exercise the powers of search and seizure in relation to the vehicle or boat as if authorised by warrant

SECTION 27(4)

Note: Section 36 of the Deer (Scotland) Act, 1996 relates to venison dealing.

SECTION 28 DEER (SCOTLAND) ACT, 1996

Arrest

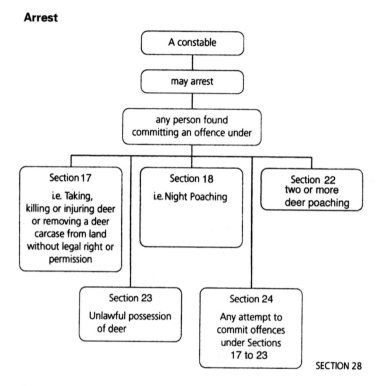

A constable

may arrest

any person found committing an offence under

Section 17

i.e. Taking, killing or injuring deer or removing a deer carcase from land without legal right or permission

Section 18

i.e. Night Poaching

Section 22 two or more deer poaching

Section 23

Unlawful possession of deer

Section 24

Any attempt to commit offences under Sections 17 to 23

SECTION 28

Cancellation of Firearm/Shotgun Certificates

SECTION 31 Deer (Scotland) Act, 1996 Where a person is convicted of an offence under Sections 17 to 23 of the Act, the court has the power to cancel any firearm or shotgun certificate held by the offender.

Deer – Exemptions

DEER (SCOTLAND) ACT, 1996

It is not an offence under the Act

During close season (subject to certain conditions)
- The owner of agricultural land or enclosed woodland and the owner's employees - authorised by the occupier of such land.
- Occupier of such land
- Occupier's employees or any other person normally resident on such land
- Any person approved in writing by the Red Deer Commission as a fit and competent person for the purpose may take, kill and sell or otherwise dispose of any deer found on agricultural land (other than moorland) or on enclosed woodland where the occupier reasonaby believes that serious damage will be caused to crops, pasture or human foodstuffs on the agricultural land or to that woodland, if the deer are not taken or killed.
S26

To carry out an act (which might otherwise be an offence) to prevent suffering to an injured or diseased deer or to any deer calf, fawn or kid deprived of its mother or about to be deprived of its mother.
S25

During night time - the occupier of agricultural land or woodland or any person nominated by the occupier in writing may, if authorised by the Red Deer Commission, take or kill and sell or otherwise dispose of any deer on the land where satisfied that:-
a) the taking or killing is necessary to prevent serious damage to crops, pasture, human or animal foodstuffs or to woodland and
b) no other means of control which might reasonably be adopted in the circumstances would be adequate.
S18 (2)

Salmon and Freshwater Fish

SALMON AND FRESHWATER FISHERIES (PROTECTION)(SCOTLAND) ACT, 1951

Illegal fishing SECTION 1

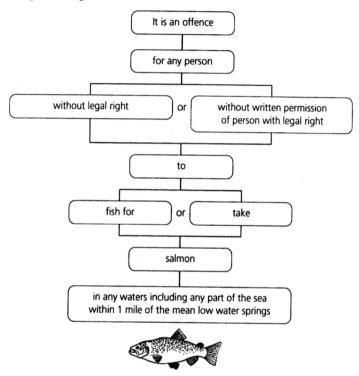

It is an offence

for any person

without legal right   or   without written permission of person with legal right

to

fish for   or   take

salmon

in any waters including any part of the sea within 1 mile of the mean low water springs

Note 1: `Salmon' means all migrating fish of the species Salmo Salar (Salmon) and Salmo Trutta (Sea Trout) or any part of any such fish.

Note 2: Anyone convicted under Section 1 and any fish illegally taken by him or found in his possession at the time of the offence are liable to be forfeited.

Note Regulation 2 Conservation of Salmon (Prohibition of Sale) (Scotland) Regulations, 2002 provides that no person shall sell, offer or expose for sale any salmon that has been taken by rod and line. 'Rod and line' means single rod and line with such bait or lure as is lawful on 1 October 2002.

Methods of Fishing

SECTION 2 SALMON AND FRESHWATER FISHERIES
(PROTECTION) (SCOTLAND) ACT, 1951

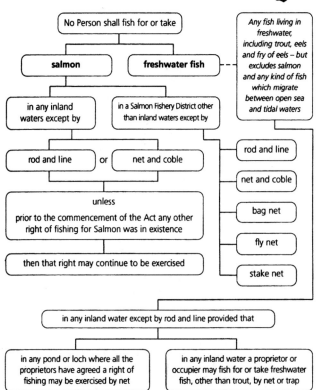

No Person shall fish for or take

salmon   **freshwater fish**

Any fish living in freshwater, including trout, eels and fry of eels – but excludes salmon and any kind of fish which migrate between open sea and tidal waters

in any inland waters except by

in a Salmon Fishery District other than inland waters except by

rod and line   or   net and coble

rod and line

net and coble

bag net

fly net

stake net

unless

prior to the commencement of the Act any other right of fishing for Salmon was in existence

then that right may continue to be exercised

in any inland water except by rod and line provided that

in any pond or loch where all the proprietors have agreed a right of fishing may be exercised by net

in any inland water a proprietor or occupier may fish for or take freshwater fish, other than trout, by net or trap

Note: Nothing in Section 2 prohibits the use of a gaff, tailer or landing-net to the taking of salmon or freshwater fish by rod and line.

Offence

Any person who contravenes Section 2 commits an offence.

Inland Waters includes all rivers above estuary limits and their tributary streams, and all waters, watercourses, lochs whether natural or artificial draining into the sea.

Gang Poaching

SECTION 3 SALMON AND FRESHWATER FISHERIES
(PROTECTION) (SCOTLAND) ACT, 1951

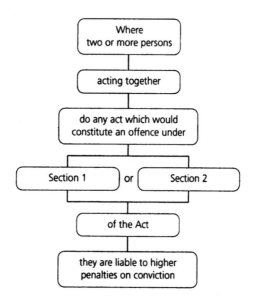

Where
two or more persons

acting together

do any act which would
constitute an offence under

Section 1 or Section 2

of the Act

they are liable to higher
penalties on conviction

Destruction of Fish by Explosives

SECTION 4 SALMON AND FRESHWATER FISHERIES
(PROTECTION) (SCOTLAND) ACT, 1951

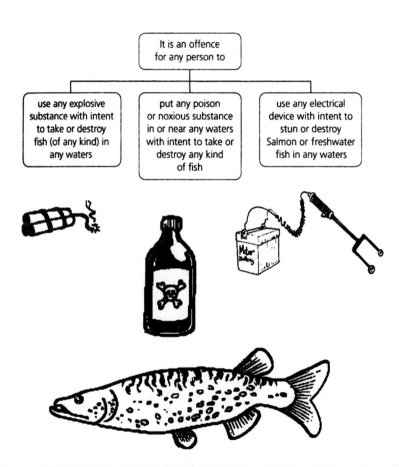

It is an offence
for any person to

use any explosive substance with intent to take or destroy fish (of any kind) in any waters

put any poison or noxious substance in or near any waters with intent to take or destroy any kind of fish

use any electrical device with intent to stun or destroy Salmon or freshwater fish in any waters

Note: `Any waters' means any waters including the sea within the
fishery limits of the British Isles.

Taking of Dead Salmon or Trout

SECTION 6 SALMON AND FRESHWATER FISHERIES
(PROTECTION) (SCOTLAND) ACT, 1951

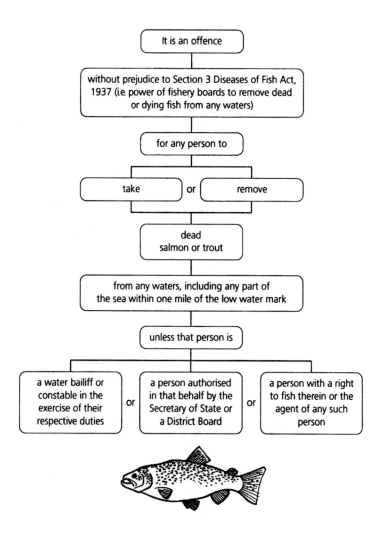

It is an offence

without prejudice to Section 3 Diseases of Fish Act, 1937 (i.e. power of fishery boards to remove dead or dying fish from any waters)

for any person to

take **or** remove

dead salmon or trout

from any waters, including any part of the sea within one mile of the low water mark

unless that person is

a water bailiff or constable in the exercise of their respective duties **or** a person authorised in that behalf by the Secretary of State or a District Board **or** a person with a right to fish therein or the agent of any such person

Illegal Possession of Salmon or Trout

SECTION 7 SALMON AND FRESHWATER FISHERIES
(PROTECTION) (SCOTLAND) ACT, 1951

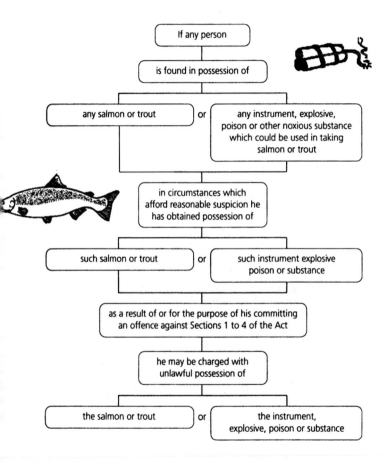

If any person

is found in possession of

any salmon or trout   **or**   any instrument, explosive, poison or other noxious substance which could be used in taking salmon or trout

in circumstances which afford reasonable suspicion he has obtained possession of

such salmon or trout   **or**   such instrument explosive poison or substance

as a result of or for the purpose of his committing an offence against Sections 1 to 4 of the Act

he may be charged with unlawful possession of

the salmon or trout   **or**   the instrument, explosive, poison or substance

Note: It is lawful to convict a person under Section 7 on the evidence of one person.

Possession of Salmon which have been Illegally Taken SECTION 7A SALMON AND FRESHWATER

FISHERIES (PROTECTION) (SCOTLAND) ACT, 1951

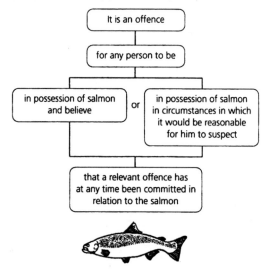

An offence is a relevant offence in relation to a salmon if:

- It is committed by taking, killing or landing that salmon either in Scotland or in England or Wales; or

- That salmon is taken, killed or landed, either in Scotland or in England and Wales in the course of the commission of the offence.

Defence

An accused has a defence to the above offence to show that no relevant offence has in fact been committed in relation to the salmon.

Note 1: A person shall not be guilty of an offence under Section 7A in respect of conduct which constitutes a relevant offence in relation to any salmon or in respect of anything done in good faith for the purposes connected with the prevention or detection of crime or the investigating or treatment of disease.

Note 2: It is lawful to convict a person charged under Section 7A on the evidence of one witness.

Fish – Attempts

SECTION 8 SALMON AND FRESHWATER FISHERIES
(PROTECTION) (SCOTLAND) ACT, 1951

Any person who attempts to commit or does any act preparatory to the commission of an offence under Sections 1 to 7 shall be guilty of an offence.

Fish – police powers

SECTION 10 SALMON AND FRESHWATER FISHERIES
(PROTECTION) (SCOTLAND) ACT, 1951

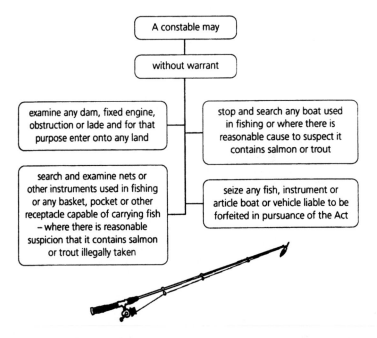

A constable may

without warrant

examine any dam, fixed engine, obstruction or lade and for that purpose enter onto any land

stop and search any boat used in fishing or where there is reasonable cause to suspect it contains salmon or trout

search and examine nets or other instruments used in fishing or any basket, pocket or other receptacle capable of carrying fish – where there is reasonable suspicion that it contains salmon or trout illegally taken

seize any fish, instrument or article boat or vehicle liable to be forfeited in pursuance of the Act

It is an offence for any person to refuse to allow a constable to exercise his powers in pursuance of the Act or obstruct a constable in the exercise of these powers.

Fish – Warrants

SECTION 11 SALMON AND FRESHWATER FISHERIES
(PROTECTION) (SCOTLAND) ACT, 1951

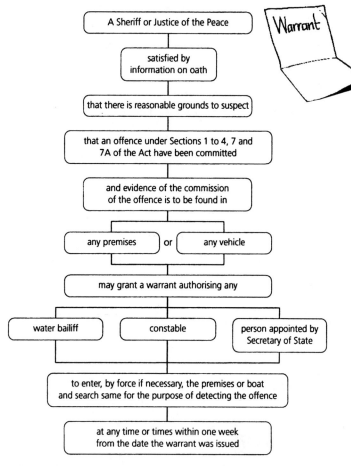

A person authorised by such a warrant may search every person who
is found in or whom he has reasonable grounds to believe has
recently left or is about to enter these premises or that vehicle.

Fish – Urgency

SECTION 11 SALMON AND FRESHWATER FISHERIES
(PROTECTION) (SCOTLAND) ACT, 1951 CONTINUED

Where a constable has reasonable suspicion that an offence against
any of the provisions of Sections 1 to 4, 7 and 7A has been committed
and that evidence of the commission of the offence is to be found in
any vehicle, but because of urgency or for other good reason it is
impracticable to obtain a warrant to search such vehicle, the constable
may stop and search that vehicle and any person who is found in, or
whom he has reasonable grounds to believe to have recently left, or
to be about to enter the said vehicle.

Weekly close time

SECTION 13 SALMON AND FRESHWATER FISHERIES
(PROTECTION) (SCOTLAND) ACT, 1951 CONTINUED

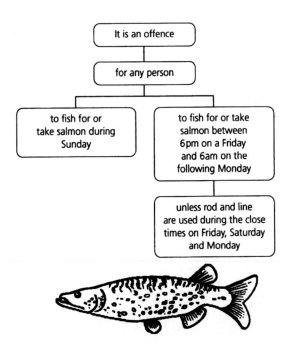

It is an offence

for any person

to fish for or
take salmon during
Sunday

to fish for or take
salmon between
6pm on a Friday
and 6am on the
following Monday

unless rod and line
are used during the close
times on Friday, Saturday
and Monday

Badgers

PROTECTION OF BADGERS ACT, 1992

Killing S 1(1)

It is an offence to wilfully kill, injure, take or
attempt to kill, injure or take a badger. *See next page for exceptions.*

Firearms S 2

It is an offence to use for killing a badger any firearm except a
smoothbore weapon of not less than 20 bore, or a rifle using
ammunition of muzzle energy not less than 217 joules (160 ft/lb) or
bullet weighing not less than 2.46 g (38 grains). *See next page for
exceptions.*

Sale and possession S 4

It is an offence to sell, offer for sale, or have in possession or under
control, any live badger. *See next page for exceptions.*

Possession S 1(3)

It is an offence to have in possession or under control any dead badger
or any part of, or anything derived from a dead badger unless it was
not killed in contravention of this Act. *See next page for exceptions.*

Cruelty

It is an offence to:

- Cruelly ill-treat a badger. S 2

- Use any badger tongs in the course of taking or killing a badger. S 2

- Dig for a badger. S 2

- Mark or ring a badger, unless authorised by a licence. S 5

- Interfere with a badger sett by:
  a) Damaging a sett or part of it
  b) Destroying a sett
  c) Obstructing access to any entrance of a sett
  d) Causing a dog to enter a badger sett
  e) Disturbing a badger when it is occupying a sett.

Except: if necessary to prevent serious damage to crops, land or
poultry (but licence must have been applied for); obstructing for fox
hunting purposes (but only if done by hand); or incidental and
unavoidable result of a lawful operation.

Exceptions

A person will not be guilty of the offences of killing, etc if:

- He is a 'licensed person'. S 10
- A badger is found disabled and it is taken for the purpose of tending it. S 6
- A badger is so seriously injured or in such a condition that to kill it would be an act of mercy. S 6
- Where the killing or injuring was an unavoidable result of a lawful action. S 6
- Authorised under the Animals (Scientific Procedures) Act, 1986. S 6
- The act was necessary to prevent serious damage to land, crops or poultry (but if such damage was foreseeable then a licence must have been applied for).

A person shall not be guilty of having a live badger in his possession under S 4 if:

- He has possession of it in the course of his business as a carrier
- He is a licensed person
- It is necessary to keep it in possession for the purpose of tending to its disability.

Police powers

Where a police constable has reasonable cause to suspect that an offence against the Act has been or is being committed he may without warrant:

- Stop and search that person and search any vehicle or article he may have with him
- Seize and detain anything which may be evidence of the commission of an offence or may be liable to be forfeited under Section 12(4) namely any badger or badger skin in respect of which an offence was committed or any weapon or article used in commission of the offence
- Arrest an offender if he fails to give his full name and address to the constable's satisfaction.

Birds

WILDLIFE AND COUNTRYSIDE ACT, 1981

The law relating to birds broadly covers restrictions on killing and taking wild birds; the prohibition of certain methods of killing or taking them; restrictions on the sale of birds and their eggs; and the prevention of disturbance to nesting birds. The various aspects are discussed in the following pages but for ease of reference the four categories into which birds are placed may be exemplified at this point.

Schedule 1

These are birds which are protected by special penalties.

Part 1   At all times - for example, barn owl, eagle, purple heron, osprey, stone curlew.

Part 2   During the close season - for example, wild duck, wild goose.

Schedule 2

These are birds which may be killed or taken.

Part 1   Outside the close season - for example, moorhen, wild duck, wild goose, woodcock.

Part 2   At any time by authorised persons - for example, crow, magpie, pigeon, sparrow, starling, wood pigeon.

Schedule 3

These are birds which may be sold.

Part 1   Alive at all times - for example, blackbird, chaffinch, magpie, barn owl, starling.

Part 2   Dead at all times - for example feral pigeon, wood pigeon.

Part 3   Dead from 1 September to 28 February - for example, tufted duck, mallard, snipe, woodcock.

Schedule 4

These are birds which must be registered and ringed if kept in captivity - for example stone curlew, falcon, hawk, kingfisher, osprey, crested tit.

'Wild bird' means one which is ordinarily resident in or is a visitor to Great Britain in a wild state but does not include poultry or game.

If the bird in question is listed in the first schedule, a greater penalty may be imposed.

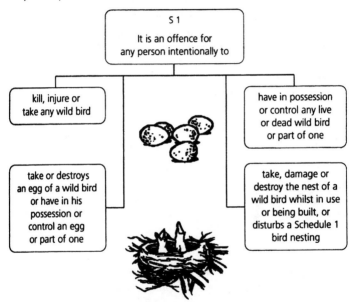

S 1

It is an offence for any person intentionally to

kill, injure or take any wild bird

take or destroys an egg of a wild bird or have in his possession or control an egg or part of one

have in possession or control any live or dead wild bird or part of one

take, damage or destroy the nest of a wild bird whilst in use or being built, or disturbs a Schedule 1 bird nesting

Note 1: Where an accused takes or destroys the egg of a wild bird, he may be convicted on the evidence of one person.

Note 2: 'Poultry' means domestic fowl, geese, ducks, guinea fowls, pigeons, quails and turkeys.

Note 3: 'Game bird' means pheasant, partridge, grouse (or game), black (or heath) game or ptarmigan.

*See next page for **exceptions**.*

Birds – Exceptions

Killing

A person shall not be guilty of an offence under Section 1 by reason of the killing or taking of a bird included in Part 2 of Schedule 2 or the injuring of such a bird in an attempt to kill it; or the taking, damaging or destruction of a nest of such a bird, or the taking or destruction of an egg of such a bird, when done in any case by an authorised person.

A person shall not be guilty of an offence under Section 1 by reason of the killing, injuring or taking of a bird included in Part 1 of Schedule 2 outside the close season for that bird.

Close season

Capercaillie: 1 February to 30 September

Snipe: 1 February to 11 August

Wild duck or wild geese (in any area below high water mark of ordinary spring tides): 21 February to 31 August

Any other case: 1 February to 31 August

Authorised persons

An authorised person will not be guilty of an offence of killing or injuring a wild bird, other than a bird included in Schedule 1, if he shows that it was necessary:

- For preserving public health or public or air safety
- For preventing the spread of disease
- Preventing serious damage to livestock, foodstuffs for livestock, crops, vegetables, fruit, growing timber or fisheries.

General

A person shall not be guilty of an offence by reason of:

- Taking a wild bird which has been disabled and which was taken to tend it and release when no longer disabled
- Killing a wild bird so seriously disabled that it would not recover, or
- Any act which was the incidental result of a lawful operation and could not have been avoided. S 4

Prohibited Methods of Killing Birds

SECTION 5 WILDLIFE AND COUNTRYSIDE ACT, 1981

Unless authorised by licence, it is an offence for any person to:

- Set in position any article to cause bodily injury to any wild bird coming into contact with it, for example springs; traps; snares; net; hook and line; any poisoned, poisonous or stupefying substance; floating container holding explosives; or any electrical device to frighten birds (except when done in the interests of public health, agriculture, forestry, fisheries or nature conservation for the purpose of lawful killing of wild animals when all reasonable precautions were taken to prevent injury to wild birds)

- Use for the purpose of taking or killing any wild bird any article as aforesaid, or any net, baited board, gas, bird-lime or other like substance

- Use as a decoy, for the purpose of killing or taking a wild bird, any sound recording or any live bird or other animal which is tethered or similarly secured, or which is blind, maimed or injured

- Use for the purpose of killing or taking any wild bird:

  a) a bow or crossbow

  b) explosive other than ammunition

  c) an automatic weapon

  d) shotgun over $1^3/_4$″ diameter barrel

  e) an illuminating or night sighting device

  f) a lighting or dazzling device

  g) gas or smoke

  h) a chemical wetting agent.

- Use any mechanically propelled vehicle in immediate pursuit of a wild bird for the purpose of killing or taking it.

But it shall not be unlawful:

- For an authorised person to use a cage-trap or net to take a bird included in Part 2 of Schedule 2

- To use nets for taking wild duck in a duck decoy which was in use immediately before the passing of the Protection of Birds Act, 1954

- To use a cage-trap or net for taking any game bird for the purpose of breeding.

But it will not be lawful to use a net for taking birds in flight, or a projected or propelled net for taking birds on the ground.

Restrictions on Sale of Birds

SECTION 6 WILDLIFE AND COUNTRYSIDE ACT, 1981

It is an offence to sell, offer or expose for sale, or have in possession or transport for the purpose of sale, or advertise the buying or selling of

Live birds

other than a bird included in Part 1 of Schedule 3

(see page 225)

Dead birds

other than a bird included in Part 2 or 3 of Schedule 3, or any part of, or anything derived from, such a wild bird

unless he is for the time being registered so to do

Eggs

of a wild bird or any part of such an egg

It is an offence to show or cause or permit to be shown in a competition any live bird other than a bird included in Part 1 of Schedule 3; or a bird one of whose parents was such a wild bird

Birds – Specific Offences

WILDLIFE AND COUNTRYSIDE ACT, 1981

Disturbing nesting birds S 1

It is an offence to intentionally disturb any wild bird
included in Schedule 1 while it is building a nest or is in,
on or near a nest containing eggs or young; or to
disturb dependant young of such a bird.

Confining S 8

It is an offence to keep or confine any bird in any cage or receptacle
which does not allow sufficient room for the bird to stretch its wings
freely.

But this offence does not apply to:

- Domestic fowl, ducks, geese, guinea fowl, pigeons and turkeys

- Any bird while being conveyed, publicly exhibited (provided
  the time does not exceed 72 hours), or while undergoing
  veterinary treatment.

Shooting events S 8

It is an offence to be in any way involved in any event
in which captive birds are liberated for the purpose
of being shot immediately after their liberation.

Birds – Police Powers

SECTION 19 WILDLIFE AND COUNTRYSIDE ACT, 1981

In relation to any offence against the Act (this includes taking or killing birds or eggs; using illegal methods of taking or killing, etc; unlawful selling etc; confining; and disturbing nesting birds) a constable may without warrant

stop and search

that person if the constable reasonably suspects that evidence of the commission of the offence is to be found on that person

and examine anything which that person may then be using or have in his possession if the constable reasonably suspects that evidence of the commission of the offence is to be found on that thing; arrest that person if he fails to give his name and address to the constable's satisfaction

seize and detain

for the purpose of proceedings, any thing which may be evidence of the commission of the offence or may be liable to be forfeited under this Act

for the purpose of exercising these powers the constable may enter any land other than a dwelling house

a Sheriff or Justice of the Peace may grant a warrant to enter and search premises if there is reasonable suspicion that an offence attracting a special penalty has been committed and evidence of its commission is to be found

CHAPTER 7
People

Children and Young Persons

SECTION 110 CHILDREN AND YOUNG PERSONS (SCOTLAND) ACT, 1937

Terms

Child	Young person	Guardian
Under the age of 14	Attained the age of 14 years but under 17 years.	Any person who, in the opinion of the courts has, for the time being, charge of or control over the child or young person.

Street:
Any highway and any public bridge, road, lane, footway, square, court, alley or passage, whether a thoroughfare or not.

Public place:
Any public park, garden, sea beach, railway station, and any ground to which the public have or are permitted to have access, whether a thoroughfare or not.

Cruelty to Children and Young Persons

SECTION 12 CHILDREN & YOUNG PERSONS (SCOTLAND) ACT, 1937

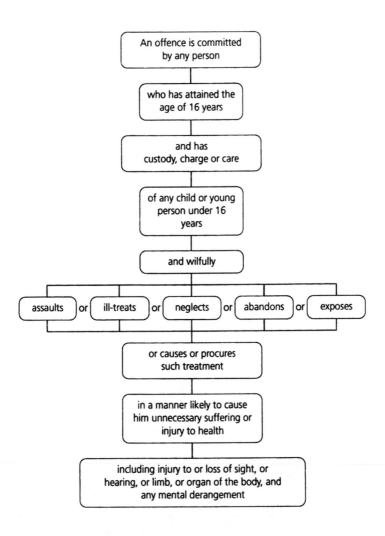

Children and Employment
SECTION 28 CHILDREN AND YOUNG PERSONS (SCOTLAND) ACT, 1937
as amended

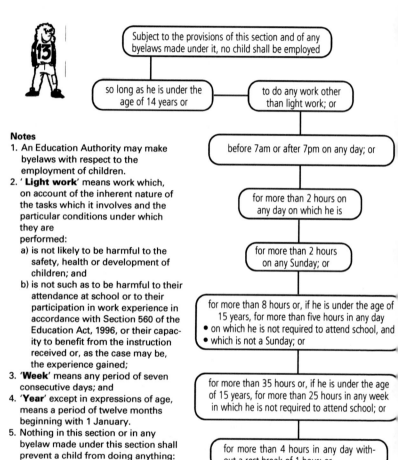

Subject to the provisions of this section and of any byelaws made under it, no child shall be employed

so long as he is under the age of 14 years or

to do any work other than light work; or

before 7am or after 7pm on any day; or

for more than 2 hours on any day on which he is

for more than 2 hours on any Sunday; or

for more than 8 hours or, if he is under the age of 15 years, for more than five hours in any day
- on which he is not required to attend school, and
- which is not a Sunday; or

for more than 35 hours or, if he is under the age of 15 years, for more than 25 hours in any week in which he is not required to attend school; or

for more than 4 hours in any day without a rest break of 1 hour; or

at any time in a year unless at that time he has had, or could still have, during a period in the year in which he is not required to attend school, at least 2 consecutive weeks without employment

Notes

1. An Education Authority may make byelaws with respect to the employment of children.
2. ' **Light work**' means work which, on account of the inherent nature of the tasks which it involves and the particular conditions under which they are performed:
    a) is not likely to be harmful to the safety, health or development of children; and
    b) is not such as to be harmful to their attendance at school or to their participation in work experience in accordance with Section 560 of the Education Act, 1996, or their capacity to benefit from the instruction received or, as the case may be, the experience gained;
3. '**Week**' means any period of seven consecutive days; and
4. '**Year**' except in expressions of age, means a period of twelve months beginning with 1 January.
5. Nothing in this section or in any byelaw made under this section shall prevent a child from doing anything:
    a) under the authority of a licence granted under this part of this Act; or
    b) in a case where by virtue of Section 37(3), Children and Young Persons Act, 1963, no licence under that section is required for him to do it.

Children and Tobacco

SECTION 18 CHILDREN AND YOUNG PERSONS (SCOTLAND) ACT, 1937

It is an offence for a person to sell a person **apparently** under the age of 16 years any tobacco or cigarette papers, whether for his own use or not.

It is the duty of a constable in uniform to seize any tobacco or cigarette papers from persons apparently under 16 years found smoking in a street or public place.

An order may be made by a court for the removal of any automatic cigarette machine which has been used by any person under 16 years.

Children and alcohol

SECTION 16 CHILDREN AND YOUNG PERSONS (SCOTLAND) ACT, 1937

It is an offence for any person to give or cause to be given to any child under the age of 5 years any alcoholic liquor (except under the order of a doctor or in the case of sickness or apprehended sickness, or other urgent case).

Children and Education

SECTION 21 CHILDREN AND YOUNG PERSONS (SCOTLAND) ACT, 1937

If a person habitually wanders from place to place and takes with him any child who has attained the age of 5 years, or any young person who is of compulsory school age, he will commit an offence unless he can prove that the child or young person is not being prevented from receiving an efficient education, suitable to his age, ability and aptitude.

Children and Begging

SECTION 15 CHILDREN AND YOUNG PERSONS (SCOTLAND) ACT, 1937

It is an offence for any person to cause or procure any child or young person under 16 years, or having custody, charge or care of such a child or young person, to allow him to be in any street, premises or place for the purpose of begging or receiving or inducing the giving of alms (whether or not there is any singing etc).

Children and Burning

SECTION 22 CHILDREN AND YOUNG PERSONS (SCOTLAND) ACT, 1937

If a person who has attained the age of 16 years, has custody, charge or care of any child under the age of 12 years

allows the child to be in any room containing an open fire grate

not sufficiently protected to guard against the risk of being burnt or scalded, without taking reasonable precautions against the risk

and by reason thereof the child is killed or suffers serious injury

then that person commits an offence

Children Residing in Brothels

SECTION 12 CRIMINAL LAW (CONSOLIDATION) (SCOTLAND) ACT, 1995

It is an offence for a person

having parental responsibilities in relation to

or

having custody, charge or care of

a child

who has attained the age of 4 years and is under the age of 16 years

to allow that person to reside in or frequent a brothel

Emergency protection of children where child protection order not available and Duties of a constable when a child is removed to a Place of Safety

SECTION 61(5) CHILDREN (SCOTLAND) ACT, 1995 AND REGULATIONS 3 & 4 EMERGENCY CHILD PROTECTION MEASURES (SCOTLAND) REGULATIONS, 1996

Where a constable has reasonable cause to believe that

i.e. There are reasonable grounds to believe that a child:
is being so treated (or neglected) that he is suffering significant harm
or
will suffer such harm if he is not removed to and kept in a place of safety, or if he does not remain in the place where he is then being accommodated (whether or not he is resident there)
and
an order under this section is necessary to protect that child from such harm (or such further harm)

the conditions for the making of a child protection order laid down in Section 57(1) are satisfied and

that it is not practicable in the circumstances for the constable to make an application for such an order to the Sheriff or for the Sheriff to consider such an application and

that, in order to protect the child from significant harm (or further such harm), it is necessary for the constable to remove the child to a place of safety

the constable may remove the child to such a place and keep him there. S 61(5)

As soon as reasonably practicable after a child has been removed by a constable to a place of safety a constable shall, take such steps as are reasonably practicable to inform the following persons

continued on next page

continued from previous page

a) any relevant person in relation to the child;
b) any person, other than a relevant person, with whom the child was residing immediately before being removed to the place for safety;
c) the Local Authority for the area in which the place of safety to which the child was removed is situated;
d) where not falling within paragraph c) above, the Local Authority for the area in which the child is ordinarily resident;
e) the Local Authority for the area in which the child was residing immediately before being removed to a place of safety (where they are not the authority under c) or d); and
f) the Principal Reporter (Reg 3)

of
a) the removal of the child by a constable to a place of safety;
b) the place of safety at which the child is being, or is to be, kept;
c) the reasons for the removal of the child to a place of safety;

and

d) any other steps which a constable has taken or is taking to safeguard the welfare of the child while in a place of safety. Reg 4.

Note Where the constable considers it necessary to safeguard the welfare of the child, he may withhold any of the information specified in Regulation 4(b) and d) above.

Children Requiring Compulsory Measures of Supervision

SECTION 52 CHILDREN (SCOTLAND) ACT, 1995

The question of whether compulsory measures of supervision are necessary in respect of a child arises if at least one of the conditions mentioned below is satisfied with respect to him:-
a) is beyond the control of any relevant person;
b) is falling into bad associations or is exposed to moral danger;
c) is likely
   i) to suffer unnecessarily; or
   ii) be impaired seriously in his health or development, due to a lack of parental care;
d) is a child in respect of whom any of the offences mentioned in Schedule 1 to the Criminal Procedure (Scotland) Act, 1975 has been committed;
e) is, or is likely to become, a member of the same household as a child in respect of whom any of the offences referred to in paragraph d) above has been committed;
f) is, or is likely to become, a member of the same household as a person who has committed any of the offences referred in paragraph d) above;
g) is, or is likely to become, a member of the same household as a person in respect of whom an offence under Sections 2A to 2C of the Sexual Offences (Scotland) Act, 1976 (incest and intercourse with a child by a step-parent or person in position of trust) has been committed by a member of that household;
h) failed to attend school regularly without reasonable excuse;
i) committed an offence;
j) misused alcohol or any drug, whether or not a controlled drug within the meaning of the Misuse of Drugs Act, 1971;
k) has misused a volatile substance by deliberately inhaling its vapour, other than for medicinal purposes;
l) is being provided with accommodation by a Local Authority under Section 25, or is the subject of a parental responsibilities order obtained under Section 86, of this Act and, in either case, his behaviour is such that special measures are necessary for his adequate supervision in his interest or the interest of others.

Note '**Supervision**' in relation to compulsory measures of supervision may include measures taken for the protection, guidance, treatment or control of the child.

Note: Schedule 1 Offence relates to those offences contained in Schedule 1 Criminal Procedure (Scotland) Act, 1995 namely:

- *Any offence contained in Part 1 of Criminal Law (Consolidation) (Scotland) Act, 1995 (for example sexual offences);*

- *Any offence under Sections 12, 15, 22 or 33 of Children and Young Persons (Scotland) Act, 1937;*

- *Any offence involving bodily injury to a child under 17 years; and*

- *Any offence involving lewd, indecent or libidinous practices or behaviour towards a child under 17 years.*

Preliminary and Investigatory Measures

SECTION 52 CHILDREN (SCOTLAND) ACT, 1995

Where information is received by a Local Authority which suggests that compulsory measures of supervision may be necessary in respect of a child, they shall cause inquiries to be made into the case unless they are satisfied that such inquiries are unnecessary; and

if it appears to them after such inquiries, or after being satisfied that such inquiries are unnecessary, that such measures may be required in respect of the child, give to the Principal Reporter such information about the child as they have been able to discover.

A person, other than a Local Authority, who has reasonable cause to believe that compulsory measures of supervision may be necessary in respect of a child

a) shall, if he is a constable, give to the Principal Reporter such information about the child as he has been able to discover;

b) in any other case, may give the Principal Reporter that information.

A constable shall make any report required to be made under Section 17(1) of the Police (Scotland) Act, 1967 (duty to make reports in relation to commission of offences) in relation to a child to the Principal Reporter as well as to the appropriate prosecutor.

Where an application has been made to the Sheriff by the Principal Reporter in accordance with a direction given by a children's hearing under Section 65(7) or (9) of the Act; or by any person entitled to make an application under Section 84 of the Act - the Principal Reporter may request any prosecutor to supply him with any evidence lawfully obtained in the course of, and held by the prosecutor in connection with, the investigation of a crime or suspected crime, being evidence which may assist the Sheriff in determining the application; and, it shall be the duty of the prosecutor to comply with such a request unless the prosecutor reasonably believes that it is necessary to retain the evidence for the purposes of any proceedings in respect of a crime, whether the proceedings have been commenced or are to be commenced by him.

The Lord Advocate may direct that in any specified case or class of cases any evidence lawfully obtained in the course of an investigation of a crime or suspected crime shall be supplied, without the need for a request to the Principal Reporter.

Armed Forces

Absentees and deserters
SECTION 186 ARMY ACT, 1955; SECTION 186 AIR FORCE ACT, 1955;
SECTION 105 NAVAL DISCIPLINE ACT, 1957

A constable may arrest without warrant any person whom he has
reasonable cause to suspect of being a member of the regular forces
who has deserted or is absent without leave. This provision also
applies to **visiting forces** but only where a request is made by the
appropriate authority of the country to which he belongs. S 13 VISITING
FORCES ACT, 1952

Uniforms
SECTION 3 UNIFORMS ACT, 1894

It is an offence for any person
not serving in Her Majesty's forces
to wear without Her Majesty's
permission any dress having the
appearance, or bearing any of
the regimental or other distinctive
marks of any such uniform

but there is an exemption in
the case of stage plays in properly
authorised places for public
performances, music halls, circus
performances or any bona fide
military representation

Decorations and badges, etc
SECTION 197 ARMY AND AIR FORCE ACTS, 1955

> An offence is committed by any person who

> without authority uses or wears any military decoration or badge, wound stripe or emblem supplied or authorised by the defence council; or wears any decoration, etc. so nearly resembling an official one as to be calculated to deceive; or falsely represents himself to be a person who is or has been entitled to wear any official decoration etc

> but this does not prohibit the use or wearing of ordinary regimental badges or of broaches or ornaments representing them

and

> a person shall be guilty of an offence if he

> purchases, takes in pawn, solicits or procures any person to sell or pledge

> or acts for any person in the sale or pledging of

> medals, medal ribbons, clasps and good conduct badges

> any naval, military or air forces decoration awarded to any member of Her Majesty's forces. But it shall be a defence to prove that at the time of the alleged offence the person to whom the decoration was awarded was dead or had ceased to be a member of those forces

Aliens
SECTIONS 1-3 IMMIGRATION ACT, 1971

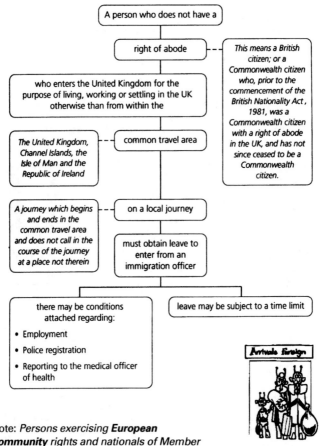

A person who does not have a

right of abode

> This means a British citizen; or a Commonwealth citizen who, prior to the commencement of the British Nationality Act, 1981, was a Commonwealth citizen with a right of abode in the UK, and has not since ceased to be a Commonwealth citizen.

who enters the United Kingdom for the purpose of living, working or settling in the UK otherwise than from within the

common travel area

> The United Kingdom, Channel Islands, the Isle of Man and the Republic of Ireland

on a local journey

> A journey which begins and ends in the common travel area and does not call in the course of the journey at a place not therein

must obtain leave to enter from an immigration officer

there may be conditions attached regarding:

- Employment
- Police registration
- Reporting to the medical officer of health

leave may be subject to a time limit

Note: *Persons exercising **European Community** rights and nationals of Member States (currently Austria, Belgium, Denmark, Finland, France, Germany, Greece, Italy, Luxembourg, Netherlands, Portugal, Spain, Sweden, Czech Republic, Estonia, Latvia, Lithuania, Hungary, Poland, Slovenia, the Slovak Republic and the Republic of Cyprus - plus Ireland and the United Kingdom) do not require leave to enter or remain.*

Aliens - offences
SECTIONS 24 & 25 IMMIGRATION ACT, 1971

A person will commit an offence if he

is knowingly concerned with making or carrying out arrangements for securing or facilitating illegal entry

knowingly harbours anyone whom he knows or has reasonable cause to believe to be an illegal entrant or to have exceeded his time limit or failed to observe a condition of entry

enters the UK without leave, remains beyond any time limit, fails to comply with any conditions

a constable or immigration officer may arrest without warrant anyone who has, or whom he, with reasonable cause, suspects to have, committed or attempted to commit any of the above offences (except for failing to report to a medical officer of health or harbouring)

Hotels, etc
ARTICLES 3 & 4 IMMIGRATION (HOTEL RECORDS) ORDER, 1972

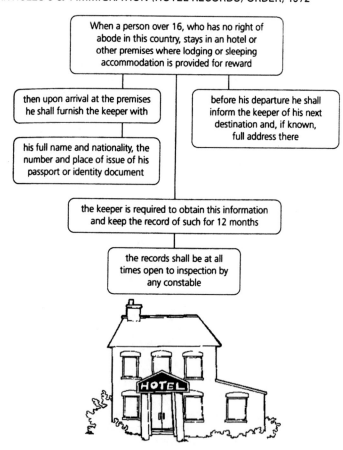

When a person over 16, who has no right of abode in this country, stays in an hotel or other premises where lodging or sleeping accommodation is provided for reward

then upon arrival at the premises he shall furnish the keeper with

before his departure he shall inform the keeper of his next destination and, if known, full address there

his full name and nationality, the number and place of issue of his passport or identity document

the keeper is required to obtain this information and keep the record of such for 12 months

the records shall be at all times open to inspection by any constable

Mental Health
SECTION 118 MENTAL HEALTH (SCOTLAND) ACT, 1984

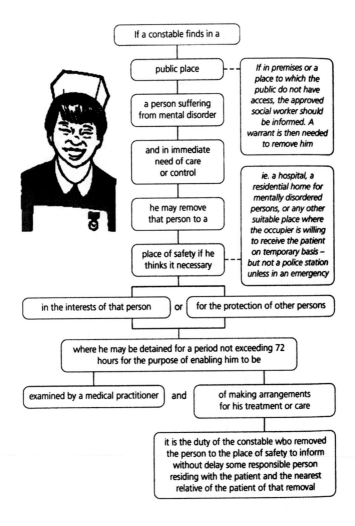

If a constable finds in a

public place

If in premises or a place to which the public do not have access, the approved social worker should be informed. A warrant is then needed to remove him

a person suffering from mental disorder

and in immediate need of care or control

ie. a hospital, a residential home for mentally disordered persons, or any other suitable place where the occupier is willing to receive the patient on temporary basis – but not a police station unless in an emergency

he may remove that person to a

place of safety if he thinks it necessary

in the interests of that person   **or**   for the protection of other persons

where he may be detained for a period not exceeding 72 hours for the purpose of enabling him to be

examined by a medical practitioner   **and**   of making arrangements for his treatment or care

it is the duty of the constable who removed the person to the place of safety to inform without delay some responsible person residing with the patient and the nearest relative of the patient of that removal

Pedlars

PEDLARS ACT, 1871

A `pedlar' is defined as any pedlar, hawker, petty chapman, tinker, caster of metals, mender of chairs, or other persons who, without any horse or other beast bearing or drawing burden, **travels and trades on foot**, and goes from town to town or to other men's houses, carrying to sell, or exposing for sale any goods, wares or merchandise, or procuring orders for goods immediately to be delivered, or selling or offering for sale his skill in handicraft. S3

The Act does not apply to commercial travellers or other persons selling or seeking orders for goods to or from dealers for resale; or to agents authorised by publishers selling or seeking orders for books; or sellers of vegetables, fish, fruit or victuals; or persons selling at any public market, etc. S 23

Any person who acts as a pedlar must obtain a certificate. It is an offence to act without one. S 4

It is an offence to fail to produce the certificate to a justice, police officer, person to whom he offers goods, or a person on whose private grounds or premises he is found. S 17

It is also an offence to lend, transfer or assign, borrow or make use of another person's certificate, or forge a certificate. SS 10, 11 AND 12

Metal Dealers

CIVIC GOVERNMENT (SCOTLAND) ACT, 1982

A metal dealer is defined as a person carrying on a business which consists wholly or partly of buying and selling for scrap old, broken, worn out, defaced or partly manufactured articles made wholly or partly of metal, (whether the metal sold is in the form in which it is bought or otherwise), but does not include and itinerant metal dealer. SS 36 AND 37

'Metal' means any metal (including precious metal) and any metal alloy (old or new) including manufactured articles (old or new) made wholly or partly of metal; of the material commonly known as hard metal, or of cemented or sintered metallic carbides. S 36

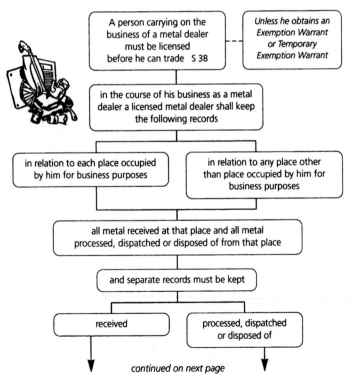

A person carrying on the business of a metal dealer must be licensed before he can trade   S 38

Unless he obtains an Exemption Warrant or Temporary Exemption Warrant

in the course of his business as a metal dealer a licensed metal dealer shall keep the following records

in relation to each place occupied by him for business purposes

in relation to any place other than place occupied by him for business purposes

all metal received at that place and all metal processed, dispatched or disposed of from that place

and separate records must be kept

received

processed, dispatched or disposed of

continued on next page

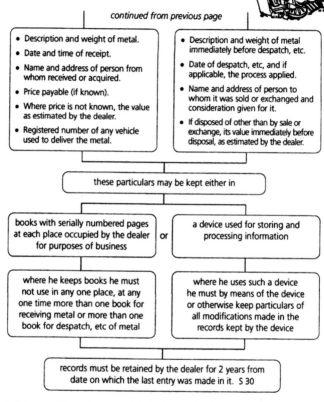

continued from previous page

- Description and weight of metal.
- Date and time of receipt.
- Name and address of person from whom received or acquired.
- Price payable (if known).
- Where price is not known, the value as estimated by the dealer.
- Registered number of any vehicle used to deliver the metal.

- Description and weight of metal immediately before despatch, etc.
- Date of despatch, etc, and if applicable, the process applied.
- Name and address of person to whom it was sold or exchanged and consideration given for it.
- If disposed of other than by sale or exchange, its value immediately before disposal, as estimated by the dealer.

these particulars may be kept either in

books with serially numbered pages at each place occupied by the dealer for purposes of business

or

a device used for storing and processing information

where he keeps books he must not use in any one place, at any one time more than one book for receiving metal or more than one book for despatch, etc of metal

where he uses such a device he must by means of the device or otherwise keep particulars of all modifications made in the records kept by the device

records must be retained by the dealer for 2 years from date on which the last entry was made in it. S 30

Note 1: It is an offence for a metal dealer to dispose of or acquire from a person apparently under 16 years, whether that person was acting on his own behalf or on behalf of another. S 34

Note 2: A constable has a right at all reasonable times to enter a licensed metal dealer's business premises and require production of and inspect equipment, plant, stock in trade, records, documents etc, and take copies of or extracts from any record or document. S 5

Note 3: It is an offence to obstruct the powers of entry and inspection conferred by these provisions. S 5

Lodging on Premises, etc Without Permission

TRESPASS (SCOTLAND) ACT, 1865

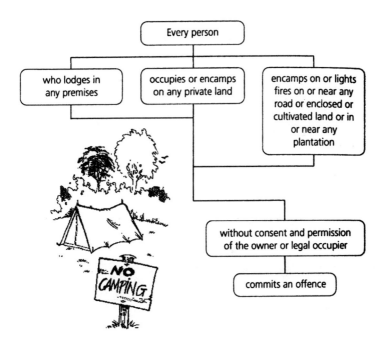

Power of arrest

Any person found in the act of committing this offence by a constable may be arrested by the constable.

Prosecutions

Must be commenced within one month of the offence being committed.

Premises

Means any house, barn, stable, shed, loft, granary, outhouse, garden, stockyard, court, close or enclosed space.

Police

SECTION 43 POLICE (SCOTLAND) ACT, 1967

Uniform

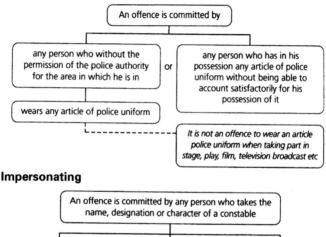

An offence is committed by

any person who without the permission of the police authority for the area in which he is in

or

any person who has in his possession any article of police uniform without being able to account satisfactorily for his possession of it

wears any article of police uniform

It is not an offence to wear an article police uniform when taking part in stage, play, film, television broadcast etc

Impersonating

An offence is committed by any person who takes the name, designation or character of a constable

for the purpose of obtaining admission into any house or other place

or

of doing or procuring to be done any act which such person would not entitled to do or procure to be done of his own authority

or

for any other unlawful purpose

Note: Article of police uniform means any article of uniform or any distinctive badge or mark usually issued by a police authority to constables, or anything having the appearance of such.

Assault, etc S 41

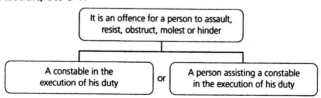

It is an offence for a person to assault, resist, obstruct, molest or hinder

A constable in the execution of his duty

or

A person assisting a constable in the execution of his duty

Protection of Insecure Premises

SECTION 61 CIVIC GOVERNMENT (SCOTLAND) ACT, 1982

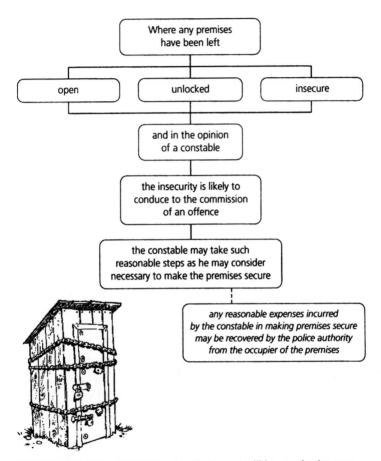

Where any premises have been left

open

unlocked

insecure

and in the opinion of a constable

the insecurity is likely to conduce to the commission of an offence

the constable may take such reasonable steps as he may consider necessary to make the premises secure

any reasonable expenses incurred by the constable in making premises secure may be recovered by the police authority from the occupier of the premises

Note: Where there is no occupier, the tenant will be required to pay and where there is no tenant, the owner of the premises will have this obligation.

CHAPTER 8
Public Order

Litter

SECTION 87 ENVIRONMENTAL PROTECTION ACT, 1990

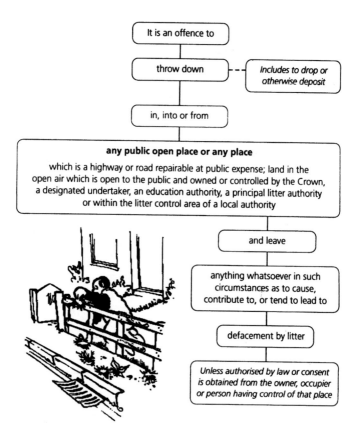

It is an offence to

throw down — — Includes to drop or otherwise deposit

in, into or from

any public open place or any place

which is a highway or road repairable at public expense; land in the open air which is open to the public and owned or controlled by the Crown, a designated undertaker, an education authority, a principal litter authority or within the litter control area of a local authority

and leave

anything whatsoever in such circumstances as to cause, contribute to, or tend to lead to

defacement by litter

Unless authorised by law or consent is obtained from the owner, occupier or person having control of that place

Note: A person who drops litter and picks it up again does not commit an offence. The police are not required to give a person who throws down litter an opportunity to pick it up before he can be charged with an offence.

Abandoning Vehicles

SECTION 2 REFUSE DISPOSAL (AMENITY) ACT, 1978

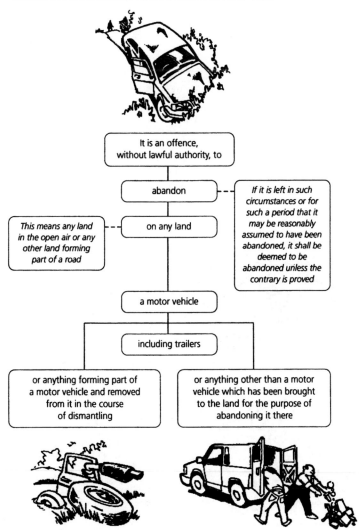

It is an offence,
without lawful authority, to

abandon

If it is left in such circumstances or for such a period that it may be reasonably assumed to have been abandoned, it shall be deemed to be abandoned unless the contrary is proved

on any land

This means any land in the open air or any other land forming part of a road

a motor vehicle

including trailers

or anything forming part of a motor vehicle and removed from it in the course of dismantling

or anything other than a motor vehicle which has been brought to the land for the purpose of abandoning it there

Noise
SECTION 62 CONTROL OF POLLUTION ACT, 1974

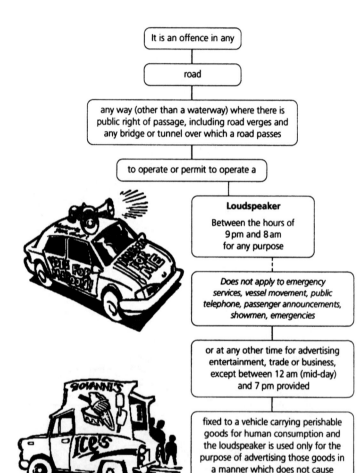

It is an offence in any

road

any way (other than a waterway) where there is public right of passage, including road verges and any bridge or tunnel over which a road passes

to operate or permit to operate a

Loudspeaker

Between the hours of
9 pm and 8 am
for any purpose

Does not apply to emergency services, vessel movement, public telephone, passenger announcements, showmen, emergencies

or at any other time for advertising entertainment, trade or business, except between 12 am (mid-day) and 7 pm provided

fixed to a vehicle carrying perishable goods for human consumption and the loudspeaker is used only for the purpose of advertising those goods in a manner which does not cause annoyance. Words may not be used

Playing Musical Instru...
Annoyance of Others

SECTION 54 (I) CIVIC GOVERNMENT (SCOTLAN...

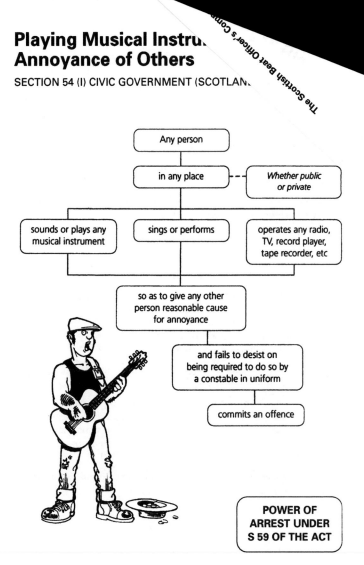

Any person

in any place ---- *Whether public or private*

sounds or plays any musical instrument

sings or performs

operates any radio, TV, record player, tape recorder, etc

so as to give any other person reasonable cause for annoyance

and fails to desist on being required to do so by a constable in uniform

commits an offence

POWER OF ARREST UNDER S 59 OF THE ACT

Section 54 (1) of the Act does not apply to the operation of a loudspeaker –

   a) for police, fire brigade or ambulance purposes, by a water authority in the exercise of any of its functions, or by a local authority within its area

   b) for communicating with persons on a vessel for the purpose of directing the movement of that or any other vessel

   c) if the loudspeaker forms part of a public telephone system

   d) if the loudspeaker –

      i) is in or fixed to a vehicle, and

      ii) is operated solely for the entertainment of or for communicating with the driver or a passenger of the vehicle or, where the loudspeaker is or forms part of the horn or similar warning instrument of the vehicle, solely for giving warning to other traffic, and

      iii) is so operated as not to give reasonable cause for annoyance to persons in the vicinity

   e) otherwise than on a road, by persons employed in connection with a transport undertaking used by the public in a case where the loudspeaker is operated solely for making announcements to passengers or prospective passengers or to other persons so employed

   f) by a travelling showman on land which is being used for the purposes of a pleasure fair

   g) in case of emergency

SECTION 54 (2A) CIVIC GOVERNMENT (SCOTLAND) ACT, 1982
(INSERTED BY CRIME AND DISORDER ACT, 1998)

Seizure of musical instruments and other sound producing devices

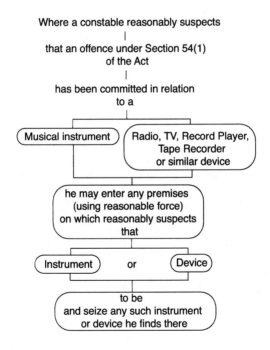

Where a constable reasonably suspects

that an offence under Section 54(1)
of the Act

has been committed in relation
to a

| Musical instrument | Radio, TV, Record Player, Tape Recorder or similar device |

he may enter any premises
(using reasonable force)
on which reasonably suspects
that

| Instrument | or | Device |

to be
and seize any such instrument
or device he finds there

Trade Disputes

SECTION 241 TRADE UNION AND LABOUR RELATIONS
(CONSOLIDATION) ACT, 1992

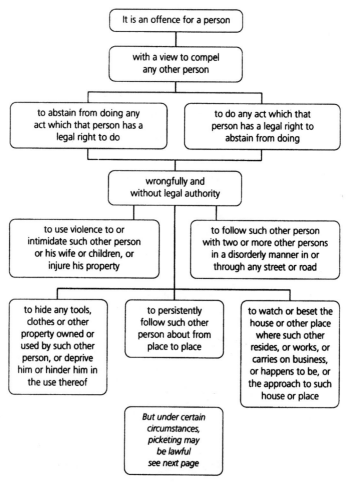

It is an offence for a person

with a view to compel
any other person

to abstain from doing any
act which that person has a
legal right to do

to do any act which that
person has a legal right to
abstain from doing

wrongfully and
without legal authority

to use violence to or
intimidate such other person
or his wife or children, or
injure his property

to follow such other person
with two or more other persons
in a disorderly manner in or
through any street or road

to hide any tools,
clothes or other
property owned or
used by such other
person, or deprive
him or hinder him in
the use thereof

to persistently
follow such other
person about from
place to place

to watch or beset the
house or other place
where such other
resides, or works, or
carries on business,
or happens to be, or
the approach to such
house or place

*But under certain
circumstances,
picketing may
be lawful
see next page*

*Note: A constable may arrest without warrant anyone he reasonably
suspects is committing one of the above offences.*

Peaceful Picketing

SECTION 220 TRADE UNION AND LABOUR RELATIONS
(CONSOLIDATION) ACT, 1992

Breach of the Peace

Crime at common law.

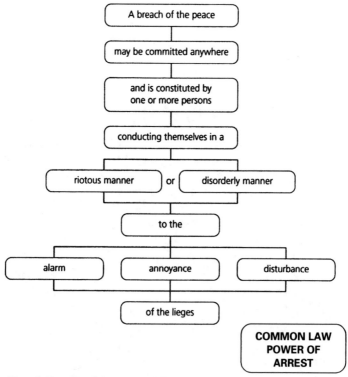

A breach of the peace

may be committed anywhere

and is constituted by
one or more persons

conducting themselves in a

riotous manner | or | disorderly manner

to the

alarm | annoyance | disturbance

of the lieges

**COMMON LAW
POWER OF
ARREST**

Note 1: Brawling is not essential.

*Note 2: Insulting or abusive words do not constitute a breach of the
peace unless unduly persisted in or accompanied by threats or violent
gestures, but, threatening, abusive or insulting language or behaviour
with intent or calculated to provoke a breach of the peace or whereby
a breach of the peace may be occasioned is a crime at common law.*

Mobbing and Rioting

Crime at common law.

Definition
Mobbing and rioting is committed when a number of persons assemble and combine for a common purpose to the alarm of the lieges and in breach of the peace.

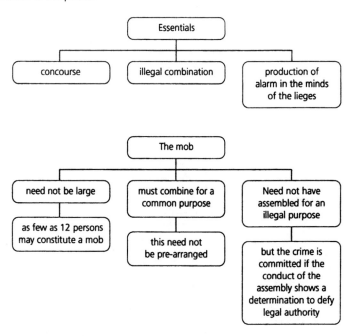

Violence and so on, not essential
The mob need not commit acts of violence, noise, tumult or threatening behaviour – it is sufficient if the mob assembles for the purpose of intimidating people in the lawful performance of their duties.

Art and part

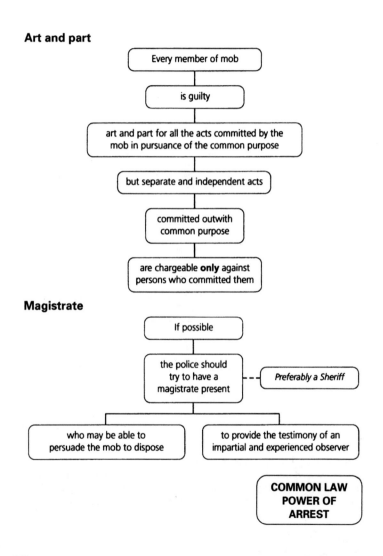

Every member of mob

is guilty

art and part for all the acts committed by the mob in pursuance of the common purpose

but separate and independent acts

committed outwith common purpose

are chargeable **only** against persons who committed them

Magistrate

If possible

the police should try to have a magistrate present

Preferably a Sheriff

who may be able to persuade the mob to dispose

to provide the testimony of an impartial and experienced observer

COMMON LAW POWER OF ARREST

Touting
SECTION 55 CIVIC GOVERNMENT (SCOTLAND) ACT, 1982

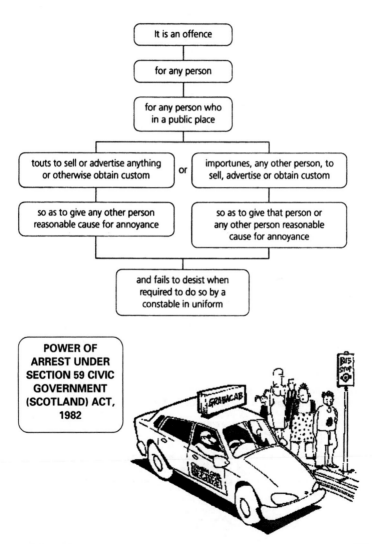

It is an offence

for any person

for any person who
in a public place

touts to sell or advertise anything
or otherwise obtain custom

or

importunes, any other person, to
sell, advertise or obtain custom

so as to give any other person
reasonable cause for annoyance

so as to give that person or
any other person reasonable
cause for annoyance

and fails to desist when
required to do so by a
constable in uniform

**POWER OF
ARREST UNDER
SECTION 59 CIVIC
GOVERNMENT
(SCOTLAND) ACT,
1982**

Offensive Weapons

SECTION 47 CRIMINAL LAW (CONSOLIDATION) (SCOTLAND) ACT, 1995

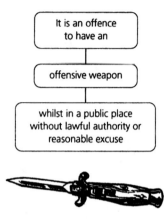

It is an offence
to have an

offensive weapon

whilst in a public place
without lawful authority or
reasonable excuse

Offensive weapons fall into one of three categories:

1) Articles made for causing injury

2) Articles adapted for causing injury

3) Articles intended by the person having them to cause injury

Public place includes any road as defined in the Roads (Scotland) Act, 1984 and any other premises or place to which at the material time the public have or are permitted access, whether on payment or otherwise.

Power of arrest

A constable may arrest without warrant a person whom he has reasonable cause to believe has committed the above offence, if:

- The constable is not satisfied as to that person's identity or place of residence; or

- The constable has reasonable cause to believe that it is necessary to arrest him to prevent the commission by him of **any** other offence in the course of committing which an offensive weapon might be used.

Search for Offensive Weapons

SECTION 48 CRIMINAL LAW (CONSOLIDATION) (SCOTLAND) ACT, 1995

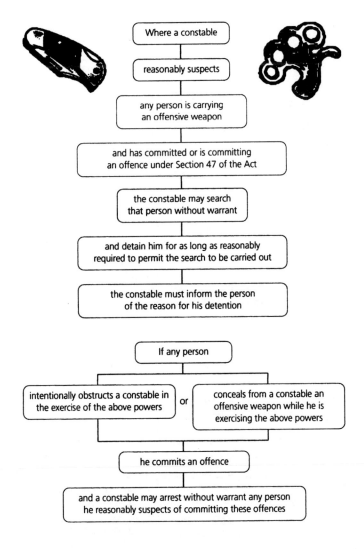

Where a constable

reasonably suspects

any person is carrying
an offensive weapon

and has committed or is committing
an offence under Section 47 of the Act

the constable may search
that person without warrant

and detain him for as long as reasonably
required to permit the search to be carried out

the constable must inform the person
of the reason for his detention

If any person

intentionally obstructs a constable in
the exercise of the above powers

or

conceals from a constable an
offensive weapon while he is
exercising the above powers

he commits an offence

and a constable may arrest without warrant any person
he reasonably suspects of committing these offences

Possession of Articles with Blade or Point

SECTION 49 CRIMINAL LAW (CONSOLIDATION) (SCOTLAND) ACT, 1995

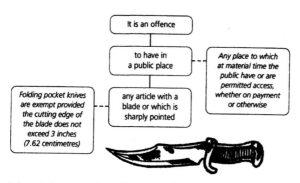

It is an offence

to have in a public place

Any place to which at material time the public have or are permitted access, whether on payment or otherwise

Folding pocket knives are exempt provided the cutting edge of the blade does not exceed 3 inches (7.62 centimetres)

any article with a blade or which is sharply pointed

It is a defence to show that he had good reason or lawful authority for having it, or he had it with him for use at work, or for religious reasons or as part of a national costume.

Police powers

Search: A constable may search without warrant a person if he has reasonable grounds for believing that the person has or is committing an offence under Section 49 and detain him for such a time as is reasonably required to permit the search to be carried out.

The constable must inform the person detained the reason for his detention.

Arrest: Section 49 provides a similar power of arrest to that detailed in Section 47.

Obstruction and concealment

Section 49 provides that it is an offence to obstruct or conceal articles to which Section 49 applies, when a constable is exercising his powers under Section 49 and gives a constable power to arrest without warrant persons committing these offences.

The Offensive Weapons Act, 1996 came into force on 1 January 1997 and makes provisions about persons having knives, articles with blades or sharp points and offensive weapons; and about selling

Offensive Weapons Act, 1996

knives and so on, to persons under 16 years of age.

Offensive weapons on school premises

Section 4(3) of the Offensive Weapons Act, 1996 adds Section 49A to the Criminal Law (Consolidation) (Scotland) Act, 1995 which provides:

SECTION 49A(1), (2)

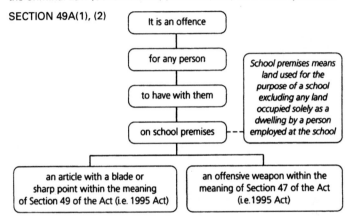

It is an offence

for any person

to have with them

on school premises

School premises means land used for the purpose of a school excluding any land occupied solely as a dwelling by a person employed at the school

an article with a blade or sharp point within the meaning of Section 49 of the Act (i.e. 1995 Act)

an offensive weapon within the meaning of Section 47 of the Act (i.e. 1995 Act)

Defences
SECTION 49A(3), (4)

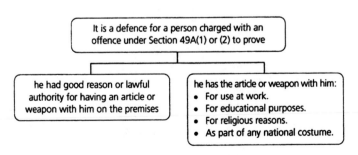

It is a defence for a person charged with an offence under Section 49A(1) or (2) to prove

he had good reason or lawful authority for having an article or weapon with him on the premises

he has the article or weapon with him:
- For use at work.
- For educational purposes.
- For religious reasons.
- As part of any national costume.

Power of Entry to School Premises

SECTION 4(3) OF THE OFFENSIVE WEAPONS ACT, 1996 ADDS
SECTION 49B TO THE CRIMINAL LAW (CONSOLIDATION) (SCOTLAND)
ACT, 1995

SECTION 49B(1) TO (3)

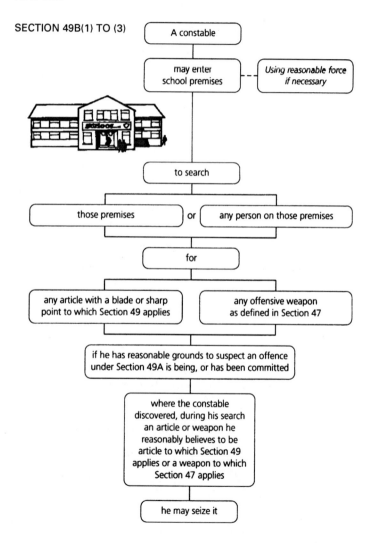

A constable

may enter
school premises — *Using reasonable force
if necessary*

to search

those premises — or — any person on those premises

for

any article with a blade or sharp
point to which Section 49 applies

any offensive weapon
as defined in Section 47

if he has reasonable grounds to suspect an offence
under Section 49A is being, or has been committed

where the constable
discovered, during his search
an article or weapon he
reasonably believes to be
article to which Section 49
applies or a weapon to which
Section 47 applies

he may seize it

Sale of Knives to Persons Under 16

SECTION 141A, CRIMINAL JUSTICE ACT, 1988 AS INSERTED BY
SECTION 6 OF THE OFFENSIVE WEAPONS ACT, 1996

SECTION 141A(1) TO (2)

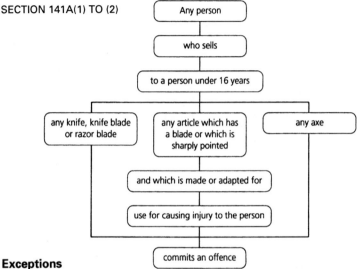

Any person

who sells

to a person under 16 years

| any knife, knife blade or razor blade | any article which has a blade or which is sharply pointed | any axe |

and which is made or adapted for

use for causing injury to the person

commits an offence

Exceptions

SECTION 141A(3)

Section 141A does not apply to any article described in:

* Section 1 of the Restriction of Offensive Weapons Act, 1959 (for example knife and gravity knife)

* An order made under Section 141(2) of the Criminal Justice Act, 1988 (for example knuckle-duster, swordstick, handlaw, belt buckle knife, push dagger and so on)

* An order made by the Secretary of State under this section (to date, no order has been made)

Defence

SECTION 141A(4)

It is a defence for a person charged with an offence under Section 141A to prove he took all reasonable precautions and exercised all due diligence to avoid committing the offence.

Combat Knives

KNIVES ACT, 1997 (*see note 1 below*)

Unlawful marketing SECTION 1

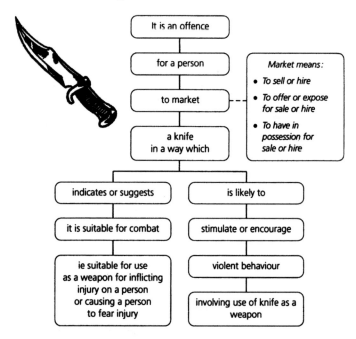

It is an offence

for a person

to market

a knife
in a way which

Market means:
- *To sell or hire*
- *To offer or expose for sale or hire*
- *To have in possession for sale or hire*

indicates or suggests

it is suitable for combat

ie suitable for use
as a weapon for inflicting
injury on a person
or causing a person
to fear injury

is likely to

stimulate or encourage

violent behaviour

involving use of knife as a
weapon

Note 1: An indication or suggestion that a knife may be suitable for combat may, in particular, be given or made by a name or description:

- *Applied to knife*

- *On knife or packaging in which it is contained; or*

- *Included in any advertisement which, expressly or by implication, relates to the knife*

KNIVES ACT, 1997 continued

Publications SECTION 2

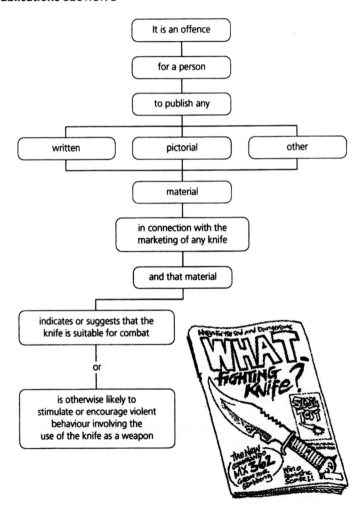

It is an offence

for a person

to publish any

| written | pictorial | other |

material

in connection with the marketing of any knife

and that material

indicates or suggests that the knife is suitable for combat

or

is otherwise likely to stimulate or encourage violent behaviour involving the use of the knife as a weapon

Combat Knives – Statutory Defences to Section 1 Offence

SECTION 3(1) KNIVES ACT, 1997

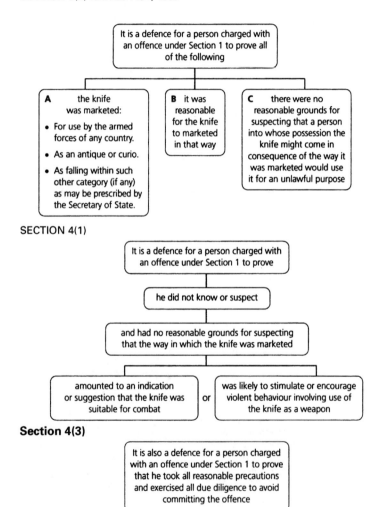

It is a defence for a person charged with an offence under Section 1 to prove all of the following

A the knife was marketed:

- For use by the armed forces of any country.
- As an antique or curio.
- As falling within such other category (if any) as may be prescribed by the Secretary of State.

B it was reasonable for the knife to marketed in that way

C there were no reasonable grounds for suspecting that a person into whose possession the knife might come in consequence of the way it was marketed would use it for an unlawful purpose

SECTION 4(1)

It is a defence for a person charged with an offence under Section 1 to prove

he did not know or suspect

and had no reasonable grounds for suspecting that the way in which the knife was marketed

amounted to an indication or suggestion that the knife was suitable for combat

or

was likely to stimulate or encourage violent behaviour involving use of the knife as a weapon

Section 4(3)

It is also a defence for a person charged with an offence under Section 1 to prove that he took all reasonable precautions and exercised all due diligence to avoid committing the offence

Combat Knives – Statutory Defences to Section 2 Offence

SECTION 3(2) KNIVES ACT, 1997

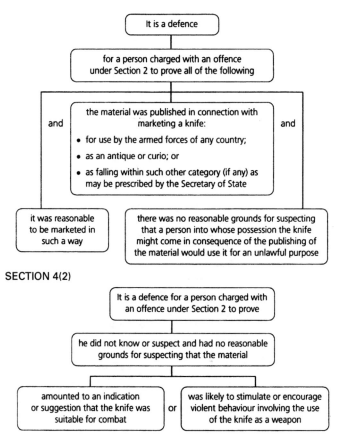

It is a defence

for a person charged with an offence under Section 2 to prove all of the following

and

the material was published in connection with marketing a knife:

- for use by the armed forces of any country;
- as an antique or curio; or
- as falling within such other category (if any) as may be prescribed by the Secretary of State

and

it was reasonable to be marketed in such a way

there was no reasonable grounds for suspecting that a person into whose possession the knife might come in consequence of the publishing of the material would use it for an unlawful purpose

SECTION 4(2)

It is a defence for a person charged with an offence under Section 2 to prove

he did not know or suspect and had no reasonable grounds for suspecting that the material

amounted to an indication or suggestion that the knife was suitable for combat

or

was likely to stimulate or encourage violent behaviour involving the use of the knife as a weapon

Section 4(3)

It is also a defence for a person charged with an offence under Section 2 to prove that he took all reasonable precautions and exercised all due diligence to avoid committing the offence.

Combat Knives – Warrants

SECTION 5 KNIVES ACT, 1997

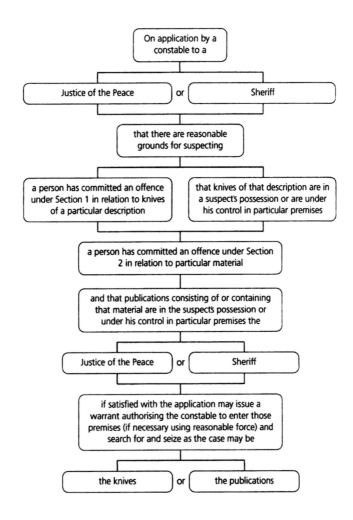

Combat Knives – Stopping and Searching

Section 8 Knives Act, 1997 amends Section 60 of the Criminal Justice and Public Order Act, 1994 as indicated below and extends it to include Scotland.

Authorisation
SECTION 60 (1), (2)

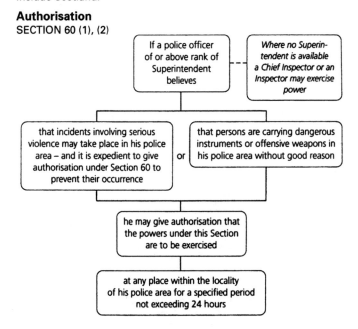

Extension of authorisation
SECTION 60(3)

If it appears to the officer who gave the authorisation under Section 60(1) or to a Superintendent that it is expedient to do so – having regard to offences which have, or are reasonably suspected to have, been committed in connection with any incident falling within the authorisation – he may continue the authorisation for a further 24 hours.

Combat Knives – Search

SECTION 60(4) CRIMINAL JUSTICE AND PUBLIC ORDER ACT, 1994

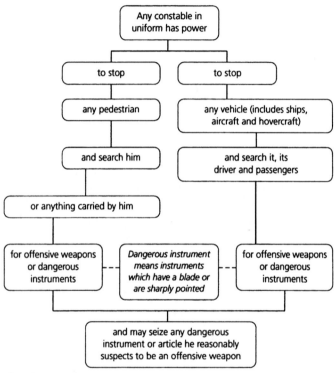

Section 60(5)

A constable (in uniform) may in the exercise of his powers under Section 60(4) stop any person, any vehicle (includes ships, aircraft and hovercraft) and make any search he thinks fit.

Whether or not he has any reasonable grounds for suspecting that person or vehicle is carrying offensive weapons or dangerous instruments and he may seize any dangerous instrument or articley he reasonably suspects to be an offensive weapon.

Section 60 – Offence

SECTION 60(8) CRIMINAL JUSTICE AND PUBLIC ORDER ACT, 1994

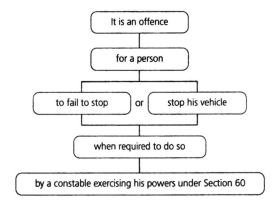

Authorisation must be in writing

SECTION 60(9)

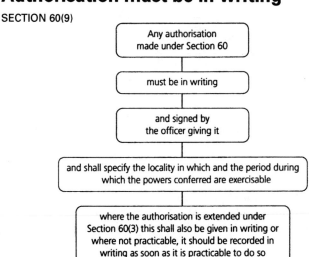

Section 60 - Written Statement of Search

SECTION 60(10) CRIMINAL JUSTICE AND PUBLIC ORDER ACT, 1994

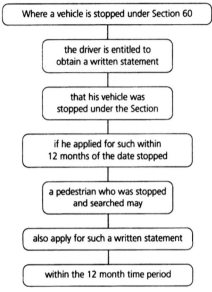

Where a vehicle is stopped under Section 60

the driver is entitled to obtain a written statement

that his vehicle was stopped under the Section

if he applied for such within 12 months of the date stopped

a pedestrian who was stopped and searched may

also apply for such a written statement

within the 12 month time period

Possession
SECTION 60(11A)

For the purposes of Section 60, a person carries a dangerous instrument or an offensive weapon if he has it in his possession.

Offensive weapons
RESTRICTION OF OFFENSIVE WEAPONS ACTS, 1959 and 1961

It is an offence for any person to manufacture, import, sell, hire, offer for sale or hire, expose or have in possession for the purpose of sale or hire, or to lend or give any other person a flick knife or gravity knife.

Crossbows

CROSSBOWS ACT, 1987

Offences

Sale

To sell or hire a crossbow or part of a crossbow to a person under the age of 17 years, unless he believes and has reasonable grounds to believe him to be 17 years

Purchase

For a person under 17 years to buy or hire a crossbow or part of a crossbow

Possession

For a person under 17 years to have with him a crossbow (whether assembled or not) capable of discharging a missile unless under the supervision of a person of 21 years or older.

Note: The Act does not apply to crossbows with a draw weight of less than 1.4 kg

Police powers

Search

Where a constable suspects with reasonable cause, that a person is committing, or has committed an offence of unlawful possession, he may search that person, any vehicle, or anything in or on a vehicle, and may detain the person or vehicle for that purpose

Seizure

A constable may seize and retain for the purpose of proceedings any crossbow or part of a crossbow discovered in the course of the search

Entry

For the purpose of exercising the above powers, a constable may enter any land other than a dwelling house.

Fireworks

FIREWORKS ACT, 2003. FIREWORKS REGULATIONS, 2004 (AS AMENDED)

Any person who contravenes a prohibition imposed by these Regulations commits an offence (S 11)

Possession under 18
No person under the age of 18 years shall possess an adult firework in a public place. (Reg. 4).

'Public Place' Includes any place to which at the material time the public have or are permitted access, whether on payment or otherwise. (Reg. 4).

'Adult firework' means any firework (except for a cap, cracker snap, novelty match, party popper, serpent, sparkler or throwdown) which does not comply with BS 7114. (Reg. 3).

Possession of Category 4 firework
No person shall possess a category 4 firework. (Reg. 5). This does not apply to a person transporting fireworks in the course of employment in, or trade or business of, transporting fireworks. (Reg. 6).

'Category 4 firework' means classified as such by B.S. 7114.

Exceptions to Regs. 4 & 5
a) Professional operator or organiser of firework displays;
b) Manufacturer of fireworks or assemblies;
c) Supplier of fireworks or assemblies;
d) Local authority employee for a firework display, national public celebration or national commemorative event;
e) Special effects in theatre, film or TV;
f) A body having enforcement powers;
g) Government department for firework display, national public celebration, national commemorative event, or research or investigation;
h) Supplier of goods used for fireworks or assemblies, for testing purposes; or
i) Navy, military or air force employees for firework display, national public celebration or national commemorative event. (Reg. 6).

Use of fireworks at night
No person shall use an adult firework during night hours (11 pm to 7 am) except:
a) during a permitted fireworks night; or
b) a person employed by a local authority putting on a firework display, national public celebration or national commemorative event. (Reg.7).

'Permitted fireworks night' means a period:
a) beginning at 11 pm on the first day of the Chinese New Year and ending at 1 am the following day;
b) beginning at 11 pm and ending at midnight on 5 November;
c) beginning at 11 pm on the day of Diwali and ending at 1 am the following day; or
d) beginning at 11 pm on 31 December and ending at 1 am the following day.

Enforcement
The above offences concerning possession and use are enforced by the police (Reg. 12). A power to stop, search and seize prohibited firearms was inserted into S1 PACE by the Serious Organised Crime and Police Act, 2005 (see later).

Racial Hatred

SECTIONS 17-23 PUBLIC ORDER ACT, 1986

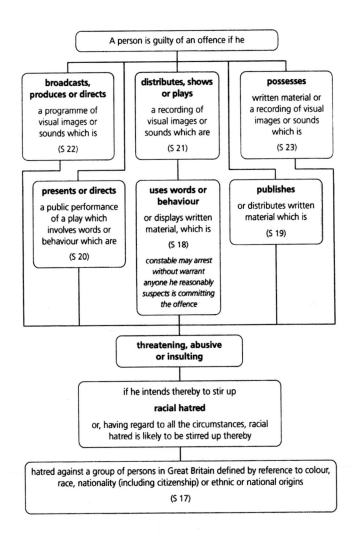

A person is guilty of an offence if he

broadcasts, produces or directs

a programme of visual images or sounds which is

(S 22)

distributes, shows or plays

a recording of visual images or sounds which are

(S 21)

possesses

written material or a recording of visual images or sounds which is

(S 23)

presents or directs

a public performance of a play which involves words or behaviour which are

(S 20)

uses words or behaviour

or displays written material, which is

(S 18)

constable may arrest without warrant anyone he reasonably suspects is committing the offence

publishes

or distributes written material which is

(S 19)

threatening, abusive or insulting

if he intends thereby to stir up

racial hatred

or, having regard to all the circumstances, racial hatred is likely to be stirred up thereby

hatred against a group of persons in Great Britain defined by reference to colour, race, nationality (including citizenship) or ethnic or national origins

(S 17)

Racially Aggravated Harassment

SECTION 50A OF THE CRIMINAL LAW (CONSOLIDATION) (SCOTLAND) ACT, 1995 INSERTED BY THE CRIME AND DISORDER ACT, 1998

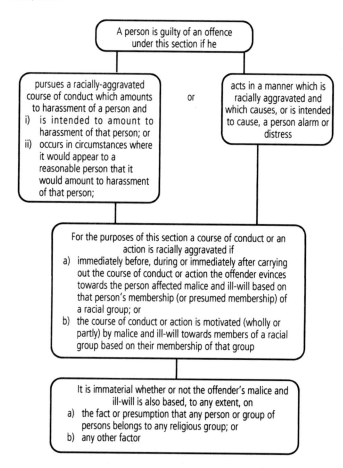

A person is guilty of an offence under this section if he

pursues a racially-aggravated course of conduct which amounts to harassment of a person and
i) is intended to amount to harassment of that person; or
ii) occurs in circumstances where it would appear to a reasonable person that it would amount to harassment of that person;

or

acts in a manner which is racially aggravated and which causes, or is intended to cause, a person alarm or distress

For the purposes of this section a course of conduct or an action is racially aggravated if
a) immediately before, during or immediately after carrying out the course of conduct or action the offender evinces towards the person affected malice and ill-will based on that person's membership (or presumed membership) of a racial group; or
b) the course of conduct or action is motivated (wholly or partly) by malice and ill-will towards members of a racial group based on their membership of that group

It is immaterial whether or not the offender's malice and ill-will is also based, to any extent, on
a) the fact or presumption that any person or group of persons belongs to any religious group; or
b) any other factor

Trespassers on Land

SECTIONS 61 and 62 CRIMINAL JUSTICE AND PUBLIC ORDER ACT, 1994

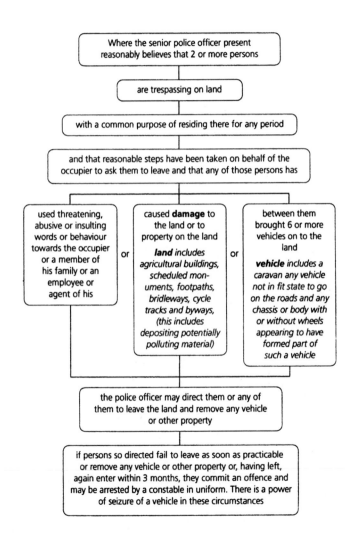

Where the senior police officer present reasonably believes that 2 or more persons

are trespassing on land

with a common purpose of residing there for any period

and that reasonable steps have been taken on behalf of the occupier to ask them to leave and that any of those persons has

| used threatening, abusive or insulting words or behaviour towards the occupier or a member of his family or an employee or agent of his | or | caused **damage** to the land or to property on the land

land includes agricultural buildings, scheduled monuments, footpaths, bridleways, cycle tracks and byways, (this includes depositing potentially polluting material) | or | between them brought 6 or more vehicles on to the land

vehicle includes a caravan any vehicle not in fit state to go on the roads and any chassis or body with or without wheels appearing to have formed part of such a vehicle |

the police officer may direct them or any of them to leave the land and remove any vehicle or other property

if persons so directed fail to leave as soon as practicable or remove any vehicle or other property or, having left, again enter within 3 months, they commit an offence and may be arrested by a constable in uniform. There is a power of seizure of a vehicle in these circumstances

Aggravated Trespass

SECTION 68 CRIMINAL JUSTICE AND PUBLIC ORDER ACT, 1994

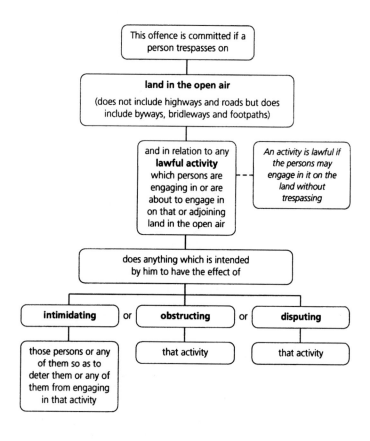

This offence is committed if a person trespasses on

land in the open air

(does not include highways and roads but does include byways, bridleways and footpaths)

and in relation to any **lawful activity** which persons are engaging in or are about to engage in on that or adjoining land in the open air

An activity is lawful if the persons may engage in it on the land without trespassing

does anything which is intended by him to have the effect of

intimidating or **obstructing** or **disputing**

those persons or any of them so as to deter them or any of them from engaging in that activity

that activity

that activity

Note: A constable in uniform who reasonably suspects that a person is committing this offence may arrest him without a warrant.

Aggravated Trespass – Removal of Persons

SECTION 69 CRIMINAL JUSTICE AND PUBLIC ORDER

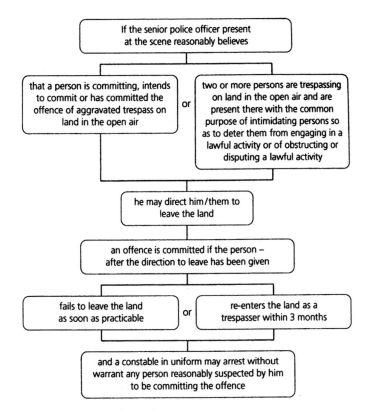

If the senior police officer present at the scene reasonably believes

that a person is committing, intends to commit or has committed the offence of aggravated trespass on land in the open air

or

two or more persons are trespassing on land in the open air and are present there with the common purpose of intimidating persons so as to deter them from engaging in a lawful activity or of obstructing or disputing a lawful activity

he may direct him/them to leave the land

an offence is committed if the person – after the direction to leave has been given

fails to leave the land as soon as practicable

or

re-enters the land as a trespasser within 3 months

and a constable in uniform may arrest without warrant any person reasonably suspected by him to be committing the offence

Note: The direction to leave may be communicated by a constable at the scene.

Defence

If a person shows he was not trespassing or that he had a reasonable excuse for not leaving or for re-entering.

Trespassory Assemblies

SECTION 14A PUBLIC ORDER ACT, 1986 INSERTED BY SECTION 70
CRIMINAL JUSTICE AND PUBLIC ORDER ACT, 1994

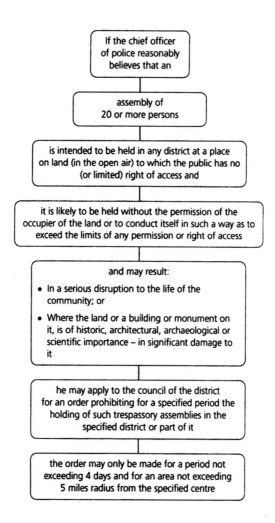

If the chief officer
of police reasonably
believes that an

assembly of
20 or more persons

is intended to be held in any district at a place
on land (in the open air) to which the public has no
(or limited) right of access and

it is likely to be held without the permission of the
occupier of the land or to conduct itself in such a way as to
exceed the limits of any permission or right of access

and may result:

- In a serious disruption to the life of the
  community; or

- Where the land or a building or monument on
  it, is of historic, architectural, archaeological or
  scientific importance – in significant damage to
  it

he may apply to the council of the district
for an order prohibiting for a specified period the
holding of such trespassory assemblies in the
specified district or part of it

the order may only be made for a period not
exceeding 4 days and for an area not exceeding
5 miles radius from the specified centre

Trespassory Assemblies – Powers

SECTIONS 14B and 14C PUBLIC ORDER ACT, 1986 INSERTED BY
SECTIONS 70-71 CRIMINAL JUSTICE AND PUBLIC ORDER ACT, 1994

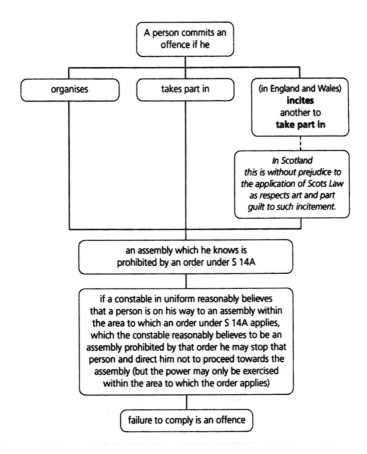

*Note: A constable in uniform may arrest without warrant any person he
reasonably suspects to be committing an offence under SS 70 or 71.*

Raves

SECTION 63 CRIMINAL JUSTICE AND PUBLIC ORDER ACT, 1994

A 'rave' is defined as a:

gathering of 100 or more persons — *whether or not trespassers*

on land in the open air — *includes places partly open to the air*

at which amplified music is played — *includes sounds wholly or predominantly characterised by the emission of a succession of repetitive beats*

during the night

and is such as by reason of its **loudness and duration and the time at which it is played**, is likely to cause **serious distress** to the inhabitants of the locality

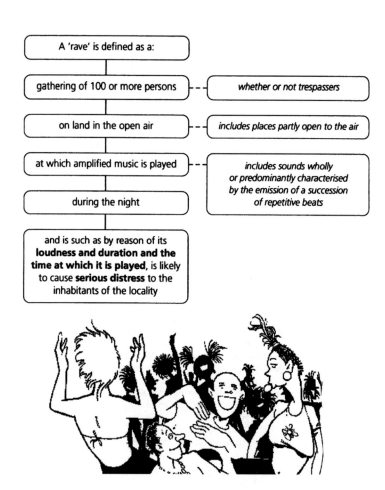

Raves – Powers

SECTIONS 63-65 CRIMINAL JUSTICE AND PUBLIC ORDER ACT, 1994

Removal of persons S 63

A police officer of at least the rank of Superintendent who reasonably believes that:

- Two or more persons are making preparations for a rave

- 10 or more persons are waiting for it to begin; or

- 10 or more persons are attending a rave in progress, may **direct** those persons and any other persons who arrive, to leave the land and remove any vehicles or other property that they have with them. The direction may be communicated by any constable at the scene. It will be treated as having been communicated if reasonable steps have been taken to bring it to their attention. Failure to leave or re-entry within 7 days is an offence arrestable by a constable in uniform who reasonably suspects a person to be committing the offence.

Entry and seizure S 64

A Superintendent or above who believes the above direction would be justified in the circumstances, may authorise any constable to enter the land for the purposes of ascertaining whether such circumstances exist and to exercise any of the above powers and to seize and remove a vehicle or sound equipment which the person to whom a direction has been given has failed to remove and which appears to the constable to belong to him or to be in his possession or control. Also applies where a person has re-entered the land with a vehicle and/or sound equipment within 7 days.

Stopping persons from attending S 65

If a constable in uniform reasonably believes that a person is on his way to a gathering to which S 63 applies and in respect of which a direction is in force, he may stop that person and direct him not to proceed in the direction of that gathering. This power may be exercised within 5 miles of the boundary of the site of the gathering. Failure to comply is an offence and a constable in uniform who reasonably suspects that a person is committing the offence may arrest him without warrant.

Public Meetings

S 1 PUBLIC MEETING ACT, 1908

Any person who at a lawful

public meeting

acts in a disorderly manner for the purpose of preventing the transaction of the business of the meeting shall be guilty of an offence

It is the duty of the police to prevent any action likely to result in a breach of the peace. Refusing to desist is an obstruction of the police in the execution of their duty

POWER OF ENTRY

The police have a right to enter premises at which the public have been invited to attend if they reasonably apprehend a **breach of the peace**

Any person who incites a person to commit such an offence shall be guilty of a like offence

If a constable reasonably suspects a person to be committing such an offence he may, if requested by the chairman of the meeting, request the offender to give his name and address. If he fails or refuses or gives a false name and address he shall be guilty of an offence

Uniforms

S 1 PUBLIC ORDER ACT, 1936

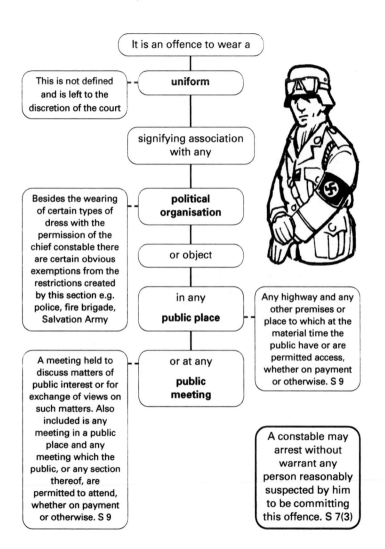

It is an offence to wear a

uniform

This is not defined and is left to the discretion of the court

signifying association with any

political organisation

Besides the wearing of certain types of dress with the permission of the chief constable there are certain obvious exemptions from the restrictions created by this section e.g. police, fire brigade, Salvation Army

or object

in any **public place**

Any highway and any other premises or place to which at the material time the public have or are permitted access, whether on payment or otherwise. S 9

or at any **public meeting**

A meeting held to discuss matters of public interest or for exchange of views on such matters. Also included is any meeting in a public place and any meeting which the public, or any section thereof, are permitted to attend, whether on payment or otherwise. S 9

A constable may arrest without warrant any person reasonably suspected by him to be committing this offence. S 7(3)

Organisations

S 2 PUBLIC ORDER ACT, 1936

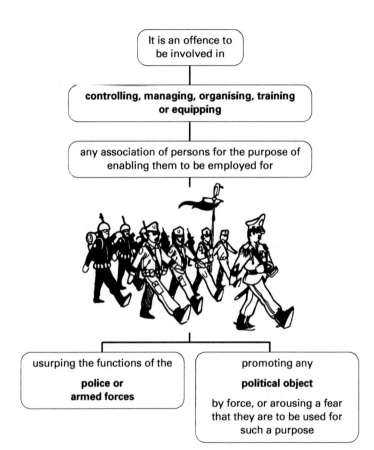

It is an offence to be involved in

controlling, managing, organising, training or equipping

any association of persons for the purpose of enabling them to be employed for

usurping the functions of the

police or armed forces

promoting any

political object

by force, or arousing a fear that they are to be used for such a purpose

But this section does not prevent the employment of a reasonable number of stewards to assist in the preservation of order at any public meeting held on private premises, or giving them instruction in their duties, or giving them badges, etc

Terrorism – Interpretation

S 1 TERRORISM ACT, 2000

Terrorism means the use or threat of action which

1. involves serious violence against a person,

2. involves serious damage to property,

3. endangers a person's life, other than that of the person committing the action,

4. creates a serious risk to the health or safety of the public or a section of the public, or

5. is designed seriously to interfere with or seriously to disrupt an electronic system

and the use or threat is designed to influence the government or to intimidate the public, or a section of the public

But the use or threat of action which involves the use of firearms or explosives is 'terrorism' whether or not this part is satisfied

and the use or threat is made for the purpose of advancing a political, religious or ideological cause

'action' includes action outside the United Kingdom

the reference to any person or property means wherever situated

'public' includes the public of a country other than the United Kingdom

'government' means the government of the UK, or a part of the UK or of a country other than the UK

Terrorism – Offences

SS 11 – 12 TERRORISM ACT, 2000

Offences are committed in the following circumstances:

MEMBERSHIP (S 11): Belonging to or professing to belong to a proscribed organisation.

It is a **defence** to prove:
a) that the organisation was not proscribed on the last occasion he became a member or began to profess to be a member, and
b) that he has not taken part in the activities of the organisation at any time while it was proscribed.

SUPPORT (S 12(1)): Inviting support for a proscribed organisation, and the support is not, or is not restricted to, the provision of money or other property.

ARRANGING MEETINGS (S 12(2)): Arranging, managing or assisting in arranging or managing a meeting which he knows is:

a) to support a proscribed organisation,
b) to further the activities of a proscribed organisation, or
c) to be addressed by a person who belongs or professes to belong to a proscribed organisation (but it would be a defence at a private meeting to prove that he had no reasonable cause to believe that the address would support a proscribed organisation or further its activities).

ADDRESSING MEETINGS (S 12(3)): Addressing a meeting and the purpose of the address is to encourage support for a proscribed organisation or to further its activities.

'Meeting' means a meeting of 3 or more persons, whether or not the public are admitted. A meeting is *private* if the public are not admitted.

SS 13 & 15 TERRORISM ACT, 2000

Offences are committed in the following circumstances:

UNIFORM (S 13)

In a public place if a person:

a) wears an item of clothing, or
b) wears, carries or displays an article,

in such a way or in such circumstances as to arouse reasonable suspicion that he is a member or supporter of a proscribed organisation.

A constable in Scotland may arrest a person if he has reasonable grounds to suspect the person to be guilty of this offence.

FUND-RAISING (S 15(1))

Inviting another to provide money or other property, intending that it should be used, or having reasonable cause to suspect that it may be used, for the purposes of terrorism.

RECEIVING MONEY OR OTHER PROPERTY (S 15(2))

Receiving money or other property intending that it should be used, or having reasonable cause to suspect that it may be used, for the purposes of terrorism.

PROVIDING MONEY OR OTHER PROPERTY (S 15(3))

Providing money or other property, knowing or having reasonable cause to suspect that it will or may be used for the purposes of terrorism.

Provision of money or other property means being given, lent or otherwise made available, whether or not for consideration.
Purposes of terrorism includes for the benefit of a proscribed organisation (see later).

The offence will be committed even if the act is done outside the UK (S 63)

Terrorism – Offences – continued

SS 16 – 18 & 21 TERRORISM ACT, 2000

Offences are committed in the following circumstances:

USE AND POSSESSION (S 16)

a) Using money or other property for the purposes of terrorism.
b) Possessing money or other property, intending that it should be used, or having reasonable cause to suspect that it may be used, for the purposes of terrorism.

The offence will be committed even if the act is done outside the UK (S 63)

FUNDING ARRANGEMENTS (S 17)

Entering into or becoming concerned in an arrangement as a result of which money or other property is made available or is to be made available to another, knowing or having reasonable cause to suspect that that it will or may be used for the purposes of terrorism.

MONEY LAUNDERING (S 18)

Entering into or becoming concerned in an arrangement which facilitates the retention or control by or on behalf of another person of terrorist property:

a) by concealment,
b) by removal from the jurisdiction,
c) by transfer to nominees, or
d) in any other way.

It is a defence to prove that he did not know and had no reasonable cause to suspect that the arrangement related to terrorist property.

'TERRORIST PROPERTY' MEANS:

a) money or other property which is likely to be used for the purposes of terrorism (including any resources of a proscribed organisation),
b) proceeds of the commission of acts of terrorism, and
c) proceeds of the acts carried out for the purposes of terrorism (S 14).

CO-OPERATION WITH THE POLICE (S 21)

A person does not commit an offence under Ss 15 to 18 if he is acting with the express consent of a constable. Neither does he commit an offence under those sections by involvement in a transaction or arrangement relating to money or other property if he discloses to a constable:

a) his suspicion or belief that the money or other property is terrorist property, and
b) the information on which his suspicion or belief is based.

But the above only applies where he makes the disclosure

a) after he becomes concerned in the transaction,
b) on his own initiative, and
c) as soon as reasonably practicable.

S 54 TERRORISM ACT, 2000

Offences are committed in the following circumstances:

WEAPONS TRAINING (S 54)

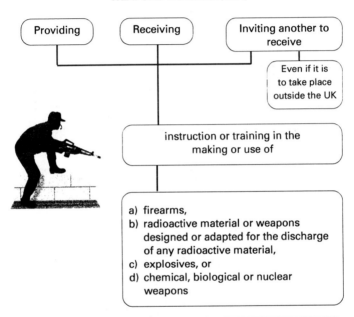

Providing

Receiving

Inviting another to receive

Even if it is to take place outside the UK

instruction or training in the making or use of

a) firearms,
b) radioactive material or weapons designed or adapted for the discharge of any radioactive material,
c) explosives, or
d) chemical, biological or nuclear weapons

'Providing instruction' and 'inviting' includes making it available either generally or to one or more specific persons.

It will be a defence to prove that his action or involvement was for a purpose other than terrorism.

Terrorism – Offences – continued

SS 56 – 58 TERRORISM ACT, 2000

Offences are committed in the following circumstances:

DIRECTING ORGANISATIONS (S 56)

Directing, at any level, the activities of a terrorist organisation.

POSSESSION OF ARTICLES (S 57)

Possessing an article in circumstances which gave rise to a reasonable suspicion that it was connected with the commission, preparation or instigation of an act of terrorism.

It is a defence to prove that it was not for a terrorist purpose.

It will be assumed that the person *possessed* the article if it was:

a) on any premises at the same time as that person, or

b) on premises which the person occupied or habitually used other than as a member of the public, unless he proves that he did not know of its presence or that he had no control over it.

'Article' includes substance and any other thing (S 121)

COLLECTION OF INFORMATION (S 58)

Collecting or making a record of	Possessing a document or record containing

information likely to be useful to a person committing or preparing an act of terrorism

'record' includes a photographic or electronic record

It is a defence to prove that he had a reasonable excuse for his action or possession.

SS 59 – 63 TERRORISM ACT, 2000

Offences are committed in the following circumstances:

INCITING TERRORISM OVERSEAS (S 61)
Inciting a person to commit an act of terrorism wholly or partly outside the UK, and the act would, if committed in Scotland, constitute one of the following offences:
a) murder,
b) assault to severe injury, and
c) reckless conduct which causes actual injury.

It is immaterial whether or not the person incited is in the UK at the time of the incitement.

ACTS OF TERRORISM OUTSIDE THE UK
(S 62)
Doing anything outside the UK as an act of terrorism or for the purposes of terrorism, and the action would, if done in the UK, constitute one of the following offences:

a) explosions, etc (S 2, 3 or 5 Explosive Substances Act, 1883),
b) biological weapons (S 1 Biological Weapons Act, 1974)
c) chemical weapons (S 2 Chemical Weapons Act, 1996)

Terrorism – Disclosure of Information

TERRORISM ACT, 2000, SS 19 & 20

Where a person :

a) believes or suspects that another person has committed an offence under Sections 15 to 18 (see earlier), and

b) bases his belief or suspicion on information which comes to his attention in the course of a trade, profession, business or employment

the person commits an offence if he does not disclose to a constable as soon as reasonably practicable:

a) his belief or suspicion, and
b) the information on which it is based.

This does not require disclosure by a professional legal adviser of

a) information which he obtains in privileged circumstances, or
b) a belief or suspicion based on information which he obtains in privileged circumstances.

This does not apply if the information came to the person in the course of a business in the regulated sector. (Sched. 3A lists the types of business which are 'regulated'. These include national savings, credit unions, banking, building societies, investments, life insurance, etc) However, a similar offence of failure to disclose in the regulated sector is provided by Section 21 A.

but it is a defence to prove that he had a reasonable excuse for not making the disclosure.

It is also a defence where:

a) a person is in employment,
b) his employer has established a procedure for the making of disclosures of such matters, and
c) he is charged with such an offence,

to prove that he disclosed the matters in accordance with the procedure.

A person may make such disclosures to a constable notwithstanding any restriction on disclosing it imposed by statute or otherwise (S 20).

Terrorism – Investigations

SS 33 – 39 TERRORISM ACT, 2000

CORDONED AREAS (Ss 33 – 36)

If considered expedient for the purposes of a terrorist investigation, a Superintendent (or lower rank in the case of urgency) may designate an area to be cordoned.

A constable in uniform may:

a) order a person in a cordoned area to leave it immediately;

b) order a person immediately to leave premises which are wholly or partly in or adjacent to a cordoned area;

c) order the driver or person in charge of a vehicle in a cordoned area to move it from the area immediately;

d) arrange for the removal of a vehicle from a cordoned area;

e) arrange for the movement of a vehicle within a cordoned area;

f) prohibit or restrict access to a cordoned area by pedestrians or vehicles.

A person commits an offence if he fails to comply with an order, prohibition or restriction imposed as above. But it is a defence to prove that he had a reasonable excuse for his failure.

FAILURE TO DISCLOSE INFORMATION (S 38B)

Where a person has information which he knows or believes might be of material assistance:

a) in preventing an act of terrorism, or

b) in securing the apprehension, prosecution or conviction of another person in the UK, for an offence of terrorism,

he commits an offence if he does not disclose the information as soon as reasonably practicable to a constable or (in Northern Ireland) a member of HM Forces.

It is a defence to prove that he had a reasonable excuse for not making the disclosure.

DISCLOSURE OF INFORMATION (S 39)

Where a person knows or has reasonable cause to suspect that a constable is conducting or proposes to conduct a terrorist investigation, he commits an offence if he:

a) discloses to another anything which is likely to prejudice an investigation, or

b) interferes with material which is likely to be relevant to the investigation.

He would also commit an offence by a similar disclosure or interference where a disclosure had been or was to be made under the aforementioned Sections 19, 21 or 38B.

It would be a defence to prove that:

a) he did not know and had no reasonable cause to suspect that the disclosure or interference was likely to affect a terrorist investigation, or

b) that he had a reasonable excuse for the disclosure or interference.

An offence would not be committed in the case of a professional legal adviser.

Terrorism – Police Powers

SS 40 – 43 TERRORISM ACT 2000

ARREST WITHOUT WARRANT (S 41)

A constable may arrest without warrant anyone he reasonably suspects to be a terrorist.

'Terrorist' is defined as a person who:

a) has committed any offence under any of Sections 11 (membership), 12 (support), 15 (fund raising), 16 (use and possession), 17 (funding), 18 (money laundering), 54 (weapon training), 56 (directing organisations), 57 (possession of articles), 58 (collection of information), 59 (inciting overseas), 60 (Northern Ireland), 61 (Scotland), 62 (bombing outside UK) or 63 (finance outside UK), or

b) is or has been concerned in the commission, preparation or instigation of acts of terrorism.

SEARCH OF PREMISES (S 42)

A Justice of the Peace and a Sheriff may issue a warrant for a constable to search specified premises if he is satisfied that there are reasonable grounds to suspect that a person to whom para b) in the above definition applies is to be found there.

SEARCH OF PERSONS (S 43)

A constable may stop and search a person whom he reasonably suspects to be a terrorist (see above definition) or a person arrested under S 41 above to discover whether he has in his possession anything which may constitute evidence that he is a terrorist.

The search must be carried out by a person of the same sex.

A constable may seize and retain anything discovered in the course of the search which he reasonably suspects may constitute evidence that the person is a terrorist.

GENERAL (S 114)

Any power conferred by this Act is additional to any other powers at common law or other enactment, and will not affect those powers. A constable may use reasonable force if necessary in exercising the powers under this Act.

Terrorism – Stop and Search

SS 44 - 45 TERRORISM ACT, 2000

A constable in uniform may be authorised to **stop**

a vehicle
and to *search-*
a) the vehicle;
b) the driver of the vehicle;
c) a passenger in the vehicle;
d) anything in or on the vehicle or carried by the driver or a passenger.

a pedestrian
and to *search-*
a) the pedestrian;
b) anything carried by him.

Authorisation may be given:
by an ACC, a commander in London or the metropolitan area, or an ACC in Northern Ireland.
Authorisation may be given by an ACC of the BTP or MOD police but only in relation to BTP or MOD premises respectively.

if he considers it expedient for the prevention of acts of terrorism.

Exercise of Power
The power may be exercised only for the purpose of searching for articles of a kind which could be used in connection with terrorism, whether or not the constable has grounds for suspecting the presence of such articles.

Seizure
Articles which are discovered and which are reasonably suspected to be intended to be used in connection with terrorism may be seized and retained.

Removal of Clothing
A constable may not require a person to remove any clothing in public except head-gear, footwear, an outer coat, a jacket or gloves.

Detention
A constable may detain the person or vehicle for such time as is reasonably required to permit the search to be carried out.

Offences
A person will be guilty of an offence if he fails to stop, or if he fails to stop the vehicle, when required to do so, or if he wilfully obstructs the constable.

Terrorism – Restrictions on Parking

SS 48 - 52 TERRORISM ACT, 2000

A constable in uniform may be authorised to prohibit or restrict the parking of vehicles on a road specified in the authorisation.

Authorisation may be given

by an ACC, a commander in London or the metropolitan area, or an ACC in Northern Ireland, if he considers it expedient for the prevention of acts of terrorism.

Exercise of Power

The power is exercised by placing a traffic sign on the road concerned. A constable may suspend a parking place and this will be treated as a restriction for the purposes of removal of vehicles illegally parked or for the purposes of committing offences (see below).

Duration of Authorisation

The period of authorisation shall not exceed 28 days but it may be renewed.

Offences

A person commits an offence if:

a) he parks a vehicle in contravention of a prohibition or restriction.

b) he is the driver or other person in charge of the vehicle which has been permitted to remain at rest in contravention of a prohibition or restriction and he fails to remove the vehicle when ordered to do so by a constable in uniform.

It will be a defence to prove that he had a reasonable excuse for the act or omission. Possession of a disabled person's badge shall not itself constitute a reasonable excuse.

No Parking

Terrorism – Proscribed Organisations

S 3 & SCHED 2 TERRORISM ACT, 2000

An organisation is **'proscribed'** if it is mentioned in the list below or operates under the same name as an organisation so mentioned:

The Irish Republican Army
Cumann na mBan
Fianna na hEireann
The Red Hand Commando
Saor Eire
The Ulster Freedom Fighters
The Ulster Volunteer Force
The Irish National Liberation Army
The Irish People's Liberation Organisation
The Ulster Defence Association
The Loyalist Volunteer Force
The Continuity Army Council
The Orange Volunteers
The Red Hand Defenders
Al-Qaeda
Egyptian Islamic Jihad
Al-Gama'at al-Islamiya
Armed Islamic Group (GIA)
Salafist Group for Call and Combat (GSPC)
Babbar Khalsa
International Sikh Youth Federation
Harakat Mujahideen
Jaish e Mohammed
Lashkar e Tayyaba
Liberation Tigers of Tamil Eelam (LTTE)
Hizballah External Security Organisation
Hamas-Izz al-Din al-Qassem Brigades
Palestinian Islamic Jihad – Shaqaqi
Abu Nidal Organisation
Islamic Army of Aden
Mujaheddin e Khalq
Kurdistan Worker's Party (PKK)
Revolutionary People's Liberation Party – Front (DHKP-C)
Basque Homeland and Liberty (ETA)
17 November Revolutionary Organisation (N17)
Abu Sayyaf Group
Asbat Al-Ansar
Islamic Movement of Uzbekistan
Jemaah Islamiyah

Terrorism – Nuclear Weapons

S 47 ANTI-TERRORISM, CRIME AND SECURITY ACT, 2001

A person commits an offence if he:

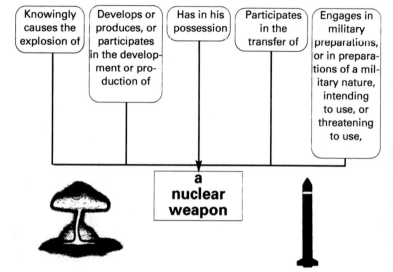

| Knowingly causes the explosion of | Develops or produces, or participates in the development or production of | Has in his possession | Participates in the transfer of | Engages in military preparations, or in preparations of a military nature, intending to use, or threatening to use, |

a nuclear weapon

'Participates in the development or production' means doing any act which:
a) facilitates the development by another of the capability to produce or use, a nuclear weapon; or
b) facilitates the making by another of a nuclear weapon knowing or having reason to believe that his act has (or will have) that effect.

'Participates in the transfer' means:
a) buying or otherwise acquiring it or agreeing with another to do so;
b) selling or otherwise disposing of it or agreeing with another to do so; or
c) making arrangements under which another person either acquires or disposes of it or agrees with a third person to do so.

Terrorism – Use of Noxious Substances

S 113 ANTI-TERRORISM, CRIME AND SECURITY ACT, 2001

A person commits an offence if he takes any action which:

involves the use of a noxious substance or other noxious thing;

which has or is likely to have the effect of:
a) causing serious violence against a person anywhere in the world;
b) causing serious damage to real or personal property anywhere in the world;
c) endangers human life or creates a serious risk to the health or safety of the public or a section of the public; or
d) induces in members of the public the fear that the action is likely to endanger their lives or create a serious risk to their health or safety;

but any effect on the person taking the action is to be disregarded; and

is designed to influence a government or to intimidate the public or a section of the public

An offence will also be committed if a person:
a) makes a threat that he or another will take any action which constitutes the above offence; and
b) intends thereby to induce in a person anywhere in the world the fear that the threat is likely to be carried out.

'substance' includes any biological agent and any other natural or artificial substance (whatever its form, origin or method of production).
'government' means the government of the UK, of a part of the UK or of a country other than the UK.
'public' includes the public of a country other than the UK.

Terrorism – Hoaxes Involving Noxious Substances

S 114 ANTI-TERRORISM, CRIME AND SECURITY ACT, 2001

A person commits an offence if he

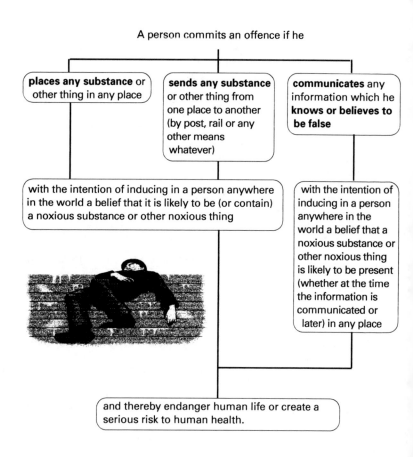

places any substance or other thing in any place

sends any substance or other thing from one place to another (by post, rail or any other means whatever)

communicates any information which he **knows or believes to be false**

with the intention of inducing in a person anywhere in the world a belief that it is likely to be (or contain) a noxious substance or other noxious thing

with the intention of inducing in a person anywhere in the world a belief that a noxious substance or other noxious thing is likely to be present (whether at the time the information is communicated or later) in any place

and thereby endanger human life or create a serious risk to human health.

For meaning of **'substance'** see previous page.

Terrorism – Control Orders

PREVENTION OF TERRORISM ACT, 2005

S 1. A **Control Order** means an order against an individual that imposes **obligations** on him for purposes connected with protecting members of the public from a risk of terrorism. It may be made by the Secretary of State or a court.

Obligations may include a **prohibition or restriction** on

a) possession or use of specified articles or substances;
b) specified services or specified facilities, or specified activities;
c) work, occupation or business;
d) association or communication with other persons;
e) place of residence, or to whom he gives access;
f) presence at specified places, areas, times and days;
g) movement to, from or within the UK

or the following **requirements**

h) to comply with restrictions on other movements for a period not exceeding 24 hours;
i) to surrender his passport or anything specified in the order;
j) to give access to specified persons to his residence or other place;
k) to allow specified persons to search premises to ascertain contravention of obligations;
l) to allow specified persons to remove anything found in the premises;
m) to allow himself to be photographed;
n) to co-operate with specified arrangements to allow his movements, communications or other activities to be monitored by electronic or other means;
o) to comply with a demand to provide information to a specified person;
p) to report to a specified person at specified times and places.

S 5. **Arrest and detention pending derogating control order** may be made by a constable if the Secretary of State has made an application to the court for such an order, and the constable believes arrest is necessary to ensure he is available to be given notice of the order. He must be taken to a designated place, where he may be held for not more than 48 hours (extendable by a court for a further 48 hours)

S 9. **Offences**
a) contravention of an obligation imposed by a control order (arrestable offence (5 years));
b) failing to report to a specified person on his re-entry to the UK after an order has expired (arrestable offence (5 years));
c) obstructing a person carrying out a search of premises for a person on whom a notice of a control order is to be served (arrestable offence (Sched. 1A PACE)).

Fraudulent Use Of Telecommunications System

SS 42 TELECOMMUNICATIONS ACT, 1984

A person who dishonestly obtains a licensed telecommunications service with intent to avoid payment of any charge shall be guilty of an offence.

Possession of Equipment for Fraudulent Use

S 42A

Where a person has in his custody or under his control anything which may be used to obtain a licensed telecommunications service, he commits an offence if he intends:

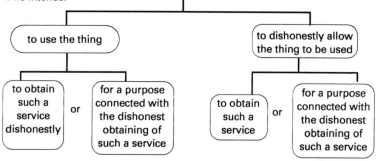

An offence is also committed if a person supplies or offers to supply anything which may be used for the above purposes if he knows or believes the person to whom it is supplied or offered intends to use it for such a purpose.

Post Office and Telecommunications Offences

SECTIONS 42 AND 43 TELECOMMUNICATIONS ACT, 1984

Fraudulent use S 42

It is an offence to make use of any service which is provided by means of a telecommunications system with the intention to avoid payment of any charge.

Grossly Offensive, Indecent Messages, etc. S43

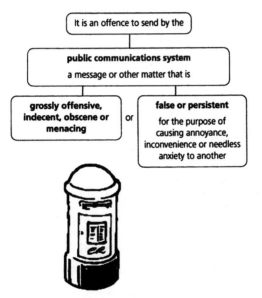

It is an offence to send by the

public communications system

a message or other matter that is

| **grossly offensive, indecent, obscene or menacing** | or | **false or persistent** for the purpose of causing annoyance, inconvenience or needless anxiety to another |

Communications Act, 2003

DISHONESTLY OBTAINING ELECTRONIC COMMUNICATIONS
SERVICES – SECTION 125

A person who
a) dishonestly obtains an electronic communications service, and
b) does so with intent to avoid payment of a charge applicable to the provision of that service, is guilty of an offence.

It is not an offence under Section 125 to obtain a service mentioned in section 297(1) of the Copyright, Designs and Patents Act, 1988 (dishonestly obtaining a broadcasting or cable programme service provided from a place in the UK).

Possession or Supply of apparatus etc for Contravention Section 125 (Section 126)

1) A person is guilty of an offence if, with an intention:
    i) to use the thing to obtain an electronic communications service dishonestly;
    ii) to use the thing for a purpose connected with the dishonest obtaining of such a service;
    iii) dishonestly to allow the thing to be used to obtain such a service; or
    iv) to allow the thing to be used for a purpose connected with the dishonest obtaining of such a service he has in his possession or under his control anything that may be used-
        a) for obtaining an electronic communications service; or
        b) in connection with obtaining such a service.

2) A person is guilty of an offence if
    a) he supplies or offers to supply anything which may be used as mentioned in subsection (1); and
    b) he knows or believes that the intentions in relation to that thing of the person to whom it is supplied or offered fall within (i) to (iv) of subsection (1) above.

Improper Use of Public Electronic Communications Network – (Section 127)

1) A person is guilty of an offence if he
    a) sends by means of a public electronic communications network a message or other matter that is grossly offensive or of an indecent, obscene or menacing character; or
    b) causes any such message or matter to be so sent.

2) A person is guilty of an offence if, for the purpose of causing annoyance, inconvenience or needless anxiety to another, he
    a) sends by means of a public electronic communications network, a message that he knows to be false,
    b) causes such a message to be sent; or
    c) persistently makes use of a public electronic communications network.

Postal Offences

POSTAL SERVICES ACT, 2000

Prohibition on sending certain articles by post (S 85)

A person commits an offence if he sends by post a postal packet:

- which encloses any creature, article or thing of any kind which is likely to injure other postal packets in course of their transmission by post or any person engaged in the business of a postal operator (does not apply to things allowed by the operator);
- which encloses any indecent or obscene print, painting, photograph, lithograph, engraving, cinematograph film or other record of a picture or pictures, book, card or written communication, or any other indecent or obscene article; or
- which has on the packet, or on the cover of the packet, any words, marks or designs which are of an indecent or obscene character.

Prohibition of Advertisements
(S 86)

A person commits an offence if, without due authority:

- he affixes any advertisement, document, board or thing in or on any universal postal service post office, letter box or other property belonging to, or used by, a universal postal service provider, or
- he paints or in any way disfigures any such office, box or property.

Bomb Hoaxes

SECTION 51 CRIMINAL LAW ACT, 1977

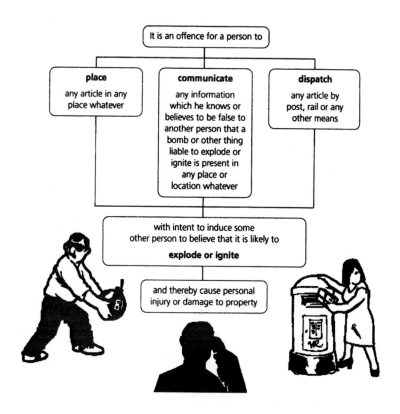

It is an offence for a person to

place
any article in any place whatever

communicate
any information which he knows or believes to be false to another person that a bomb or other thing liable to explode or ignite is present in any place or location whatever

dispatch
any article by post, rail or any other means

with intent to induce some other person to believe that it is likely to **explode or ignite**

and thereby cause personal injury or damage to property

Attempt to Pervert the Course of Justice

COMMON LAW

Definition

Taking steps to destroy in advance, evidence which might lead to the detection of a serious crime is itself a crime at common law.

Examples

```
┌──────────────────────────┐  ┌──────────────────────────┐  ┌──────────────────────────┐
│ Requesting witnesses     │  │ Witness going into       │  │ Assisting an             │
│ to refrain from          │  │ hiding to avoid giving   │  │ accused to evade the     │
│ identifying an accused   │  │ evidence at a trial      │  │ police                   │
└──────────────────────────┘  └──────────────────────────┘  └──────────────────────────┘
```

the above examples have all been held to be attempts to pervert the course of justice

however, these are by no means exhaustive of the ways in which the crime may be committed

COMMON LAW POWER OF ARREST

Wasting the Time of the Police

COMMON LAW

Definition
Any person who maliciously makes a false statement to the police with the intention and effect of causing a police investigation commits a crime at common law.

Essentials
The essence of the crime is that damage and injury to the public interest may result from causing the police to devote their time and service to the investigation of an invented story. It is not essential that any person should be named in the false statement made to the police.

> **COMMON LAW POWER OF ARREST**

Unlawful Eviction

SECTION 22 RENT (SCOTLAND) ACT, 1984

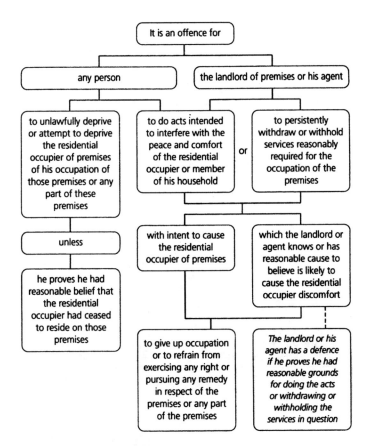

Note: **Residential occupier** is a person occupying any premises as a resident whether under a contract or by virtue of any enactment or rule of law giving him the right to remain in occupation or restricting the right of any other person to recover possession of the premises.

Police Action re Unlawful Eviction

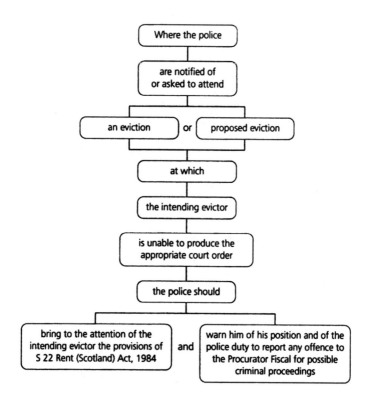

Where the police

are notified of
or asked to attend

an eviction   or   proposed eviction

at which

the intending evictor

is unable to produce the
appropriate court order

the police should

bring to the attention of the
intending evictor the provisions of
S 22 Rent (Scotland) Act, 1984

and

warn him of his position and of the
police duty to report any offence to
the Procurator Fiscal for possible
criminal proceedings

Anti-Social Behaviour Orders (ASBOs)

SECTIONS 4, 7, 9 AND 11 ANTI-SOCIAL BEHAVIOUR ETC.
(SCOTLAND) ACT, 2004

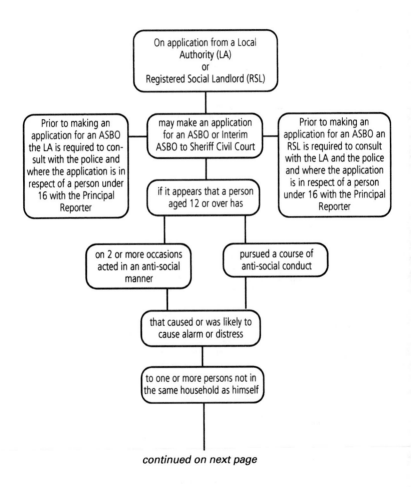

On application from a Local
Authority (LA)
or
Registered Social Landlord (RSL)

Prior to making an
application for an ASBO
the LA is required to consult with the police and
where the application is in
respect of a person under
16 with the Principal
Reporter

may make an application
for an ASBO or Interim
ASBO to Sheriff Civil Court

Prior to making an
application for an ASBO an
RSL is required to consult
with the LA and the police
and where the application
is in respect of a person
under 16 with the Principal
Reporter

if it appears that a person
aged 12 or over has

on 2 or more occasions
acted in an anti-social
manner

pursued a course of
anti-social conduct

that caused or was likely to
cause alarm or distress

to one or more persons not in
the same household as himself

continued on next page

Anti-Social Behaviour Orders (ASBOs) – continued

The Sheriff, may, if satisfied that
- that the person specified in the application is at least 12 years of age
- has engaged in antisocial behaviour towards a relevant person

and

- such order is necessary for the purpose of protecting relevant persons from further anti-social behaviour by the person specified in the application

may grant an ASBO or Interim ASBO

There are certain procedural requirements not described here which the Sheriff must follow before granting an ASBO or Interim ASBO in respect of a person under 16

An ASBO and Interim ASBO is granted on the Balance of Probability i.e. the Civil Law Standard of Proof

The ASBO or Interim ASBO will contain prohibitions, which the sheriff considers necessary to protect relevant persons from further antisocial acts or conducts by the person specified in the order

The Criminal Law Standard of Proof (i.e. Proof beyond all reasonable doubt) is required to secure a conviction for a breach of an order

If the person specified in the ASBO or Interim ASBO without reasonable excuse breaches any conditions of the Order he/she commits a criminal offence. S 9

Where a constable reasonably believes that a person is committing or has committed an offence of breaching the order the constable may arrest the person without warrant.

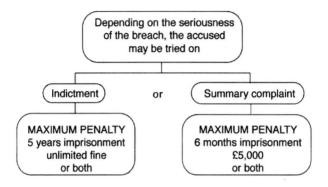

Note: Section 234AA of the Criminal Procedure (Scotland) Act ,1995 inserted by Section 118 of the Anti-social Behaviour Etc (Scotland) Act, 2004 provides:

Where an offender is convicted of an offence; and at the time when he committed the offence, the offender was at least 12 years of age; and in committing the offence, he engaged in antisocial behaviour; and the court is satisfied, on a balance of probabilities, that the making of an anti-social behaviour order is necessary for the purpose of protecting other persons from further anti-social behaviour by the offender the court may, instead of or in addition to imposing any sentence which it could impose, make an anti-social behaviour order in respect of the offender.

The power under Section 234AA is granted to all the criminal courts.

Dispersal of Groups

SECTIONS 19 TO 22 OF THE ANTI-SOCIAL BEHAVIOUR ETC (SCOTLAND) ACT, 2004

Authorisation

Where a police officer of or above the rank of superintendent has reasonable grounds for believing

a) that any members of the public have been alarmed or distressed as a result of the presence or behaviour of groups of two or more persons in public places in any locality in the officer's police area (the 'relevant locality'); and

b) that antisocial behaviour is a significant, persistent and serious problem in the relevant locality

he may authorise a constable in specific circumstances to issue directions to persons forming a group to disperse.

Note: Both conditions explained in a) and b) above have to be satisfied before authorisation can be considered.

Consultation

Where a senior police officer is considering designating a particular area, and this area adjoins another command area, division or force, the relevant officer must inform his/her opposite number (who will also be at the rank of Superintendent or above) in that adjoining area. Subject to any issues emerging from that exchange, the next step is for the senior police officer to consult the relevant local authority (or local authorities if the area extends into more than one local authority areas).

Consultation with the local authority (or authorities) should be at the level of the Chief Executive or such other senior officer in each authority as may be agreed with the Chief Executive in advance.

This consultation in no way precludes discussions at local level with elected representatives, community councils, residents/ tenants associations, community groups, local youth groups, etc. Indeed, dialogue at this level should already have taken place if anti-social behaviour is an ongoing problem in the area.

The senior police officer should take full account of the views of the local authority, and the approach outlined in the anti-social behaviour strategy for the area, before reaching a final decision on whether to authorise.

Process
The Act provides that the formal authorisation must be made in writing, signed by the senior police officer giving it, and must specify:

- The relevant locality;
- The grounds on which the authorisation is given; and
- When the powers of dispersal are exercisable, that is, the period during which the exercise of these powers is valid (including specified days and/or times).

Notification
Before any dispersal powers can be exercised by virtue of an authorisation, the senior police officer who made the authorisation is required to inform local people. Under the Act this may be done by having an **authorisation notice** either published in a local newspaper or displayed in some conspicuous place or places within the locality. An authorisation notice must state that authorisation has been given; specify the relevant locality in which the powers of dispersal are to be used; and specify when the powers may be exercised.

Constable's Direction
Once an authorisation notice has been issued, a constable who has reasonable grounds for believing that the presence or behaviour of a group of two or more persons in any public place in the relevant locality is causing or is likely to cause alarm or distress to any members of the public, to give:

a) a direction requiring the persons in the group to disperse;

b a direction requiring any of those persons whose place of residence is not within the relevant locality to leave the relevant locality or any part of the relevant locality;

c) a direction prohibiting any of those persons whose place of residence is not within the relevant locality from returning to the relevant locality or any part of the relevant locality during such period (not exceeding **24** hours) from the giving of the direction as the constable may specify.

The constable may require a direction under paragraph a) or b) above to be complied with

- immediately or by such time as the constable may specify; or
- in such way as may be so specified.

The direction given by a constable

a) may be given orally;

b) may be given to any person individually or to two or more persons together; and

c) may be withdrawn or varied by the constable who gave it.

In determining whether to exercise this power a constable shall have regard to whether the exercise of the power would be likely to result in the persons in the group causing less alarm and distress to members of the public in the relevant locality than if the power were not exercised.

Exceptions

A constable may not give a direction under these provisions in respect of a group of persons

a) who are engaged in conduct which is lawful under the Trade Union and Labour Relations (Consolidation) Act, 1992 or

b) who are taking part in a lawful procession under the provisions of the Civic Government (Scotland) Act, 1982.

Failure to Comply

A person who, without reasonable excuse, knowingly contravenes a direction given him by a constable under these provisions commits an offence and may be arrested without warrant.

Under the Anti-social Behaviour Etc (Scotland) Act 2004 - Anti-social behaviour means:

a) acting in a manner that causes or is likely to cause alarm or distress; or

(b) pursuing a course of conduct that causes or is likely to cause alarm or distress, to at least one person who is not of the same household as himself.

The term 'conduct' includes speech; and a course of conduct must involve conduct on at least two occasions.

Harassment

PROTECTION FROM HARASSMENT ACT, 1997 SECTIONS 8 AND 9

Non harassment orders etc – following the raising of a civil court action by the victim

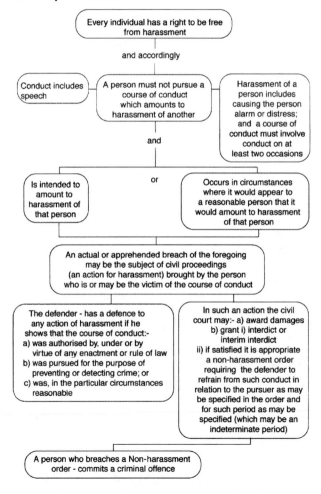

Every individual has a right to be free from harassment

and accordingly

Conduct includes speech

A person must not pursue a course of conduct which amounts to harassment of another

Harassment of a person includes causing the person alarm or distress; and a course of conduct must involve conduct on at least two occasions

and

Is intended to amount to harassment of that person

or

Occurs in circumstances where it would appear to a reasonable person that it would amount to harassment of that person

An actual or apprehended breach of the foregoing may be the subject of civil proceedings (an action for harassment) brought by the person who is or may be the victim of the course of conduct

The defender - has a defence to any action of harassment if he shows that the course of conduct:-
a) was authorised by, under or by virtue of any enactment or rule of law
b) was pursued for the purpose of preventing or detecting crime; or
c) was, in the particular circumstances reasonable

In such an action the civil court may:- a) award damages b) grant i) interdict or interim interdict ii) if satisfied it is appropriate a non-harassment order requiring the defender to refrain from such conduct in relation to the pursuer as may be specified in the order and for such period as may be specified (which may be an indeterminate period)

A person who breaches a Non-harassment order - commits a criminal offence

Harassment

SECTION 234A CRIMINAL PROCEDURE (SCOTLAND) ACT, 1995 AS
INSERTED BY SECTION 11 OF THE PROTECTION FROM
HARASSMENT ACT, 1997

Non harassment orders granted by a criminal court

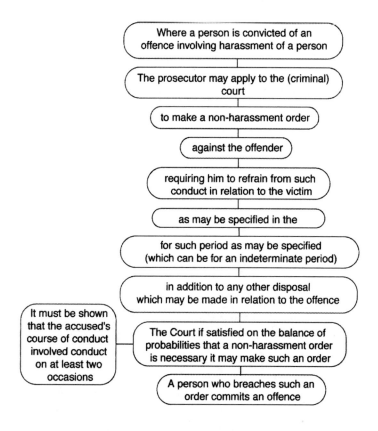

Where a person is convicted of an offence involving harassment of a person

The prosecutor may apply to the (criminal) court

to make a non-harassment order

against the offender

requiring him to refrain from such conduct in relation to the victim

as may be specified in the

for such period as may be specified (which can be for an indeterminate period)

in addition to any other disposal which may be made in relation to the offence

It must be shown that the accused's course of conduct involved conduct on at least two occasions

The Court if satisfied on the balance of probabilities that a non-harassment order is necessary it may make such an order

A person who breaches such an order commits an offence

Control of Alcohol, etc at Sporting Events

CRIMINAL LAW (CONSOLIDATION) (SCOTLAND) ACT, 1995

Designation of sports grounds and sporting events S 18

This section empowers the Secretary of State, by order, to designate:

- A sports ground or class of sports ground.

- A sporting event, or a class of sporting event, at that ground or at any of that class of ground.

- A sporting event or class of sporting event, taking place outside Great Britain.

Provided that a sporting event at which all the participants take part without financial or material reward and to which all spectators are admitted free of charge shall not be subject to an order under this section; but this proviso is without prejudice to the order's validity as respects any other sporting event.

At the time of writing the Secretary of State has designated:

- All Scottish League and Highland League football grounds and Edinburgh's Murrayfield Stadium.

- Association football matches in the Scottish and Highland Football Leagues.

- Association football matches relating to:
  a) Scottish Association Cup
  b) Scottish Football League Cup
  c) Scottish Association Qualifying Cup (North)
  d) European Cup
  e) European Cup Winners' Cup
  f) UEFA Cup

- International Association football matches in Scotland.

- Association football matches coming within jurisdiction of the SFA.

- International Rugby Union Football matches.

- Association football matches at a sports ground outside Great Britain in which one of the participating teams represents: the Scottish Football Association, or a club which is a member of the Scottish Football League or the Highland Football League.

Alcohol on Passenger Vehicles Travelling to and from Sporting Events

SECTION 19 CRIMINAL LAW (CONSOLIDATION) (SCOTLAND) ACT, 1995

Section 19(1)

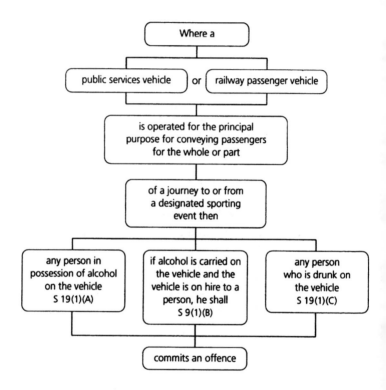

Where a

public services vehicle — or — railway passenger vehicle

is operated for the principal purpose for conveying passengers for the whole or part

of a journey to or from a designated sporting event then

any person in possession of alcohol on the vehicle
S 19(1)(A)

if alcohol is carried on the vehicle and the vehicle is on hire to a person, he shall
S 9(1)(B)

any person who is drunk on the vehicle
S 19(1)(C)

commits an offence

Section 19(2)

If the operator of a PSV which is being operated as described in S 19(1), either by himself or by employee or agent permits alcohol to be carried on the vehicle, the operator and as the case may be the employee or agent commits an offence.

SECTION 19(3) to (6) CRIMINAL LAW (CONSOLIDATION) (SCOTLAND) ACT, 1995

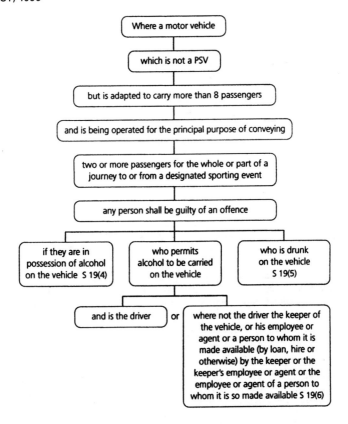

Defence in relation to carriage of alcohol in vehicles S 19(7)

Where a person is charged with an offence under S 19(1)(b), (2); or (6), it shall be a defence for that person to prove that the alcohol was carried on the vehicle without his consent or connivance and that he did all he reasonably could do to prevent such carriage.

Possession of Alcohol at a Sporting Event

SECTION 20 CRIMINAL LAW (CONSOLIDATION) (SCOTLAND) ACT, 1995

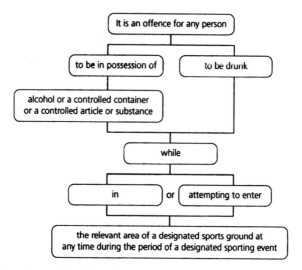

*Note 1: **Controlled Container** means any bottle, can or other portable container (open or sealed) which is, or was in its original manufactured state, capable of containing liquid and is made of such material or is of such construction, or is so adapted, that if thrown or propelled against a person it would be capable of causing some injury but excludes medicinal containers holding medicines.*

*Note 2: **Controlled Article or Substance** means: a) Any article or substance the main purpose of which is the emission of a flare to illuminate or signal (as opposed to igniting or heating) or the emission of smoke or visible gas - including distress capsules intended as fumigators for testing pipes, but not matches, cigarette lighters or heaters; and b) Any firework.*

*Note 3: **Period of Designated Sporting Event** means: The 2 hours before the start until 1 hour after the end of the event. Except that where the event is to start at a particular time but is delayed or postponed it includes, and where it does not take place, it means, the period commencing 2 hours before, and ending 1 hour after, that particular time.*

Possession of Alcohol at Sports Event – Police Powers

SECTION 20 CRIMINAL LAW (CONSOLIDATION) (SCOTLAND) ACT, 1995

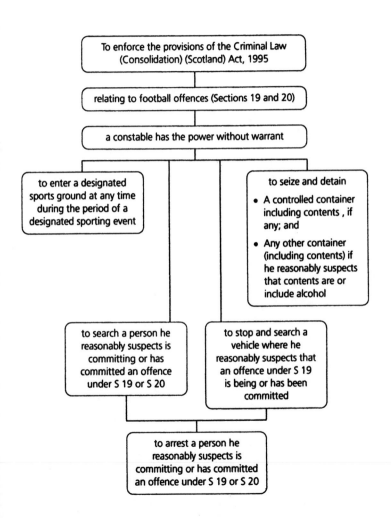

To enforce the provisions of the Criminal Law (Consolidation) (Scotland) Act, 1995

relating to football offences (Sections 19 and 20)

a constable has the power without warrant

to enter a designated sports ground at any time during the period of a designated sporting event

to seize and detain

- A controlled container including contents , if any; and
- Any other container (including contents) if he reasonably suspects that contents are or include alcohol

to search a person he reasonably suspects is committing or has committed an offence under S 19 or S 20

to stop and search a vehicle where he reasonably suspects that an offence under S 19 is being or has been committed

to arrest a person he reasonably suspects is committing or has committed an offence under S 19 or S 20

Index

A

NOTES

NOTES

NOTES

NOTES

NOTES

NOTES

NOTES

NOTES

NOTES

NOTES

NOTES